Civil Liberties

Policy and Policy Making

Edited by
Stephen L. Wasby

Southern Illinois University Press
Carbondale and Edwardsville

Feffer & Simons, Inc.
London and Amsterdam

Library of Congress Cataloging in Publication Data
Main entry under title:

Civil liberties.

   Includes bibliographical references and index.
    1. Civil rights—United States—Addresses, essays, lectures.   2. Policy
sciences—Addresses, essays, lectures.   I. Wasby, Stephen L., 1937-
JC599.U5C55 1977   323.4'0973   76-43318   ISBN 0-8093-0817-7

Southern Illinois University Press paperback edition May 1977
Printed by offset lithography in the United States of America

Contents

List of Figures and Tables

Figures

Tables

ex post facto Laws -
penumbra -

Introduction:
Civil Liberties Policy and
Policy Making

Stephen L. Wasby

What is civil liberties policy? To say it is "everything in the Bill of Rights
plus the Fourteenth Amendment" is underinclusive, because other constitutional provisions—the prohibition of ex post facto laws and the Thirteenth, Fifteenth, Nineteenth, and Twenty-sixth amendments—relate to
civil liberties. It is also ambiguous because new civil liberties, such as the
right to privacy, are being developed in the penumbra of existing provisions. Yet, it is not inaccurate to say that civil liberties policy consists
primarily of the package of First Amendment rights (free speech, press, and
association; religious freedom and church-state separation), of equal protection of the laws, and of proper procedure (due process). Thus, it includes
what some call "civil rights" (related to racial and ethnic discrimination);
we make no attempt here to engage in the generally futile exercise of
distinguishing between civil liberties and civil rights.   *futile in exercise*

13th
14th
19th
26th

Amendment

This book does not include chapters on all the subjects just noted.
Criminal justice has been covered in an earlier book in this series (Gardiner
and Mulkey 1975). In addition, the contents of this book were consciously
chosen to overrepresent writing on new developments in civil liberties
policy and on the process by which civil liberties policy is made. Our
intention is to indicate the direction in which work in this field should move,
to stimulate work in neglected areas, and particularly to encourage more
explicit policy analysis in subsequent work on civil liberties policy.

While the selections here are the result of a process of "tilting," it is
important to comment on the apparent interests of scholars in the civil
liberties policy subfield, particularly as those interests became evident in
the process of selecting and editing chapters for this book. Those working
in the field seem to focus their greatest attention on various aspects of free
speech and press and the newer right-to-privacy area. Church-state relations, in spite of recent heated controversy over aid to parochial schools,
provokes less interest. Most surprising is the apparent lack of interest in
racial equality (but see Bullock and Rodgers 1975). Apparently, attention
has shifted from the less glamorous, unfinished work of implementing
provisions prohibiting racial discrimination to women's rights and gender
discrimination. Receiving virtually no attention are a number of areas at the
cutting edge of civil libertarians' concerns; for example, the problems

posed by trying to "treat" or "help" people through the rehabilitative
model (including problems of mental commitment, psychosurgery, and
chemotherapy) appear not to have become grist for the scholarly mill (but
see *The Civil Liberties Review*).

Scholars writing about civil liberties policy seem far more interested in
the substance of that policy than in the process by which it is made. The
policies are discussed as if they were "self-contained, easily demarcated
units" (Graham and Graham 1976, p. 79), with little attempt made to show
the interrelation or intersection of policies—just as there has been insufficient attention to conflicts between civil liberties values (for example, free
press v. fair trial). Similarly, that the process by which particular civil
liberties policy is made may affect the making of policy with respect to
another topic seems to go unattended. Examination of civil liberties policy
making is still largely tied to doctrinal analysis of court rulings, particularly
those of the U.S. Supreme Court, as is usually the case with most college-
level civil liberties courses, and often is little more than a catalog of rulings;
material from outside the United States is assiduously avoided. (Seldom do
constitutional law casebooks present more than the "leading decisions";
only one really integrates the cases with judicial process materials and a
policy concern [Grossman and Wells 1972]). Furthermore, quite unlike
policy analysts working on other policy areas, those attending to civil
liberties show an abundant lack of interest in methodological problems
affecting their subject area. It almost seems to be the case that civil liberties
has joined the field of policy analysis in little more than name; the separation between courses on the law of civil liberties and policy analysis has not
narrowed noticeably.

Disproportionate attention to court rulings, with some (but considerably less) attention to forces producing them, results in a view of the
policy process noted by Thomas J. Anton: policy makers appear as reactive
or passive, responding primarily to pressures from the environment. The
conventional wisdom that judges must wait for cases has not been touched
by the view that policy is affected by organizational routines or by courts'
strategic choices. Policy decisions are also seen as final, just as they are in
other areas of policy analysis (Anton 1976, p. 91). In spite of ample evidence from impact studies (Becker and Feeley 1972; Wasby 1970) that the
impact of judicial rulings is substantially attenuated, implementation is not
a central focus. Perhaps writers on civil liberties policy are beguiled by the
"myth of rights" idea that statements of rights are self-implementing
(Scheingold 1974; see also Casper 1972); the complementary idea of the
"politics of rights" gets a back seat. That civil liberties policy making is no
longer the courts' sole preserve but is shared by legislative and executive
branches as well is not seen, nor do we find an appreciation that "policy

Card carrying member of the ACLU
American Civil Liberties Union .

arrangements are fragmented and multicentered," with any choice "structured by many decision centers . . . not related in a prescribed hierarchy" (Gregg 1976, p. 3). By and large, policy making outside the government is also ignored (Nadel 1975), which means we do not see the "little old ladies in tennis shoes" directing movie boycotts or the television networks screening the shows we can see. Public opinion similarly gets some, but not much, attention (but see Zalkind 1975).

Dissatisfaction with policy leads most of those writing in the area of civil liberties policy to look closely at particular policies (and perhaps at how they were developed). Yet, in much thinking and writing on civil liberties policy, prescription has (almost) totally ousted analysis, hardly a desirable state of affairs. This is not to say that writing on civil liberties policy should not be "informed" by a prescriptive interest (true of the items included here), particularly where judgments are made about the degree to which policies are achieved or achievable given the means currently used. Such normative judgments and evaluation are not out of keeping with policy analysis in other substantive areas, and, furthermore, such judgments have been said to be necessary if policy analysis is to be "a comprehensive area of inquiry" (Graham and Graham 1976, p. 77). Overall, however, one has the feeling that those working in the field of civil liberties have not adequately "faced up" to how they should or will handle normative analysis.

Chapters dealing with four major topics are presented in this book. These topics are new developments in traditional areas of civil liberties policy; new areas of civil liberties; policy making with respect to civil liberties; and the methodology of civil liberties policy analysis. Some chapters overlap, but each generally falls into one of the categories. A number of them engage in doctrinal analysis of Supreme Court cases, several deal with the process by which policy is made, and a few try to engage in more specific policy-analytical tasks such as mapping out questions to be asked and evidence to be examined or looking critically at tests for implementing policy.

In Part I, the largest section, we present eight chapters dealing with topics in the traditional civil liberties areas of the First Amendment and equality. Four chapters deal with matters of free speech and association. Francisco J. Lewels examines the problem of media access for minorities, detailing some of the changes produced by group action. The next two chapters deal with the question of the effect of television violence on children. Meredith W. Watts, drawing on the psychological literature, explores the questions that need to be answered as policy is developed, and Deanna Campbell Robinson suggests that education of children about television may be more effective than censorship. Thomas C. Britton then

Cut + it .
Beveledge —

examines the statutory and judicial developments with respect to collective bargaining by college and university faculty, an aspect of the right of association.

Two chapters deal with church-state matters. Raleigh W. Smith looks at the concept of civil religion and its relation to our church-state doctrines, and Daryl R. Fair provides a look at both the policy process on church-state policy and the Supreme Court's doctrine on the subject. With respect to equality, Donald W. Jackson examines the guidelines used to determine whether employment tests alleged to be discriminatory are "job relevant" as well as the methodological problems involved in trying to implement the guidelines, and Werner F. Grumbaum identifies several patterns in our treatment of various minorities.

Part II contains six chapters on new areas of civil liberties policy. In the first, Stanley H. Friedelbaum looks at what he calls the New Bill of Rights, identifying a number of rights newly created in recent years and the "substantive due process" doctrine used to do so. In more specific analyses, Marilyn Falik explores the Supreme Court's abortion rulings and some of the questions those rulings left unanswered, and Larry C. Berkson turns to the Eighth Amendment, through a canvass of court rulings on corporeal and incorporeal "cruel and unusual" punishment. Jerome J. Hanus and Richard E. Morgan then look at two closely related rights—Hanus at individuals' rights to privacy with respect to information that government and private agencies maintain about them and Morgan at the right to know as implemented through the Freedom of Information Act. The section closes with Emmet V. Mittlebeeler's examination of freedom to travel abroad, in which he also looks at the justifications for restrictions and the mechanics of policy making and the issuance of passports.

In the section on civil liberties policy making, Part III, we present five chapters. Philippa Strum, noting the Supreme Court's recent policy outputs on women's rights, suggests reasons for the new "burst" of policy, particularly emphasizing changes in the legal community. Continuing this emphasis on litigation, Stephen C. Halpern questions the relative emphasis placed by the American Civil Liberties Union on different types of cases. Introducing the question of the levels at which policy is made, Richard S. Randall looks at the Supreme Court's definition of obscenity in terms of national and local communities, focusing particularly on the values implicated in such definitions. Albert L. Sturm and Kaye M. Wright, focusing on the state level, tell about the development of civil liberties in newly revised state constitutions. To provide a comparative view, Donald S. Dobkin analyzes the state of civil liberties in Canada with particular attention to the self-restrained role taken by the Canadian High Court in interpreting the Canadian Bill of Rights.

In Part IV, the last and shortest section of the book—one that should be longer if we are to be able to carry out effective civil liberties policy analysis in the future—we present two chapters. In the first, William Lee Eubank suggests how quasi-experimental time-series analysis could be usefully applied to the study of judicial policy making. Richard Pierre Claude then tells how the study of rights on a cross-national basis could tell us much about institutional development and public policy and assist us in theory building.

References

Anton, Thomas J. 1976. "The Imagery of Policy Analysis: Stability, Determinism, and Reaction," in *Problems of Theory in Policy Analysis*, ed. Philip M. Gregg (Lexington: Lexington Books, D.C. Heath and Co.), pp. 91-101.

Becker, Theodore, and Malcolm Feeley, eds. 1972. *The Impact of Supreme Court Decisions: Empirical Studies*, 2nd ed. (New York: Oxford University Press).

Bullock, Charles S., III, and Harrell R. Rodgers, Jr. 1975. *Racial Equality in America: In Search of an Unfulfilled Goal* (Pacific Palisades, Calif.: Goodyear) [the first in a series on American Politics and Public Policy].

Casper, Jonathan. 1972. *The Politics of Civil Liberties* (New York: Harper and Row).

Civil Liberties Review, The, ed. Alan F. Westin. (New York: John Wiley). Volume 1, #1, was Fall 1973; Spring 1975, was Vol. 2, #2.

Gardiner, John A., and Michael Mulkey, eds. 1975. *Crime and Criminal Justice: Issues in Public Policy Analysis* (Lexington: Lexington Books, D.C. Heath and Co.).

Graham, George J., Jr., and Scarlett G. Graham. 1976. "Evaluating Drift in Policy Systems," in *Problems of Theory in Policy Analysis*, ed. Phillip M. Gregg (Lexington: Lexington Books, D.C. Heath and Co.), pp. 77-87.

Gregg, Phillip M. 1976. "Preface: Current Problems of Policy Theory," in *Problems of Theory in Policy Analysis*, ed. Phillip M. Gregg (Lexington: Lexington Books, D.C. Heath and Co.), pp. 1-5.

Grossman, Joel B., and Richard Wells. 1972. *Constitutional Law and Judicial Policy-Making* (New York: John Wiley; 2nd ed. forthcoming).

Nadel, Mark V. 1975. "The Hidden Dimension of Public Policy: Private Governments and the Policy-Making Process," *Journal of Politics*, 37 (February), 2-34.

Scheingold, Stuart. 1974. *The Politics of Rights* (New Haven: Yale University Press).

Wasby, Stephen L. 1970. *The Impact of the United States Supreme Court: Some Perspectives* (Homewood, Ill.: Dorsey Press).

Zalkind, Sheldon, ed. 1975. "Civil Liberties," *Journal of Social Issues*, 31, #2; entire issue devoted to the topic.

Part I
New Developments in
Traditional Civil Liberties

1 Minority Access to the Media: The Free Marketplace Dilemma

Francisco J. Lewels

The Present Marketplace

One of the most burning issues facing our society today is the ability of our country to maintain a participatory democracy by ensuring that citizens receive a wide diversity of views and opinions before deciding on important issues. This concept of a free marketplace of ideas, first proposed by John Milton in *The Aereopagitica*, provides the philosophical foundation for our modern democratic society; yet the gradual deterioration of this free marketplace during the last half century has not been made a public issue. In fact, with the exception of specialized publications, the media in general have barely dealt with the problem that is beginning to cause concern among the nation's policy makers.

Growing from the small, highly competitive business of years gone by, the media of today, critics claim, are dominated by monopolistic conglomerates primarily interested in maximizing profits and satisfying advertisers. It has been pointed out that newspaper competition is almost dead, as is separate ownership of morning and afternoon dailies. Independent ownership of both newspapers and television stations is quickly being wiped out in what has been termed "capitalistic cannibalism—one group or chain swallowing another" (Bishop 1972, p. 10).

A principal charge is that these giant corporations are concerned only with serving the needs of advertisers, not the needs of the public. This charge, although disputed by media owners, has some basis in fact, particularly in broadcasting, which depends solely on advertising for its revenue. In a business where ratings dictate policy, the interests of large segments of the public inevitably are sacrificed. To understand the consequences of such policy making, one need only examine the rating system and its blatant disregard for minority audiences of all kinds. Partners in discrimination, along with blacks and browns, are the old, the very young, the highly educated, and the rural American.

When the networks cancelled the Lawrence Welk Show and Gunsmoke, the question was not only how many viewers could be amassed for the advertiser, but what kind. Both programs were high in the ratings, but the millions of devoted fans did not fit the demographic requirements.

3

4

They were too old and too rural to satisfy the big advertisers. These audiences were not interested in buying new cars or appliances, but rather the less expensive products, such as Geritol.

The rating (profit) motive causes many other conflicts with public responsibilities. Network newsmen complain that the quest for higher ratings is turning news into entertainment and that many ideas for important documentaries are killed because of the poor ratings they might receive. Parents have organized to protest the poor quality of children's programming and the high volume of commercials for unhealthy food and expensive toys. Journalism reviews criticize local stations for not being willing to spend money on documentaries and other informative programs dealing with important community issues. The Federal Trade Commission claims broadcasters do not accept responsibility for the deceptive advertisements they air. Health groups claim the broadcast industry fought to keep advertisements for cigarettes on the airwaves in spite of evidence that smoking causes cancer.

These examples of broadcasters catering to "special" or "private" interests illustrate the scope of the real marketplace problem. If, as the Federal Communications Act states, the airwaves belong to the public and broadcasters are permitted to operate only as long as they use the public airwaves to serve the public, then use of the airwaves to serve only special interests must be contrary to the *public* interest. The term *public interest* would thus simply mean putting the interests of the general public before those of private or special interests. But who ensures that broadcasters do not violate these public duties? Obviously, the job falls squarely on the shoulders of the Federal Communications Commission, an agency that has often been accused of being dominated by the broadcasting industry and of being insensitive to minority interests. Consequently, media consumer groups are attempting to prod the FCC into doing its job more effectively and bypassing that policy making body through court actions when necessary.

Using the First Amendment as a shield from criticism and government interference, the media industry has achieved what other industries have only dreamed of doing: exemption from antitrust laws through federal legislation and the almost undivided attention of the American public for its advertising messages. The first was accomplished by the passage of the 1970 Newspaper Preservation Act, which exempts 44 daily newspapers in 22 of the country's largest cities from antitrust laws by permitting allegedly failing newspapers to share facilities with economically sound ones. In its haste to pass the bill, many congressmen seemed unconcerned with the monopolistic implications stated in a Justice Department antitrust suit. They agreed not to release to the public important financial data supplied by the newspapers that supposedly proved they were in financial difficulties. There is also evidence that the 44 newspapers involved, many belonging to chains, engaged in a concerted effort to keep information of the pending legislation from the public (Lewels 1971, p. 5).

The second, phenomenal accomplishment is a result of the monopolistic hold the three commercial networks have over prime-time television viewing. During these hours each evening, Americans have virtually no choice in the type of TV programming available, due to the networks' insatiable hunger for ratings, which produces hour after hour of light entertainment in an attempt to attract the largest possible audience. Both of these accomplishments have come under unsuccessful U.S. Department of Justice attacks for antitrust violations and are but one indication that the "free" marketplace is in grave danger.

The First Amendment

The problem of the deteriorating marketplace was forcefully brought to the attention of government and media policy makers in the early 1960s by a national movement of minority groups challenging the media industry's claim that it has the exclusive privilege of using the nation's channels of communication for whatever purposes it chooses.

Led by a small army of public interest lawyers, this grass-roots movement charges that the media industry is interested in using the channels of communication only to make money; that during the past 50 years the media became concentrated in the hands of fewer and fewer persons; that views contrary to the owners' rarely get into the media; and that the First Amendment gives the government not only the right, but the obligation, to regulate the media for purposes of preserving the free marketplace.

Indeed, these same charges have been made not only by minority groups, but also by congressmen, journalists, some Federal Communications Commissioners, and many others from both sides of the political continuum. Although ethnic and racial minorities are the most vocal about the deteriorating marketplace, the issue now concerns all citizens because of the difficulty of gaining access to the media for anyone who is not in a decision-making position within the communication industry. Therefore, the term *minority* in the context of media access refers to any group whose views are not being represented through the media.

For this reason, the ultimate goal of today's movement is to restore the free marketplace by obtaining a definitive reinterpretation of the First Amendment—one that defines press freedom as the freedom of every citizen to express himself through the channels of mass communication.

Still the most hotly contested amendment to the Constitution, the First Amendment remains surrounded by a swirl of controversy and confusion.

Does it mean that the media owners are protected from any governmental interference or does it mean that the government may regulate the press to ensure that it meets its obligation to maintain an informed citizenry? The first interpretation, sometimes called the *traditional* or *negative approach*, is used by the media to argue against any governmental interference whatsoever. This definition asserts that the First Amendment was written to give the media the power to act as a watchdog over government in order to prevent corruption. If this is the document's intent, then the press must be free from any regulation or interference from government. It is a negative command for government not to regulate.

The second interpretation is known as the *citizen-oriented* or *positive approach* which states that the first and foremost purpose of the press is to prepare the people for their roles as citizens by providing an open forum for a diversity of views. Thus, the First Amendment is a positive command to the government to regulate the media to the extent necessary to keep the channels of communication open to the widest diversity of views (Francois 1975, p. 18). This definition corresponds to Milton's "free marketplace of ideas" theory, popular at the time the amendment was written. The traditional interpretation has occasionally lost ground in the courts, particularly with regard to broadcasting where, because of the scarcity of channels, the licensee is given a technological monopoly. However, it continues to be used by the courts in rulings regarding the print media.

Perhaps the foremost advocate and one of the most prestigious leaders of the movement toward a redefined First Amendment is Jerome A. Barron, who argues that our attempt to keep a participatory democracy alive will fail unless "the public, through newspapers and broadcasts, have access to all shades of opinion" (1973, p. 16). Barron believes the monopolistic tendencies of the media prevent a diversity of views from reaching the public.

Barron's philosophical argument, however, is rarely the issue at the grass-roots level. Instead, minority groups are more concerned with changing unfavorable media stereotypes, producing documentaries, challenging broadcast licenses, sensitizing media employees, infiltrating media corporations, obtaining training and scholarships, and preparing legal arguments. These are the day-to-day goals that citizen groups hope will eventually cause media policies to change regardless of court interpretations of the First Amendment.

The Fight Over Citizen Access

Today, the issue of citizen access to the media is solidly before the nation's policy makers, if not before the public, and a confrontation is taking place between those who control the media and those who seek to change media policies in favor of increased public input to communication channels. As of now, the two forces are at a stalemate, but the communications industry seems to have the long-range advantage. Citizen groups, through constant legal pressures, have been extremely successful in forcing the media to grant greater access to minorities. On the other hand, media lobby groups have been steadily working to secure governmental policies favoring the media owners' right to deny access and thereby seal up the legal loopholes being used against them. These efforts continue to be successful, with recent court rulings heavily against a constitutional right of access *(Miami Herald* v. *Tornillo; CBS* v. *Democratic National Committee)* and congressmen standing on long queues waiting to support bills proposed by media lobbies.

The movement has primarily turned its efforts toward broadcasting, which offered the path of least resistance because of the built-in access "loopholes" existing in the Federal Communications Act. The Fairness Doctrine, the Equal Time Provision (Sec. 315), the "Responsibility Clause" (requiring that broadcasters operate in the public interest, convenience, and necessity), license renewals, and license transfers became the targets of legal petitions.

The battle lines were drawn around these highly misunderstood and controversial requirements, which force broadcasters to serve something called the "public interest." Although not specifically defined by the FCC, the term is at the core of the concept of broadcast regulation as well as the free marketplace dilemma. Broadcasters argue that the term is so amorphous that it is an open invitation for every malcontent to open fire on them. To those challenging broadcasting, the term is used with religious fervor to emphasize the belief that all citizens are entitled to participate in a marketplace of ideas.

The tactics employed by these groups to ensure the public interest is served are based upon a quite simple concept: get a piece of the action and then shape policy. Already, the impact of these efforts may have altered the media irreparably and may have caused long-range social consequences. In the early days of the civil rights movement, when the tactics of violence and demonstration were employed by minorities, it became apparent that the media most easily influenced were those operating over the public airwaves. It was also evident that violence and demonstrations, although effective means of gaining access, were unsatisfactory as a primary method (see Lewels 1974).

Lacking ownership, employment, and public relations skills used by "establishment" organizations, minorities soon began to seek nonviolent alternatives. Access to the print media was seen as something less than satisfactory to civil rights leaders. Even though some newspapers supported their cause and reported on their plight, there was no assurance that an editor would agree to cover a particular story or even to accept a paid advertisement. No court of law in the land would force an editor to do this, as evidenced by the case of the Amalgamated Clothing Workers of Chicago who fought a fruitless battle to force the editors of Chicago papers to accept paid advertisements concerning a local labor dispute *(Amalgamated Clothing Workers* v. *Chicago Tribune Co.).* This inability to use the channels of communication helped spawn a new phenomenon in our society that consumer advocate Ralph Nader likes to call the *public citizen movement.* This is the idea that citizens, working directly in their communities, can control and affect governmental policy. Nader preaches an inspired vision of reforming regulatory agencies that includes the flourishing of "public citizens" who will create a new center of influence in American life.

Although Nader has not directly been associated with the widespread citizen action movement in broadcasting, there is no doubt that his efforts in the consumer movement and his philosophy for reform have helped create the right atmosphere for the movement. Public interest law firms not associated with Nader's groups emerged in the mid-1960s to aid civil rights leaders in their efforts to effect policy changes.

Working by themselves, minority groups might never have developed the legal expertise to devise tactics needed for using the existing loopholes. With the help of those who knew the inner workings of the communication system, such as former FCC Commissioner Nicholas Johnson and public interest lawyers from such organizations as the United Church of Christ and the Citizen's Communications Center, sophisticated strategies were quickly developed.

Johnson outlined the basic concept, calling it the "law of effective reform," which consists of three parts: First, the factual basis for the grievance and the specific parties involved must be given. Second, the legal principle that indicates relief is due (constitutional provision, statute, regulation, court or agency decision) must be named. Third, the precise remedy sought (new legislation or regulations, license revocation, fines or an order changing practices) must be stated (Johnson 1969, p. 202).

Yet, knowing the formula and using it effectively were two different matters, particularly in the area of license challenging, which requires tight organization, training, discipline, and unity within the minority groups. This, unfortunately, was what the groups lacked the most. For blacks and Chicanos, the skills were learned in training sessions conducted during the 1960s and 1970s by public interest lawyers who drilled the minority spokesmen on the minutest details of dealing with broadcasters, such as, "If a team bogs down on a point in the discussion, call a recess and straighten out the point in question among yourselves. Do not be divided." Armed with a list of such dos and don'ts, the spokesmen would then confront local station managers. Such advice often resulted in flurries of license challenges.

Today, nearly every major city in the nation has at least one station that has succumbed to minority pressure tactics and signed far-reaching legal agreements providing a wide variety of concessions designed to give local minority groups input into broadcast policy. Many stations, rather than continue lengthy and costly litigation, signed agreements calling for such things as minority advisory councils, employment, training, scholarships, public service announcements, programming, sensitivity training, and minority business aid. In areas where one station was challenged and negotiated an agreement, other stations have been quick to adopt similar policies voluntarily in order to ward off similar legal attacks.

When legal tactics are inadequate to achieve changes in media policies, minority groups do not hesitate to fall back on the time-tested strategies of boycott and demonstration. These methods are particularly useful in effecting changes in advertisements that use stereotypes to sell products. Perhaps the most famous case in this category is the Chicano battle against the Frito Lay Company's "Frito Bandito." This confrontation spawned a citizen group in Washington, D.C., called the National Mexican-American Anti-Defamation Committee (NMAADC), which was specifically formed to combat advertisements depicting negative stereotypes that reinforce prejudicial attitudes.

Supporting the charge that such stereotypes reinforce prejudicial attitudes is a study conducted by sociologist Ozzie G. Simmons. He found that Anglo-Americans believe Mexicans are generally improvident, undependable, irresponsible, childlike, indolent, unclean, deceitful, prone to heavy drinking and criminality, and of low morality (Simmons 1970, pp. 383-95). The Frito Bandito, although a harmless caricature on the surface, represented one more in an endless line of examples in which Mexicans are depicted as gun-toting, mustachioed, pot-bellied thieves with thick accents. Through the use of boycotts of Frito Lay Corn Chips, as well as law suits, NMAADC was able to achieve its goal of removing these and other offensive commercials from the air.

Effects of the Movement

All of these efforts to change media policies are, of course, based on the theory that the media help structure the society's morals and behavior (DeFleur 1973, pp. 129-38) and that if minority viewpoints are considered in developing policy, the outcome will be a reduction in prejudice and ignorance and a subsequent increase in understanding.

Evidence that prejudice has decreased and understanding is increasing, however, is not yet apparent. What is apparent is that media policies are changing in spite of court decisions. Today, organizations like the Newspaper Fund, the National Association of Broadcasters, and foundations supported by media corporations are spending much of their efforts developing minority policies in the areas of recruitment and training. New minority faces on the motion picture screen and on television are but one indication that things have changed, and there are indications that media owners and operators are becoming more sensitive to minority needs in general. Newspaper editors today are conscious of their inabilities to cover minority issues properly without minority reporters and editors. Many are making honest efforts to recruit, train, and give responsible positions to ethnic and racial minority members of all kinds. The influx of persons with such backgrounds into the communications industry is bound to have far-reaching effects on the media and their policies and eventually on cultural norms within the society. The nearly overwhelming force of the minority access movement has caused media owners to make policy concessions in the area of access that a decade ago would have seemed impossible.

Perhaps even more significant than personnel changes is the fact that public access is being given high priority in the development of policies regarding cable television, which is only now emerging as a significant social force. Although CATV policies are far from being finalized, the prospect for citizen access seems bright, due in part to the pressures of the access movement. On the other hand, print media policy toward access is not likely to change without a mandate from the courts, in view of recent rulings. Finally, the victories won by the movement thus far have mainly benefited racial and ethnic minorities. Other types of minorities, less desperate, will suffer in silence while those who are more impatient will resort to violence and terrorism to reach the public. For these groups the marketplace is still an expensive forum.

Cases

Chicago Joint Board, Amalgamated Clothing Workers v. Chicago Tribune Co., 307 F. Supp. 422 (N.D. Ill., 1970).

Columbia Broadcasting System, Inc. v. Democratic National Committee, 412 U.S. 94 (1973).

Miami Herald v. Tornillo, 418 U.S. 241 (1974).

References

Barron, Jerome A. 1973. *Freedom of the Press for Whom?* (Bloomington, Ind.: Indiana University Press).

Bishop, Robert L. 1972. "The Rush to Chain Ownership," *Columbia Journalism Review*, 11 (November-December), 10-19.

DeFleur, Melvin. 1973. *Theories of Mass Communication* (New York: David McKay).

Francois, William E. 1975. *Mass Media Law and Regulation* (Columbus, Ohio: Grid, Inc.).

Johnson, Nicholas. 1969. *How to Talk Back to Your Television Set* (Boston: Little, Brown).

Lewels, Francisco J. 1971. "The Newspaper Preservation Act," *Freedom of Information Center Report No. 254*, January.

_____. 1974. *Uses of the Media by the Chicano Movement* (New York: Praeger).

Simmons, Ozzie G. 1970. "The Mutual Images and Expectations of Anglo-Americans and Mexican-Americans," *Mexican-Americans in the United States*, ed. John H. Burma (Cambridge, Mass.: Canfield Press).

2

Television and Socialization to Violence: Policy Implications of Recent Research

Meredith W. Watts

Scientific research into the effects of television on social behavior has, instead of simplifying decision, in some ways made public policy decisions about regulation of the medium more difficult. A generally libertarian stance would suggest nonregulation until evidence is available and some "clear and present danger" of the medium is demonstrated, but knotty problems of scientific inference, vested interest, consumer interests, and ideology remain. When only a minimum of evidence was available, ideology and industry estimates of consumer behavior held sway. Now, even with more data available, it is hard to decide just how much evidence is needed to overcome nonregulatory ideals in a putative liberal democracy and what level of scientific certainty will resolve the differences of critics and defenders of the television industry's behavior.

In this discussion, an attempt is made to penetrate some of the mist that seems to separate rhetoric from evidence and both from implied policy decisions. We look at the evidence from the United States Surgeon General's Report and related research, discuss relevant psychological models within which the various data seem to make sense, and, finally, discuss policy alternatives. Useful in this connection is a logical scheme that crudely indicates the major approaches through the thicket of policy alternatives. (See Figure 2-1.) The chart indicates a range of viable positions:

1. Evidence is insufficient and intervention is not indicated; further research and policy considerations may or may not be warranted.
2. Evidence is sufficient, but censorship is unacceptable, although other alternatives might be acceptable.
3. Evidence is sufficient and "guidelines" are acceptable, but the selection or establishment of an appropriate and trustworthy agency must be considered.
4. Evidence is sufficient, but effectiveness of censorship is doubtful and other "positive" action ("other policy alternatives") is warranted.

The Evidence

We can approach some of the debate about regulation of television by dis-

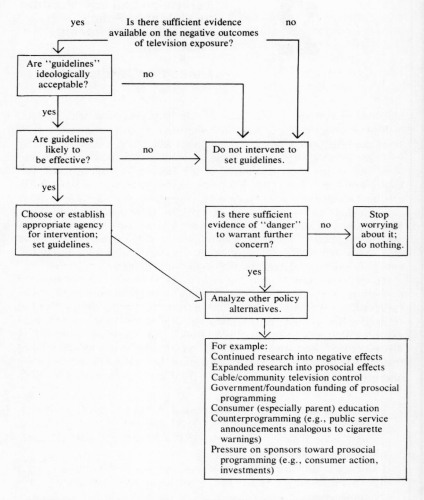

Figure 2-1. Approaches Through Evidence and Ideology to Policy

cussing first whether the evidence is very convincing. The Surgeon General's Report and the series of studies supported by the National Institute of Mental Health, plus some of the pioneering experimental studies that preceded large-scale national funding, provide some basic results:

1. Television contains a high proportion of violence, particularly in "action" programming and cartoons and there is little evidence of consistent industry attempts to reduce that proportion.

2. The amount of television viewing and the amount of violence viewed (which are highly correlated) are associated with increased aggressive attitudes and behavior of children of various ages. Although the effects vary with social class, race, age, and sex, the cumulative effect seems clear although not overly large. Statistically, the studies seem to show statistical correlations of approximately .20 to .30 (Greenberg 1975), thereby accounting for only 4 percent to 9 percent of the variance. The amount is modest to be sure, but its very ubiquity in such varied studies indicates that aggression and violence viewing are in some sense associated (Bogart 1972; Chaffee 1972; Drabman and Thomas 1974; Liebert, Neale, and Davidson 1973).

3. Experimental and quasi-experimental research indicates that exposing children to violent, aggressive social behavior tends to produce similar behavior in the young viewers; that is, children tend in some ways to imitate models of behavior that are shown them by television. Even where direct imitation does not take place, there may still be a learning effect where a behavior is "acquired" (Liebert 1972) but not performed until some later date when conditions are more favorable or social restraints less prevalent. One major program of research (Eron et al. 1972; Lefkowitz et al. 1972) found that media viewing at a young age seems to have a latency or "sleeper" effect—the behavior may emerge later in the person's life after being in the individual's repertoire or behavior for some years. Another possibility is that early viewing sets into motion a sequence of interconnected changes in the individual that results in an increased acceptance of violence as a means for solving personal and social problems. Thus, viewing may produce aggressive behavior through direct imitation or by "planting the seed," which may have later aggressive consequences. Even though the behavior may not actually be performed, repeated exposure may "disinhibit" or actually encourage the use of *other* types of aggression through the process often termed "response generalization." (Scherer, Abeles, and Fischer 1975 review this concept.)

4. Specific incidents portrayed on television have been emulated in real life by individuals predisposed toward sociopathic or criminal behavior (see, for example, Bandura 1973). Novel modes of airplane skyjacking, physical assault, robbery, and other crimes have on several occasions flourished after being widely shown on television.

5. Television can provide a distorted view of the social world by its emphasis on some aspects of life rather than others, and individuals can come to adopt a set of perceptions that may be maladaptive or inappropriate for dealing with social reality. For example, high television viewing is

associated with greater fears of victimization, exaggerated estimates of the crime rate, heightened apprehension of being personally assaulted, and a high estimate of the general use of aggression to solve social problems. That television creates a symbolic world, which many accept as real, is revealed in the tendency for heavy viewers to estimate the amount of domestic violence nearer the vastly higher proportion of television than to that of the real world. In other words, the medium deeply influences their perceptions of the real world (Gerbner and Gross 1974).

The Surgeon General's Report emphasized that television viewing of violence or aggressive behavior might be more influential for those already "predisposed" toward aggression. This might suggest that only a deranged or sociopathic few would be likely to adopt antisocial behavior as a result of TV viewing, and even then that television would be only one of the influences that would make the person violent. However, it has already been demonstrated that television very likely has *some* effect on both short- and long-term social learning. It is therefore important to recognize explicitly that the effects are not limited to a few pathological, criminal, dramatic examples but are likely to be evident in many individuals who have had a steady diet of television violence. This is better understood if we consider two of the major psychological or social learning models that have influenced researchers.

One model is the *arousal* or *activation model* in which, as described above, the television presentation is simply one stimulus that enters the life of the individual and contributes in some way to aggressive or violent behavior. That model has been expanded to suggest that physiological arousal of any kind, whether induced by erotic stimuli, drugs, or violent models, may *instigate* aggressive behavior. If such a thesis is valid, television programs that provide aggressive, arousing cues are likely to influence attitudes and behavior among a large segment of the viewing audience (Tannenbaum 1972).

Another model suggests that individuals undergo a *catharsis* or release of hostility or aggressive impulse when viewing aggressive scenes. Bolstered largely by psychoanalytic theory, this notion moves much of the action to the subconscious or unconscious motivation of the individual. Some individuals may be gratified or "released" by experiencing brutality vicariously and therefore be less likely to behave aggressively. (See Feshbach and Singer 1971; Hokanson 1970; Scherer, Abeles, and Fischer 1975, chaps. 2 and 3.) Experimental and correlational evidence indicates, however, that learning and emulation of aggression tend to increase with exposure. Therefore, while some catharsis might actually take place for some viewers, the repeated viewing of such behavior might result in decreased empathy for the victimized and greater acceptance of violence as a normal part of human social life (Drabman and Thomas 1974; Liefer,

Gordon, and Graves 1974). Thus, while catharsis *may* be psychologically useful in the short-term sense, learning and imitation seem to produce more important long-term effects.

A more short-term perspective of change sometimes is supported by a *phenomenological* or *subjectively personal* model. Here the emphasis is on the meaning that violence has for the individual, particularly on the role that television viewing and television violence play in the individual's subjective interpretation of his/her place in society. The individual is considered the prime subject of analysis, and the researcher asks what the presentation of violent content means to him or her. In such an analysis, the results are likely to be a bit different from the long-term modeling perspective discussed above.

To illustrate how such a discussion might proceed, imagine two youths viewing a violent episode on television. One has been tested on some instrument of "violence acceptance" and found to be very accepting of violence as a social solution; the scores of the other youth are in the opposite direction. We might then wonder what emotional reactions would occur during exposure. We find that the emotional reaction at the time of exposure is related to (1) the predisposition of the individual toward violence at the time of exposure, and (2) the likelihood of subsequent violence (Watts and Sumi 1975).

Supporting the first finding is the idea of selective perception of information, probably governed by attitudes, in which the individual subconsciously keeps certain noxious stimuli from rising to explicit cognitive awareness or at least lessens their impact. Emotional reactions to violent scenes may range from "stimulus intake" to "stimulus rejection," depending on the attitude of the individual viewer, suggesting that the individual consciously or unconsciously has some control over the intake and interpretation of violent stimuli such as those presented on television. For example, low violence acceptors tend to reject aggressive stimuli, while high violence acceptors tend to accept and attend more carefully to such stimuli (Watts and Sumi 1975). In other words, the mental "set" or attitude of the individual plays a large part in how the person interprets television violence. Such findings offer short-run hope that children "innoculated" against violent social behavior would react negatively when seeing it presented on television, but the findings are based on cross-sectional analysis dealing with only one brief point in time (the experimental session, generally of less than an hour's duration). What of the long-term effects of exposure, or the performing of aggressive acts after seeing the presentations?

At least one study has shown that emotional reaction is related to subsequent aggression—that, as gauged by facial expressions, the more pleased, the more attentive, the more approving the child while watching

(Ekman et al. 1972), the more likely the child is to behave aggressively later. Those who are more negative to violence will be less aggressive than the high acceptors. However, the long-term or "longitudinal" evidence noted above indicates that exposure to violence tends to have an overall effect of increasing violence acceptance no matter what the initial disposition. Thus, the short-term effects of violence presentation may show the impact of immediate attitudes, but those attitudes eventually may produce more acceptance of violence as a result of television exposure.

Therefore, it seems most reasonable at this stage of the scientific evidence to operate on the assumptions that (1) television exposure to violent incidents can produce long-term effects on social attitudes and behavior; that (2) the impact will vary with the influences to which the individual is exposed elsewhere in his/her environment (e.g., parents, peers, occupation); and that (3) the effects are filtered through the psychological "set" or mental framework of the individual (Edgar and Edgar 1971). While some negative effect from exposure to violence is generally to be expected, there are a host of other influences that affect the individual's social attitudes and behavior, and television is by no means a prime causal agent. This means that television's effects can be moderated, minimized, negated, augmented, intensified, or otherwise changed by the other influences to which a person is subject. Taking this as an operating assumption (but one supported by much empirical validation) we can turn to a discussion of practical policy alternatives for dealing with the effects of television.

Policy Implications

To the first question in Figure 2-1 ("Is there sufficient evidence on the negative outcomes of television exposure?"), the answer seems to be a tentative "yes"—at least if the goal is only to document that there is some deleterious effect. For many, the evidence is enough. However, because of the political and psychological significance of the research question, much remains to be studied. For example, the nature of predispositions and their mediating effects on television's influence need to be explored further. The emotional reactions of viewers, their physiological responses, and the relationship between arousal and subsequent learning and behavior are important research foci that require more work. In addition, more evidence on the effects of other factors—especially parental effects, peer interactions, developmental level, cognitive sophistication—would assist in determining where the most effective intervention might be made to modify any negative influence of television.

As indicated in the evidence cited earlier, much headway has been made by the researchers who participated in the work on the Surgeon General's Report, the associated studies funded by the National Institute for Mental Health, and other related research. Yet, the need for continuing analysis and research of media effects has not been obviated by the Surgeon General's Report; more can be done to develop a set of social indicators of violence levels in society. Actual levels of violence in society are sometimes subject to the vagaries of changes in crime statistics, and are further hampered by the lack of an adequate set of social indicators of the prevalence of violence. Standardized nationwide reporting of violence as well as the development of adequate social indicators would certainly add vital knowledge, but we need more information on the number of unreported crimes and interpersonal acts of aggression. Also helpful would be further measurement of actual levels of violence depicted on television. Gerbner's continuing study of the latter is highly important; any additional effort to monitor trends and provide "consumer information" to viewers, parents, and governmental agencies with responsibility for communications policy would similarly help. However, we must keep in mind that these few general areas by no means exhaust the research possibilities of importance.

The next question ("Is censorship ideologically acceptable?"), involving as it does the classic debate over media freedom versus governmental control, is difficult. If one conceded the ideological question, the feasibility problem does not seem to be insuperable. The Federal Communications Commission has "invited" broadcast executives to present plans for self-regulation. That agency and a special legislative watchdog committee (like that chaired by Senator Pastore at the time of the Surgeon General's Report) could perform an important monitoring function; perhaps a federal panel of social scientists would provide another acceptable format. Such groups would be increasingly important in the future to ensure that systematic observation of media violence and related social trends are the clear-cut responsibility of publicly accountable officials.

Prior censorship by a governmental agency of broadcast material would raise serious constitutional questions, but an active governmental role in recommending broadcast guidelines or in influencing guidelines set by the National Association of Broadcasters might not seriously endanger First Amendment freedoms. The exact format for such augmented powers would be complex, but with appropriate public input and controls such as legislative oversight, a designated regulatory panel, a public ombudsman, or a federal television-consumer advocate, it would be feasible to establish some arrangement.

If it were decided to have guidelines, what of their efficacy? Would they have a material effect on the level of violence in society? While such guidelines could indeed alter the amount and nature of portrayals of violence, it seems unlikely that they would produce a decline in the level of violence in society. The modification of only one influence in a multicausal sequence of social variables constitutes only a minor intervention in the total socialization of an individual; television is only one such element. Thus, the question of the effectiveness of intervention at the level of programming could probably be answered with a qualified "yes" with respect to violence portrayals in the medium, but with a "don't know" concerning social violence levels. Although we may never be able truly to measure the amount of social aggression, the development of more adequate indicators of its prevalence (as suggested above) would provide a better basis for informed guesses than we now have.

No matter what other alternative paths in Figure 2-1 we might take, only one, the conclusion that there is nothing to worry about, leads to inaction. Other conclusions seem to point to continuing analysis of alternative policy strategies. Although the implications of each cannot be worked out here, the following are some of the possibilities:

1. Continue research into negative effects of television with an aim of monitoring trends, assessing social violence levels, and "diagnosing" predispositions that may be conducive to violence. Such testing on the individual level—perhaps accomplished within the framework of an educational system—could provide information to teachers and parents that would help them prescribe audio-visual media, counselling, or simple vigilance to minimize the interaction between violent predispositions and television modeling effects.

2. The potential salutary effects of television programming have received increased attention (Liebert, Neale, and Davidson 1973; Liebert and Poulos 1974), but more research is called for within the traditional concern about children but with increased attention to impact on adults as well. The role of TV in socialization should remain a matter of high research priority. (See, e.g., Chaffee 1972; Edgar and Edgar 1971; Hyman 1973; Osborn and Endsley 1971; Roberts 1973.)

3. Consumer education, namely, education of parents and media consumers in schools and other institutions, requires ready access to current information about their children's dispositions, television content, and easily interpretable information on possible television influences. Some related "counterprogramming" in the form of public service announcements or periodic spot announcements about possible dangers of viewing certain types of programs might also be developed. A warning that "television watching might be dangerous to your social health" might seem unusual, but it is not out of the question. Alcohol advertisements are proscribed; advertising outlets for cigarettes are limited; and public service announcements concerning many types of drinking and smoking behav-

ior, social tolerance, interpersonal relations, and a variety of other matters regularly appear on television. Thus, announcements that criticized television itself would be novel, but not unthinkable. More important, however, the prime point of intervention in the process is at the point of viewing. Guidelines and censorship by parents of programming could have a decisive effect. Even more important might be the interpretation of media violence to children by parents—approval or disapproval and the discussion of ethical and moral alternatives seem important ways (perhaps *the* most important) to minimize whatever influence television may have in socializing people to violence.

4. There are also consumer action possibilities directed either at the networks or their local affiliates, although there is probably not sufficient public unanimity to ensure changes in policy. Pressure on local stations, particularly at the time of license renewal, might have more influence. For emphatic consumer action, the tactics of some Michigan parents who burned their television sets in a church parking lot may have some appeal, as might the tactics of the man who executed his set with a shotgun. A nationwide action of this type would very likely have an effect on the industry, but somehow the movement seems unlikely to generate much momentum. There are, however, other tactics that might have more appeal, such as the boycotting of products that sponsor violent programming and the channeling of investment (by private individuals, universities, foundations) away from companies that encourage such video material.

5. Perhaps a final consideration would be community-controlled television using either cable or conventional broadcast facilities to provide alternative programming. Such efforts are growing in number and impact, although they are not likely to draw a mass audience from network programming. What they can do, however, is provide an alternative for those who are apprehensive about television's effects and want a broader selection of program choices. In the absence of a viable community-controlled television capability, an alternative strategy might be to establish what is occasionally referred to as "purposive programming" designed to fulfill specific social goals and supported by public funds. Some kind of national organization involving social scientists, broadcast specialists, and federal officials would be required to develop such a policy, but sufficient public demand might bring about this kind of alternative programming. At a minimum, though, an informed approach to "purposive programming" would presuppose the existence of a reliable body of research on the prosocial effects of television; such research is still accumulating and should in itself be a priority policy item. Therefore, either community controlled video or national purposive programming should be supported by relevant research on the positive potential of television (see Liebert, Neale, and Davidson 1973, chap. 6).

22

Conclusion

Our discussion of policy alternatives in the area of television programming derives from a belief that the influence of television is limited and subject to many augmenting and countervailing influences. The overall conclusion is not, however, that the limited influence is negligible and that standard libertarian ideology is sufficient to dismiss the problem. For example, an opponent of regulation on grounds of First Amendment freedoms should recognize that many people's perceptions of social reality are strongly influenced by television. If those television-produced perceptions impel people to fear criminal victimization or political dissent inordinately, they may nurture antiheterodox social attitudes and a decreased sense of empathy with those who are unlike themselves. As a result they may become more receptive to punitive law enforcement practices and restriction of political dissent. Presumably such an outcome would be contrary to the intent of the libertarian, but would be a possible result where one value (nonregulation) is potentially in conflict with other values (such as an open and libertarian society). Such dilemmas are not simple, but their existence points up the necessity for integrating contemporary scientific evidence with traditional concerns in the area of media regulation. The purpose of the chart in Figure 2-1 was to clarify, if not resolve, some of the criteria on which policy decisions might be made. The central theme is that some viable policy decision is indicated by the research evidence and that serious thought must be given within the family, the community, and responsible political authorities to effective, alternative programming that answers a broader set of social needs than that presently available on commercial television.

References

Bandura, A. 1973. *Aggression: A Social Learning Analysis* (Englewood Cliffs, N.J.: Prentice-Hall).

Bogart, L. 1969. "Violence in the Mass Media," *Television Quarterly*, 8, 36-47.

_____. 1972. "Warning, the Surgeon General Has Determined That TV Violence is Moderately Dangerous to Your Child's Mental Health," *Public Opinion Quarterly*, 36, 491-521.

Chaffee, S.H. 1972. "Television and Adolescent Aggressiveness (Overview)," in *Television and Adolescent Aggressiveness*, ed. G.A. Comstock and E.A. Rubinstein (Vol. 3 of *Television and Social Behavior*) (Washington, D.C.: U.S. Government Printing Office), pp. 1-42.

23

Drabman, R.S., and M.H. Thomas. 1974. "Does Media Violence Increase Children's Toleration of Real-Life Aggression?" *Developmental Psychology*, 10, 418-421.

Edgar, P.M., and D.E. Edgar. 1971. "Television Violence and Socialization Theory," *Public Opinion Quarterly*, 35, 608-612.

Ekman, P., R.M. Liebert, W.V. Friesen, R. Harrison, C. Zlatchin, E.J. Malmstrom, and R.A. Baron. 1972. "Facial Expressions of Emotion While Watching Televised Violence as Predictors of Subsequent Aggression," in *Television's Effects: Further Explorations*, ed. G.A. Comstock, E.A. Rubinstein, and J.P. Murray (Vol. 5 of *Television and Social Behavior*) (Washington, D.C.: U.S. Government Printing Office), pp. 22-58.

Eron, L., L.R. Huesman, M.M. Lefkowitz, and L.P. Walder. 1972. "Does Television Cause Aggression?" *American Psychologist*, 27, 253-263.

Feshbach, S., and R. Singer. 1971. *Television and Aggression* (San Francisco: Jossey-Bass).

Gerbner, G., and L. Gross. 1974. "Violence Profile No. 6: Trends in Television Drama and Viewer Conceptions of Social Reality, 1967-1973" (Philadelphia: Annenberg School of Communications, University of Pennsylvania).

Greenberg, B.S. 1975. "British Children and Televised Violence." *Public Opinion Quarterly*, 38, 531-547.

Hokanson, J.E. 1970. "Psychophysiological Evaluation of the Catharsis Hypothesis," in *The Dynamics of Aggression*, ed. E.I. Megargee and J.E. Hokanson (New York: Harper and Row), pp. 74-86.

Hyman, H.H. 1973. "Mass Communication and Socialization." *Public Opinion Quarterly*, 37, 524-540.

Lefkowitz, M., L.D. Eron, L.O. Waldner, and L.R. Huesmann. 1972. "Television Violence and Child Aggression: A Followup Study," in *Television and Adolescent Aggressiveness*, ed. G.A. Comstock and E.A. Rubinstein (Vol. 3 of *Television and Social Behavior*) (Washington, D.C.: U.S. Government Printing Office), pp. 35-135.

Liebert, R.M. 1972. "Television and Social Learning: Some Relationships Between Viewing Violence and Behaving Aggressively (Overview)," in *Television and Social Learning*, ed. J.P. Murray, E.A. Rubinstein, and G.A. Comstock (Vol. 2 of *Television and Social Behavior*) (Washington, D.C.: U.S. Government Printing Office), pp. 1-42.

Liebert, R.M., and R.W. Poulos. 1974. "Television as a Moral Teacher," in *Man and Morality: Theory, Research, and Social Issues*, ed. T. Lickona (New York: Holt, Rinehart and Winston).

Liebert, R.M., J.M. Neale, and E.S. Davidson. 1973. *The Early Window: Effects of Television on Children and Youth* (New York: Pergamon Press).

Liefer, A.D., N.J. Gordon, and S.B. Graves. 1974. "Children's Television: More than Mere Entertainment," *Harvard Educational Review*, 44, 213-245.

Osborn, D.K., and E.R.K. Endsley. 1971. "Emotional Reactions of Young Children to TV Violence," *Child Development*, 42, 321-331.

Roberts, D.F. 1973. "Communication and Children: A Developmental Approach," in *Handbook of Communication*, ed. I. de Sola Pool and W. Schramm (Chicago: Rand McNally), pp. 174-215.

Scherer, K.R., R.P. Abeles, and C.S. Fischer. 1975. *Human Aggression and Conflict* (Englewood Cliffs, N.J.: Prentice-Hall).

Surgeon General, Scientific Advisory Committee on Television and Social Behavior. 1972. *Television and Growing Up: The Impact of Televised Violence* (Washington, D.C.: U.S. Government Printing Office.)

Tannenbaum, P.H. 1972. "Studies in Film- and Television-Mediated Arousal and Aggression: A Progress Report," in *Television's Effects: Further Explorations*, ed. G.A. Comstock, E.A. Rubinstein, and J.P. Murray (Vol. 5 of *Television and Social Behavior*) (Washington, D.C.: U.S. Government Printing Office), pp. 309-350.

U.S. Congress, Senate. 1972. Hearings before the Subcommittee on Communications of the Commerce Committee, March. Serial No. 92-52. Washington, D.C.: U.S. Government Printing Office.

Watts, M.W., and D. Sumi. 1975. "Television and the Socialization of Children to Violence: Some Emotional and Physiological Effects of Viewing," paper presented to the Southern Political Science Association, Nashville, Tennessee, November 6-9.

3

Television, Children, and Censorship

Deanna Campbell Robinson

Theoretically, we are now able to enter a new phase of media development where extant technology could invalidate the necessity for mass audiences (Maisel 1973). With the advent of video discs, cable television, satellite communication, and the attendant secondary services that those media make possible, the freedom to express and the concomitant freedom to hear/see whatever a person wants could be realized. However, because the FCC is reluctant to disturb the existing economic structure of the broadcast industry and because researchers, educators, and other private citizen groups believe the average person is either unable or unwilling to cope with certain types of media material, genuine First Amendment freedom for the average citizen is unlikely to be achieved. Here we consider how simple, but highly improbable, shifts in FCC policy and scholarly research strategy could bring about a real media revolution.

Complaints About Television

Critics of contemporary American television have three central complaints: First, as Spiro Agnew argued, the present selection of television programs does not represent a satisfactory diversity of voices (see also M. Robinson 1975; Schiller 1969). Second, American television does not represent a satisfactory diversity of taste (Rosenberg and White 1957). Third, some material shown on American television may be harmful to some viewers (Surgeon General 1972; Liebert, Neale, and Davidson 1973).

These criticisms are justified by problems inherent in the current American television system. Remedies such as the Fairness Doctrine, FCC program policy statements, and prime-time family viewing restrictions represent sincere, energetic attempts by many people to overcome some of these faults. However, the remedies are based on two erroneous assumptions: first, that scarcity of spectrum space necessitates scarcity of television programs; and, second, that because everyone must watch the same limited selection of programs, the best way to avoid possible adverse effects of some material on some viewers is to remove that material. These assumptions are the real problem in television today because they lead to censorship policies. Although such policies may have been warranted by past technology, they can no longer be justified.

If new technologies were developed adequately, consumers could be given a wide variety of audio-visual materials from which to choose and no small group of people could practically hope to restrict the selection of media products available to other people. Furthermore, current controls on televised material eventually would become counterproductive because a situation where people plan their own TV schedules requires that viewers possess evaluative skills necessary to select their own programs. Those skills cannot be developed under a system of paternalistic censorship.

Attempts to control broadcast material have come from the government, private interest groups, and social science researchers. In a situation of media scarcity each source has been able to develop a rationale for broadcast censorship. That rationale, especially in the case of children, is now outmoded.

Government Control of Broadcast Material

The origins of broadcast regulation lie in scarcity. Because only a few individuals could use the public airwaves, the government felt it somehow had to ensure both an optimum number of broadcast facility owners and a sufficient variety of programs to serve the "best" interests of all segments of the public. The FCC promulgated exacting rules as to how many broadcast outlets a single owner could purchase and, more recently, what combinations of media outlets a single owner could accumulate. Policies that regulate programming have been much more difficult to formulate because they may conflict with the First Amendment and with Section 326 of the Communications Act of 1934, which forbids FCC censorship of program material.

Perhaps the most specific policy on program content is the nebulous Fairness Doctrine, which the FCC has tried to clarify a number of times and about which there has been continuing controversy. The intent of the Fairness Doctrine is to protect the right of the public to hear all sides of an issue. Instead, it frequently discourages broadcasters from airing controversial programs for fear of violating the doctrine.

Other programming policies, such as the recent statement on children's programming, have been equally difficult to formulate without impinging upon First Amendment rights (Federal Communications Commission 1974). In essence, FCC policy has been to recommend general practices—for example, a station should reflect all sides of controversial public issues in its overall programming and a station should carry age-specific children's programming throughout the week—and then to expect station owners to develop and supply the details.

The FCC assumes a scarcity of program material because of a limited number of stations. Cable television, satellites, and video discs could invalidate the scarcity principle for television if the FCC did not feel a need to protect the economic investment of the established broadcast industry. This protective policy has been the instrumental factor in the failure of cable television interests to realize at least some of the potential new services the medium could offer. Similar protective policies prevented the efficient development of FM radio and UHF television as viable alternatives to AM and VHF (Krasnow and Longley 1973). The Committee for Economic Development recognized this attitude of the commission by stating recently that FCC "regulatory policies must be flexible enough to adapt to developing technologies" (1975, p. 83).

If new technologies were developed sufficiently, a viewer could assemble his own media entertainment or information package, choosing from as great a variety of audio-visual software as is now available in print. Mass audiences would congregate only if everyone wanted to witness events of national or international importance simultaneously. Daily news could be punched up on a two-way, home-to-cable connection or beamed in from a satellite data bank at any time a person wanted it. If the FCC encouraged such a situation of media plenty, a Fairness Doctrine to ensure a diversity of viewpoints or controls on children's programming to ensure satisfactory children's material would not be needed.

Private Interest Control of Broadcast Material

In the United States all citizens have been able to exercise some control over what they see and hear on broadcast stations. The most obvious method of censorship has been for viewers to turn off what they do not like. Since our commercial media depend upon large viewing audiences, this method might seem to be quite effective. But that assumption is fallacious for two reasons: First, what the majority of people will watch determines what various minorities have to watch. Second, the selection of television programs offered is determined by three commercial TV networks and one poorly financed public broadcasting system. In the case of commercial television the networks "counterprogram" each other. Counterprogramming means that in the networks' battle for the largest share of the audience, either three fairly good programs are pitted against each other or three bad programs are shown at the same time. Two of the good programs are as likely to be discarded as two of the bad because they do not command the largest audience segment. Thus, viewers are left wondering why so many tolerable programs disappear while intolerable ones survive. Public broadcasting, on the other hand, frequently commits the opposite error of offering programs so esoteric few people will be interested in them.

Viewers can engage successfully in consumer action. Since the 1966 *United Church of Christ* decision, the general public has been recognized as a legitimate advocate in license renewal proceedings. This right gives a determined group of consumers significant power because, even if their case against a station's license renewal is unsuccessful, they can cost a station much time and money in litigation. Stations frequently concede to consumer group demands before the FCC becomes involved in order to avoid such costs. Thus, a handful of people can convince a station to remove a program or change a minor policy.

Consumer groups also have had a direct influence on general FCC policy. For example, although the FCC did not bow absolutely to Action for Children's Television (ACT) demands that ads should be eliminated on children's programming and age-specific programming should be provided throughout the week, the commission eventually did issue a policy statement that concurred with most of ACT's suggestions and recommended that broadcasters regulate themselves accordingly. The National Association of Broadcasters responded by instituting "family viewing" during that portion of prime time when children were most likely to be in the audience and by reducing the number of commercial minutes on children's programs. The result of family viewing has been what many people have termed the worst season ever on network television.

The growing importance and success of consumer group action in broadcast policy formulation threatens our democratic society. Consumer groups often labor under the illusion that they are taking care of other people who cannot take care of themselves. Laudable as some of the changes desired by consumer groups may be, the underlying disposition is paternalistic. This attitude is especially dangerous in view of available technology and a potentially new media situation. If, for example, children do not learn through experience to deal effectively with adverse information and stimulation, as adults they will become extremely vulnerable to that same material. Thus, we risk raising a generation that may be faced with but will not be able to cope with an inundation of media software.

The Influence of Social Scientists on Broadcast Policy

Social scientists like to think they influence policy formulation. In the case of children's programming, at least, that influence has been real. Research on the effects of TV on young children since the early 1960s has indicated a positive relationship between televised violence and subsequent aggression in young children (Cater and Strickland 1975; Liebert, Neale, and Davidson 1973; Surgeon General 1972). The Surgeon General's Scientific Advisory Committee on Television and Social Behavior concluded that there is substantial evidence that some children act more aggressively after watching violence on TV.

As children grow older, however, the association between TV violence and aggressive behavior weakens. Several studies indicate that age and/or experience (exposure to TV) lessen the effects of TV on children (Cline, Croft, and Courrier 1972; Leifer and Roberts 1972; Liebert and Baron 1972; Meyer 1973). Recently, W. Collins has theorized that children pass through media comprehension stages similar to those posited by Piaget. If Collins' theory is correct, then we can afford to censor TV material viewed by young children. However, if experience rather than age-related development alone is the salient factor in increased comprehension of TV material, censoring material watched by young children is the worst policy we can adopt. Depriving children of contact with less desirable material may prolong the correlation between observed TV violence and subsequent aggressive behavior. Similar phenomena might be noticed in relation to the effects of ads and other TV content.

A New FCC Policy and a New Educational Approach

The FCC rarely makes sweeping or long-range policy changes but instead struggles with the varying interests of its many pressure groups by taking small, incremental steps that eventually add up to policies (Krasnow and Longley 1973). Even more rarely does the FCC act against the wishes of the broadcast industry. In 1963 when the FCC tried to adopt the broadcast industry's advertising code as the FCC's own policy, the industry rose in wrath to lobby powerfully in Congress. The House voted for the Rogers Bill, which prohibited FCC regulation of the length or frequency of broadcast ads and the Senate cut $400,000 from the FCC's 1964 budget.

Congressmen are interested in keeping peace with broadcasters because television and radio help candidates get elected. Since 1966, however, citizens have had much to say about formulation of broadcast policy. Congressmen are equally respectful of citizens. As a result of the competition for power between broadcasters and citizens, there currently are numerous bills in Congress that would extend the license renewal term for stations from three to either four or five years. These bills are an attempt by both broadcasters and congressmen to neutralize the new-found power citizens have over broadcasters through protests against license renewals.

Without a doubt, citizens can affect broadcast policy formulation. If citizen groups would cease to call for more control over today's restricted programming and would instead concentrate their efforts on promoting FCC policy favorable to the development of new technology, we might get rid of the white elephant broadcasting has become in this country. One suggestion is that a new system might comprise one or two dozen networks that would store their programs on satellites. Stations could choose programs they thought served local interests. Another possible plan would be to shift all entertainment TV from over-the-air broadcasting to cable, except in remote regions. The vacated spectrum space could then be used for other services, such as land-mobile communication, which badly need more frequencies. Whatever the future system looks like, the primary goal of citizens and the FCC should be to increase the audio-visual program options of Americans.

The end of program scarcity would mean the end of two of the three major criticisms of television in this country, lack of diversity of voices and taste. Satisfying the third criticism, harmful effects of some TV material for some viewers, requires additional action from researchers and educators. Shifts in FCC policy and social science research strategy go hand-in-hand.

Since Milton wrote in *Areopagitica* that men can reason if they are presented with all sides of an issue, we have recognized that his statement needs qualification. Because of heredity, varying environments, or both, not all persons can reason at the same level. Schools supposedly attempt to maximize an individual's inherited abilities and seek to provide an intellectually stimulating environment. But educators have not sought to strengthen children's viewing skills nor provided an atmosphere that is conducive to the intellectual analysis of the medium that 80 percent of Americans say is their number one source of news—TV. Because people can watch TV without learning an alphabet or spelling, school personnel have not concentrated on teaching children how to view audio-visual products in a sophisticated manner or how to communicate well through audio-visual media. This educational omission is particularly strange in a country where people assume citizens should know how to handle printed information competently if they are to function adequately as members of society.

Very few people have devoted extensive research efforts to discovering the effects of books on children. Most print media research, particularly that involving children, has been devoted to finding out how to increase children's reading and writing skills. If television researchers were really interested in helping society contend more intelligently with audio-visual media, they would stop treating television as a perverter of viewers' minds and instead look on the medium as a neutral communication vehicle that can be used well or badly. Such an attitude might produce studies on how "good" viewers process sequential audio-visual information, how they acquired those skills, and how we can teach those skills to other people. For example, researchers might investigate the differences among people in perceiving, remembering, and juxtaposing audio-visual elements and cues.

In the following section a primitive theory of how people interpret films or TV programs is presented as an illustration of the direction that television research and, subsequently, media education might take. This approach may enable us to teach people to process audio-visual information in a more complex manner and, therefore, to view critically a diverse range of television content.

A Possible Direction for Television Research and Education

According to Gardiner, complex thinkers use a large amount of information to provide many concepts (1974, p. 375). People who think complexly are more likely to be creative, empathic, democratic, and able to cope with complex environments than those who think simplistically. Along the same line of thought, H. Witkin characterizes "field independent" people as those who can extract relevant information elements from an information pool and then reassemble those elements in an innovative manner to arrive at a problem solution. The journalist I.F. Stone, who displays a similar skill, says that citizens have trouble finding out what's going on not because there is a paucity of information but because there is too much information available. Stone sees his task as picking out salient information from the massive amount of material issued by the government and the press and reassembling it in such a manner as to ascribe meaning to a situation. Gardiner's complex thinker may be someone who can recognize and pick out from a mass of information those elements that are important to interpreting a TV program or film and who can reassemble those elements in various ways to come up with a meaning for the work as a whole.

A graphic representation might help illustrate the process by which people interpret films or television programs. In Figure 3-1 "X" is the smallest bit of information stimulus that can be perceived by the source or receiver. These bits of information are labeled "elements" and they refer to a color, a shot angle, a word. Cue "A_c" (or "A_v") is the combination of elements that may be perceived all at once at a specific point in time ("Y_1") in the movie or TV program. The subscripts "c" and "v" refer to the cue as perceived by the creator (or, as often happens in TV or movies, group of creators) or viewer, respectively. An example of a cue might be one point in time during a presidential address where the camera has just

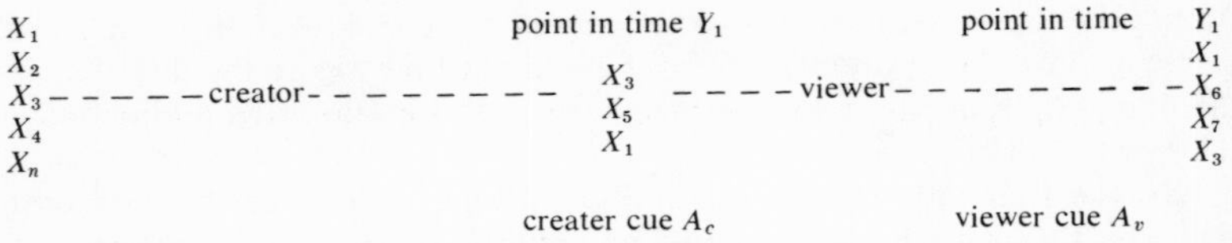

X_1 point in time Y_1 point in time Y_1

$$
\begin{array}{llcl}
X_1 & & \text{point in time } Y_1 & \text{point in time } \quad Y_1 \\
X_2 & & & X_1 \\
X_3 &----\text{creator}-------- & X_3 \quad ----\text{viewer}--------& X_6 \\
X_4 & & X_5 & X_7 \\
X_n & & X_1 & X_3 \\
\end{array}
$$

creater cue A_c viewer cue A_v

(cue Ac_{y1} + cue Bc_{y2} + cue Cc_{y3} ... + cue Nc_{yn}) = creator's product

(cue Av_{y1} + cue Bv_{y2} + cue Cv_{y3} ... + cue Nv_{yn}) = viewer's interpretation

Figure 3-1. The Interpretation of a Sequential Audio-Visual Product.

zoomed in from a long shot and high angle (which emphasized how weak and vulnerable the president looked behind his desk) to a close-up just as he loses his place on the teleprompter and starts to stutter. In spite of the other elements present in the frame that symbolize the power of the presidency such as a bust of Lincoln and an American flag, visually unaware viewers will perceive the president as weak and inept. More astute viewers will understand that the director of the TV coverage purposely created that image and that it does not necessarily reflect the president's real abilities or power.

A receiver will not always interpret a cue in the same manner as the creator. Nor will different receivers interpret the same cue in the same way, hence the difference in subscripts for the same cue as seen by creator and viewer. The reason for this discrepancy is that the elements (X_1, X_2, etc.) included in a specific cue are not the same and are not structured in the same way by the creator and viewer. The creator, through a process both conscious and subconscious, looks at the elements within his stimulus field (current, external, environmental elements or past, internal, memory-stored elements), selects some of them, and juxtaposes them in a specific manner to achieve the effect he wants. The viewer looks at the cue provided by the creator, perceives some but not all of the elements put there by the creator, perceives some elements present in the cue of which the creator may have been unaware, perhaps adds more elements from his own stimulus bank and juxtaposes these elements in an idiosyncratic fashion to come up with an original interpretation of that cue. The two equations at the bottom of Figure 3-1 describe how the creator takes all the cues and combines them in the editing room to form the whole movie or program and how the viewer stores all the cues in his mind and mentally reassembles them at the end of the movie or program in order to ascribe meaning to the entire work. Thus, a viewer becomes a creator in his own right by the process of selection and juxtaposition of elements and cues. Because the viewer actively processes rather than passively absorbs the elements and cues, his interpretation of the work will vary at least slightly, sometimes radically, from the creator's interpretation and no two viewers will interpret the same film or program exactly alike.

Delgado once remarked that "originality and invention are merely a novel combination of old data" (1966, p. 19). The relative unexpectedness of the creator's juxtaposition of elements in cues and, subsequently, of cues in the whole product introduces a degree of entropy into the product and an accompanying inability on the part of the viewer to predict what will happen next. The greater the degree of entropy, the harder it will be for a viewer to ascribe meaning to the whole product and the more disparate will be the various interpretations given the movie or TV program by different viewers. TV programs currently are quite predictable because they use standard "ingredients" and formula-like sequencing. Movies, especially fine ones, are much more entropic and, consequently, not very popular with masses of people unused to pondering meanings of audio-visual works.

Traditionally, education (and now television) has taught children to think in the ways expected within this culture. But what we really want to teach people to do if they are to cope with a quickly changing environment characterized by continually new kinds of problems and a great abundance of largely ephemeral information is to notice many more kinds of and more numbers of elements and cues than ever before and to think of many different ways to juxtapose those elements and cues in order to ascribe meaning to the world around them. Thus, teaching people to process information in new and complex ways, teaching them to cope with unexpected and often controversial juxtapositions, may encourage them to be critical of the status quo.

A Concluding Comment

The poet William Wordsworth wrote that an artist has to educate his audience to appreciate his work. Today, the artist does not just educate the audience to appreciate his work but, according to Picasso, wakes up people in order to "revolutionize their way of identifying things . . . to create images they won't accept. . . . Force them to understand that they're living in a pretty queer world. A world that's not reassuring" (Malraux 1975). But television serves to reinforce the existing culture rather than to help viewers observe critically and perhaps revise that culture. We used to be warned that new media technology could give us a world similar to that portrayed in *1984* or *F. 451,* a world where we would be programmed by media. However, the argument could be made that this is the world we have now, one supported by the FCC, citizen groups, researchers, and educators. New technology could free us from that world and lead us out of an era of controlled scarcity into an age of media abundance. All we would need to use and enjoy that abundance would be the ability to view and hear a wide range of audio-visual information ourselves without a big brother to clean it up.

Picasso told Malraux that "most painters make themselves a little cake-mold; then they make cakes. Always the same cakes." He might have been talking about contemporary American TV. What a shame if Americans continue to eat cake in blissful oblivion.

Case

Office of Communications of the United Church of Christ v. Federal Communications Commission, 359 F. 2d 994 (D.C. Cir., 1966).

References

Cater, D., and S. Strickland. 1975. *TV Violence and the Child: The Evolution and Fate of the Surgeon General's Report* (New York: Russell Sage Foundation).

Cline, V., R. Croft, and S. Currier. 1972. "The Desensitization of Children to Television Violence," *Proceedings of the Annual Convention of the A.P.A.*, 7, Part 1, 99-100.

Collins, W. 1975. "The Developing Child as Viewer," *Journal of Communication*, 25 (Autumn), 35-44.

Committee for Economic Development (Research and Policy Committee). 1975. *Broadcasting and Cable Television: Policies for Diversity and Change* (April).

Delgado, J. 1966. "Manipulation of Behavior by Direct Stimulation of the Brain." Paper presented at the Columbia University Seminars on Technology and Social Change (November), mimeo.

Federal Communications Commission. 1974. *Children's Television Programs: Report and Policy Statement.* 39 FR 39396.

Gardiner, G. 1974. "Cognitive and Motivational Development in Two Experimental Undergraduate Programs in Business," *Academy of Management Journal*, 17 (June), 326-342.

Krasnow, G., and L. Longley. 1973. *The Politics of Broadcast Regulation* (New York: St. Martin's Press).

Leifer, A., and D. Roberts. 1972. "Children's Responses to Televised Violence," *Television and Social Behavior, Vol. II: Television and Social Learning,* ed. J.P. Murray, E.A. Rubinstein, and G.A. Comstock (Washington, D.C.: U.S. Government Printing Office), pp. 43-180.

Liebert, R., and R. Baron. 1972. "Some Immediate Effects of Televised Violence on Children's Behavior," *Developmental Psychology,* 6, 469-475.

Liebert, R., J. Neale, and E. Davidson. 1973. *The Early Window: Effects of Television on Children and Youth* (New York: Pergamon Press).

Maisel, R. 1973. "The Decline of Mass Media," *Public Opinion Quarterly,* 37 (Summer), 159-170.

Malraux, A. 1975. "As Picasso Said, Why Assume That to Look Is to See?" *New York Times Magazine* (November 2), pp. 15 ff.

Meyer, T. 1973. "Children's Perceptions of Justified/Unjustified and Fictional/Real Film Violence," *Journal of Broadcasting,* 17 (Summer), 321-332.

Robinson, M. 1975. "American Political Legitimacy in an Era of Electronic Journalism: Reflections on the Evening News," *Television as a Social Force: New Approaches to TV Criticism,* ed. D. Cater and R. Adler (New York: Praeger), pp. 97-139.

Rosenberg, B., and D. White, eds. 1957. *Mass Culture: The Popular Arts in America* (Glencoe, Ill.: Free Press).

Schiller, H. 1969. *Mass Communications and American Empire* (New York: A.M. Kelley).

Surgeon General, Scientific Advisory Committee on Television and Social Behavior. 1972. *Television and Growing Up: The Impact of Televised Violence* (Washington, D.C.: U.S. Government Printing Office).

Witkin, H. 1972. "The Role of Cognitive Style in Academic Performance and in Teacher-Student Relations." Paper presented at a symposium on "Cognitive Styles, Creativity and Higher Education" sponsored by the Graduate Record Examination Board (Montreal, Canada: November 8-10).

4

Faculty Rights to Bargain Collectively

Thomas C. Britton

Since the late 1960s, the movement in higher education toward collective bargaining for college and university faculty has accelerated greatly. In 1970 the National Labor Relations Board extended the protections of the National Labor Relations Act to many private colleges and universities. There has been active debate in the states over the merits of allowing public employees, in most cases including public college and university faculty, to bargain collectively over wages, hours, and other conditions of employment. Twenty-three states have enacted laws that allow collective bargaining by faculty in public higher education. Of these 23 laws, 20 have been passed in the last three years.

This chapter is aimed at defining and analyzing the legal bases that have recently emerged upon which college and university faculty are able to join organizations that advocate collective bargaining, enter into a collective bargaining relationship with their college or university employer, and engage in strikes. The following discussion is separated into four parts: the recent focus upon the constitutionally protected union rights of college and university faculty in the public sector; the rights of faculty at public colleges and universities under the auspices of state laws explicitly enabling collective bargaining; the rights of faculty at public colleges and universities to bargain collectively with their institutions in the absence of state laws guaranteeing that right; and the rights of faculty at private colleges and universities to bargain collectively with their employer and to engage in concerted activities under federal law.

Two important areas of the developing labor law regarding faculty rights are discussed only incidentally, that is, the development of the constitutional issues surrounding the activity of picketing and the significant body of case law on boycotts in the private sector. In the following discussion, *concerted activities* means primarily the right to strike. The strike is an indispensible element in any discussion of collective bargaining since historically the strike has been used to compel bargaining. The process by which decisions are made regarding the inclusion or exclusion of employees in the group to be represented by the bargaining agent, referred to as *unit determination,* is also discussed only incidentally.

Constitutionally Protected Rights

Although the right to freedom of association is referred to as a First Amendment constitutional right, it springs from no specific language of the Constitution. The courts, by reading the First Amendment as a whole, have developed the concept of freedom of association. The states have been prevented from abridging this First Amendment right by virtue of the Fourteenth Amendment (*Gitlow* v. *New York*).

Questions regarding the right of public employees to associate have recently shifted away from those involving internal security to other questions. Included are the right of public employees to join a union, which springs from the Constitution, and rights to bargain collectively and engage in concerted activity, which exist only if created by laws enacted by the state or federal governments.

The constitutional right of public employees to associate freely has not always received judicial protection. An historical example comes in the form of an opinion written by Justice Oliver Wendell Holmes while sitting on the Supreme Court of Massachusetts (*McAuliff* v. *Mayor*). The case involved the discharge of a policeman who violated a departmental regulation that provided no policeman would be allowed to solicit money or aid any political purpose. The policeman involved had become a member of a "political committee," was discharged, and sought reinstatement. Justice Holmes wrote:

The petitioner may have a constitutional right to talk politics, but he has no constitutional right to be a policeman. There are few employments for hire in which the servant does not agree to suspend his constitutional right of free speech, as well as idleness, by the implied terms of his contract. The servant cannot complain, as he takes the employment on the terms which are offered him. On the same principle, the city may set any reasonable condition upon holding offices within its control. (at 519)

A more recent example of the same principle enunciated by Justice Holmes is found in *Adler* v. *Board of Education*, decided by the Supreme Court in 1952, in which a New York statute disqualifying persons from state public employment on the basis of membership in an organization advocating the overthrow of the government by force, violence, or any unlawful means was upheld as not violative of constitutional limitations on state action.

Both *Adler* and *McAuliff* demonstrate that the right to freedom of association is not always absolute, but may be limited by reasonable regulations promulgated by the states. These two cases involved "political" associations. Several courts have now dealt with questions of the reasonableness of restraint on freedom of association in the context of "economic" associations: unions.

In the past several years, there have been many cases involving the rights of municipal employees that serve as a basis for analogies concerning, first, public school teachers and, then, faculty at public colleges and universities. A conclusion reached with respect to municipal employees has generally been that discharge based solely on union membership violates the constitutional prohibitions against interference with the freedom of association (*Atkins* v. *City of Charlotte*). However, the courts have been quick to point out that the presence of the right of municipal employees to join a union does not confer the rights to enter into a collective bargaining agreement or to strike. The states and their political subdivisions are not constitutionally compelled to bargain or enter into a contract with a union representing faculty of public colleges or universities. The Court of Appeals for the Seventh Circuit, holding that a probationary public school teacher could not be dismissed solely on the basis of union activities, stated that it was well settled that public school teachers have the right to join unions as a part of freedom of association, and unjustifiable interference with the teachers' right to organize violates the Due Process Clause of the Fourteenth Amendment (*McLaughlin* v. *Tilendis*).

When we turn from the right to join to the right to strike, we find that strikes by public employees have long been condemned as against the public interest, and that striking is not a constitutionally protected activity. President Franklin D. Roosevelt in a letter to the president of the National Federation of Federal Employees, dated August 16, 1937, stated: "[A] strike by public employees manifests nothing less than an intent on their part to prevent or obstruct the operation of Government until their demands are satisfied. Such action, looking toward the paralysis of Government by those who have sworn to support it, is unthinkable and intolerable" (Vogel 1950, p. 612). A recent decision involving the right of postal employees to strike has reemphasized the general opinion that, in the absence of a statutorily created right, public employees may not legally strike (*Postal Clerks* v. *Blount*).

Several generalizations based on case law might be made with respect to the constitutional rights of faculty at public colleges and universities. Faculty may join organizations that advocate a collective bargaining relationship with their college or university employers and that also encourage the use of concerted activities, strikes in particular. Neither tenured or nontenured faculty may be discharged solely on the basis of union membership. However, public colleges and universities are not constitutionally compelled to bargain or enter into a contract with unions representing faculty. Strikes by faculty at public colleges and universities, although arguably a form of economic expression, may be limited by state law.

Public College and University Faculty Bargaining Under State Law

Because the National Labor Relations Act excludes public employees from its protections, faculty at public colleges and universities must look to state statutory and case law to determine their rights relating to collective bargaining and concerted activities. Many states have enacted laws that describe public employees' rights with respect to collective bargaining and concerted activities.

These state laws can generally be separated into two categories: The first is the "meet and confer" statute, which imposes no duty on the employer to bargain with the representative of employees and which creates little machinery for impasse resolution. This type of statute, represented by the Rhode Island statute (Gen. Laws of R.I., sec. 36-11-1, et seq.), provides a vehicle for communication between the organization selected by public employees and their employer without requiring adoption of any agreement they might reach. The employer retains the power unilaterally to determine the terms "agreed" upon. The second is the "collective bargaining" law, which imposes a duty on the public employer to bargain with representatives, to incorporate the agreed-upon terms into a collective bargaining agreement, and which provides machinery for impasse resolution, represented by Hawaii's statute (Hawaii Rev. Stat., secs. 89-1 - 89-20).

The Rhode Island statute is mild in terms of the duties imposed upon employers and employees and the machinery and procedures established to guide the bargaining. The act provides that employees of that state have the right to organize, designate a representative, and negotiate with the "chief executive or his designee" on matters relating to wages, hours, and working conditions. The statute also requires the chief executive to recognize an organization designated as the employees' bargaining representative.

The provision that distinguishes this statute from those in most other states provides that "it shall be the obligation of the chief executive or his designee to *meet* and *confer* in good faith with representatives of the state employees' bargaining agent. . . ." Any issues that remain unresolved after 30 days of bargaining are submitted to the state labor relations board. If within ten days after submission to the conciliator a resolution has not been reached, the conciliator makes findings of facts and recommendations to both parties. Any issues that remain unresolved voluntarily are submitted to binding arbitration. This is not as ominous as it sounds, since the arbitrator's decisions regarding wages are not binding. The act is helpful in that it establishes the right of faculty at public colleges and universities to bargain through a representative and allows the chief executive to enter into a collective bargaining agreement with the faculty representative.

The Hawaii Act, by contrast, is a comprehensive collective bargaining act granting collective bargaining rights to virtually all state employees except top-level managerial personnel, members of the National Guard, and part-time and student employees. The legislature declared that the policy of the state is to promote harmonious and cooperative relations between government and its employees and to protect the public by ensuring continuity in the operations of government. The act specifically describes the faculty at the University of Hawaii as an appropriate bargaining unit. Faculty have the right to organize and join unions and to bargain collectively with their employer. The statute further imposes a duty upon the public employer to bargain with faculty with respect to wages, hours, and other terms and conditions of employment.

Hawaii's is one of only five state collective bargaining laws that allows public employees, except guards and court personnel, the right to strike. Like the other four states, Hawaii allows strikes only after a considerable effort has been made to reach agreement. If a strike occurs after the collective bargaining processes have been completely used and exhausted, it will not be prohibited unless or until such a strike creates a clear and present danger or threat to the health, safety, or welfare of the public.

State statutes governing collective bargaining between faculty at colleges and universities and their public employers vary widely in terms of the duties imposed and the rights guaranteed. In most statutes, more attention appears to have been given to impasse resolution than any other phase of collective bargaining. One might generalize that greater attention has been paid by state legislators to avoiding interruption of public business than to securing rights for public employees comparable to those enjoyed by private sector employees.

Public Faculty Bargaining in the Absence of State Legislation

Faculty in a majority of states, if they bargain at all, do so in the absence of explicit state or federal rights. In those states without enabling legislation, collective bargaining by faculty takes place only with the consent of the public college or university employer and gives rise to two questions, both focusing on the power of the public *employers* rather than on the rights of the employees.

The first is whether the public employer has the authority to enter into a collective bargaining agreement with a union representing its employees. In some states, the courts have held that the public employer, even though desiring to bargain with public employees, lacks the authority to bargain with and enter into collective bargaining agreements with organizations representing public employees. This position has been supported by a variety of arguments; however, the most common are based upon a traditional delegation of authority rationale, that is, once the legislature has given a part of its power to a public agency, that agency may not in turn delegate that power to unelected and uncontrolled private organizations, such as unions. Applied in the context of public employee labor relations, this means that a public employer has only those powers delegated to it by the state legislature. Absent enabling legislation, the employer also has no power to bargain and cannot redelegate those powers given it to determine employee working conditions.

In 1964 the Supreme Court of Alabama held that a public agency, the Water Works Board of the City of Birmingham, could not bargain or enter into a collective bargaining agreement with a labor organization concerning wages, hours, and conditions of employment in the absence of express statutory or constitutional authority to do so (*International Union of Operating Engineers* v. *Water Works Board of City of Birmingham*). The Supreme Court of Nebraska in 1965 reached the same result as did the court in Alabama (*I.B.E.W.* v. *City of Hastings*). The case arose out of an order by the Supreme Court of Industrial Relations requiring the city of Hastings to bargain with employees of its public works department. The court was faced with interpreting the act giving powers to the Supreme Court of Industrial Relations, which was silent with respect to public employees. The court stated a general rule regarding statutory construction:

It has long been accepted in this state that the enumeration of certain powers in a statute implies the exclusion of all others not fairly incidental to those enumerated, and that an affirmative description of specific circumstances in which certain powers may be exercised implies a negative as to the exercise of such powers in circumstances not enumerated. (at 825)

The court went on to discuss collective bargaining between public employers and public employees and stated that, "However desirable extrajudicial discussion between the parties or a court encouraged settlement might seem in effectuating the policies of the statutes, the statutory grant of power does not extend to the órder here" (at 826).

In another line of cases, state courts have held that, in the absence of statutory language, public employers may bargain and enter into collective bargaining agreements with public employees concerning wages, hours, and conditions of employment. This power has been implied generally from language in statutes giving the public employer the power to hire employees and determine wages, hours, and other conditions of employment. One writer (Dole 1969) suggests that to allow a public employer to use individual form contracts applicable to a large group of employees is little different than negotiating one master contract applicable to the same group of employees, and to approve of one practice and not the other has the effect of "exalting form over substance."

Two leading cases holding that public employers have the power, in the absence of legislation, to bargain and enter into agreements with organizations representing public employees were decided by the highest state courts of Connecticut and Iowa. The Connecticut decision was rendered in 1951 and marks the beginning of a trend toward allowing public employers to enter into collective bargaining agreements in the absence of explicit legislation granting such authority (*Norwalk Teachers' Association* v. *Board of Education of City of Norwalk*). The Supreme Court of Connecticut held that a board of education could, in its discretion, choose to bargain with a representative of its teachers so long as any agreement reached did not involve the surrender of the board's legal prerogatives. That is, the board could not agree to allow binding arbitration on a subject over which the board had exclusive discretion through legislative directive. The court further held that members of the teachers' association had no right to strike.

The Iowa Supreme Court, in a case involving a dispute between the Board of Regents of the University of Northern Iowa and nonacademic employees, addressed itself to the question of the Regents' implied authority (*Board of Regents* v. *Packing House, Food and Allied Workers, Local 1258*). The Iowa court held that the Regents had the power to "confer and consult" and enter into a collective bargaining agreement with representatives of its employees by virtue of the Regents' power to hire, fix wages, and determine other conditions of employment. The court found that the signing of an agreement by the Regents involved no improper delegation of authority, as the Regents were not compelled to sign an agreement and the final decision with respect to terms of the agreement remained with the Regents.

Once it has been determined that a public employer does have the implied authority to enter into collective bargaining agreements, the second question arises, that is, whether a collective bargaining agreement entered into by a public employer and an organization representing a majority of, but not all, employees in a given unit is binding upon all employees in the unit for which the organization bargained. This question has not been dealt with substantially by the courts. The Supreme Court of Connecticut in *Norwalk* did not address itself specifically to the question of exclusive representation; however, the court's opinion can be read to imply that exclusive representation would not be permissible. The court stated, "It would seem to make no difference theoretically whether the negotiations are with a committee of the whole association or with individuals or small related groups, so long as any agreement made with the committee is confined to members of the association" (at 486). In the case involving the University of Northern Iowa, the Iowa Supreme Court deferred to the legislature to act with respect to exclusive representation and held that the judiciary would not make the concept of exclusive representation operative in the context of public employment. The Iowa court referred to exclusive representation as an "industrial concept" not necessarily applicable in public employee labor relations.

The leading case cited as being contrary to the Iowa court's determination regarding exclusive representation arose in Illinois (*Chicago Division, Illinois Education Association* v. *Board of Education*). This case involved two organizations representing public school teachers: the Board of Education for the City of Chicago and a private citizen. In the written opinion of the appellate court which heard the case, the arguments of each group and the private citizen were repeated, and without adding clarifying language of its own the court held that the Board of Education had the power to enter into a collective bargaining agreement with an exclusive representative of classroom teachers.

In general, faculty at public colleges and universities in states without a statute enabling collective bargaining must look to their public employers to determine if they will consent to bargaining, and then the employer must look to the courts to determine if they have the power to enter into a collective bargaining agreement. The question regarding exclusive representation is one to which few answers exist, but the question is important at those institutions at which a single union does not command a large majority.

Bargaining at Private Colleges and Universities

Congress enacted the National Labor Relations Act (29 U.S.C. 14l) as an exercise of its constitutional power to regulate interstate commerce. The act guarantees that employees may organize; choose representatives for purposes of collective bargaining with their employer; and engage in concerted activities, including strikes, picketing, and boycotts, aimed at enforcing bargaining demands.

There is no language in the act that would exclude the faculty of private colleges and universities from its coverage. For many years the National Labor Relations Board took the position that because the bulk of activity at private colleges and universities related only indirectly, if at all, to interstate commerce, it should not exercise jurisdiction over them (*Columbia University*). In 1970 the board in a dramatic move reversed itself in a case involving Syracuse and Cornell Universities, specifically overriding its earlier doctrine (*Cornell University*). The board took notice of the greatly increased impact that higher education had on interstate commerce and the difficulty of separating those activities that were commercial and those that were "intimately connected with the charitable purposes and educational activities of the institutions" (Finkin 1969, p. 609). The board's decision in *Cornell* and the jurisdictional regulation promulgated as the result of *Cornell* allowed the faculty at over 80 percent of the private colleges and universities in the nation to bargain and engage in the concerted activities allowable under the act.

Once the board has asserted jurisdiction, certain duties and prohibitions come into play that are aimed at preventing employers from frustrating or otherwise interfering with employees' rights guaranteed under section 7 of the act. Provisions of the act declare that it is an unfair labor practice for an employer to dominate or interfere with the employee union, to discriminate in hiring or tenure of employment on the basis of union membership, and to discharge an employee because he has filed charges or given testimony under the act. A key provision of the act makes it an unfair labor practice for an employer to refuse to bargain collectively with representatives of his employees.

Few cases involving colleges and universities have been brought before the board; however, it is clear that if jurisdictional requirements are met, the faculty at a private college and university may organize unions; force the college or university to bargain regarding wages, hours, and other terms and conditions of employment; and strike, picket, or boycott, with a few limited exceptions, in order to enforce their bargaining demands. If the college or university engages in activities designed to restrain or coerce the faculty in the exercise of rights guaranteed under the act, the faculty can seek a remedy before the National Labor Relations Board.

Since the act has been interpreted to apply to only 80 percent of private colleges and universities, the remaining 20 percent are left in a legal no-man's-land with respect to collective bargaining, looking to state labor laws for the right to bargain collectively. In many states, however, these private colleges and universities may turn to "mini-Taft-Hartley Acts" enacted to operate in such a situation.

Conclusion

Faculty at both private and public colleges and universities have the right *to form and join organizations,* the purpose of which is to advocate collective bargaining with their college or university employer. This right is guaranteed by the First Amendment and the National Labor Relations Act. In a majority of institutions, faculty have the right *to bargain collectively* with their college or university employer. This faculty right at a majority of *private* colleges and universities is the product of the National Labor Relations Act. That act also allows faculty to engage in strikes aimed at enforcing bargaining demands. If faculty at *public* colleges and universities have the right to bargain collectively and engage in concerted activities, this right has been created by state statutory law. In some of those states *without statutory law* enabling faculty to bargain, the courts have found that public colleges and universities have implied authority to allow faculty to bargain collectively and the implied authority to enter into collective bargaining agreements with faculty. The public college or university in such a state has the option to bargain; it is not required to do so. In other states without state legislation, however, the courts have held that public *employers* do not have the authority to bargain collectively with employees or to enter into collective bargaining agreements, because to do so would be to delegate to a private organization authority delegated to the employer by the legislature.

Cases

Adler v. Board of Education, 342 U.S. 485 (1952).

Atkins v. City of Charlotte, 296 F. Supp. 1068 (W.D.N.C., 1969).

Board of Regents v. Packing House, Food and Allied Workers, Local 1258, 175 N.W.2d 110 (Iowa, 1970).

Columbia University, 29 L.R.R.M. 1098 (1951).

Cornell University, 74 L.R.R.M. 1269 (1970).

Gitlow v. New York, 268 U.S. 652 (1925).

Illinois Education Association v. Board of Education, 76 Ill.App.2d 456, 222 N.E.2d 243 (1966).

I.B.E.W. v. City of Hastings, 179 Neb. 455, 138 N.W.2d 822 (1965).

International Union of Operating Engineers v. Water Works Board of City of Birmingham, 276 Ala. 462, 163 So.2d 619 (1964).

McAuliff v. Mayor, 155 Mass. 216, 29 N.E. 517 (1892).

McLaughlin v. Tilendis, 398 F.2d 287 (7th Cir., 1968).

Norwalk Teachers' Assn. v. Board of Education of City of Norwalk, 138 Conn. 269, 83 A.2d 482 (1951).

Postal Clerks v. Blount, 325 F.Supp. 879 (D.D.C., 1971); aff'd, 404 U.S. 802 (1971).

References

Richard F. Dole. 1969. "State and Local Public Employees Collective Bargaining in the Absence of Explicit Legislative Authorization," *Iowa Law Review*, 54, 539-559.

Matthew W. Finkin. 1969. "The N.L.R.B. in Higher Education," *University of Toledo Law Review*, 5, 608-655.

Isadore Vogel. 1950. "What About Rights of the Public Employee," *Labor Law Journal*, 1, 604-618.

5

The American Civil Religion and the First Amendment

Raleigh W. Smith, Jr.

We are a religious people whose institutions presuppose a Supreme Being.

Justice Douglas,
In *Zorach* v. *Clauson*

The Supreme Court, charged with interpreting the First Amendment, has had to deal with intricate questions concerning the parameters of the prohibition that "Congress shall make no law respecting an establishment of religion or prohibiting the free exercise thereof. . . ." The question is complex because the American people have a religious core that will not be denied independent expression and a government whose influence pervades all corners of life. Substantial amounts of commentary have evolved, of course, on just what the First Amendment prohibition means. There has also been considerable comment on the American civil religion in an attempt to elucidate what it means to be "a religious people whose institutions presuppose a Supreme Being." I do not propose to suggest a new reading of either. Rather, I hope to call attention to the concept of the American civil religion within the context of the interpretation of the First Amendment, thereby exploring a little-noticed relationship. (For further exploration, see Richey and Jones 1974, pp. 273-78; Garret 1974, 193-94.)

The applicability of the concept of a civil religion to America was first deliberated by Robert Bellah in 1967 in his "Civil Religion in America," an essay both soundly praised and roundly condemned. Bellah argued that one theme in the American tradition was "the obligation, both collective and individual, to carry out God's will on earth. This obligation, which served to motivate the Founding Fathers, has remained ever since" (1967, p. 25). He pointed out that this inviolable commitment, like other religions, reveals itself in its canonical scripture (the Declaration and the Constitution), its saints (Washington), and its martyrs (Lincoln). Moreover, the American civil religion is not sectarian—it has deliberately es-

49

chewed being explicitly confessional by selective borrowing from various religious traditions in such a way that "the average American saw no conflict between" the civil religion and his own sectarian religion (pp. 34-35). Indeed, the American civil religion was "never anticlerical or militantly secular" (p. 34); rather, it is a comfortable belief that God and right will prevail.

By adopting G.K. Chesterton's characterization of America as "the nation with the soul of a church" for his title, Sidney E. Mead in that same year adroitly summarized Bellah's argument. The author, a vigorous proponent of the American civil religion, further contended that this faith is synergistic because it conceives the churches as embodying "the simultaneous action of separate agencies working in combination to effect an end" (1967, p. 55). The "end," of course, is God's purpose, a design in which America has a particular place.

Will Herberg, in essence reiterating what he had propounded in *Protestant, Catholic, Jew,* has now argued that even though the American civil religion is "a noble religion, celebrating some very noble civic virtues," it is idolatry insofar as it is seen to include the biblical religions "in its overarching unity" (Herberg 1974, pp. 86-87). Others, too, have raised serious questions regarding the concept of a civil religion, such as its validity for blacks (Long 1974) and for ethnics (Greeley 1973). There are semantic problems with the very idea in itself (Garret 1974), and still other scholars propose methodological refinements (Wilson 1974; Marty 1974).

Only two premises emerge clearly from published debate: almost all writers agree that there is a civil religion and that it is accepted by most Americans. The tenets of this religion are not hard to surmise. I suggest the following: God exists. He takes an interest in human affairs and most particularly in America. And two implications immediately follow: First, what America does and how she does it are of transcendent importance; America is answerable to God. Second, acquiescence to this "faith" requires public recognition, hence the set of religious symbols that permeate our public life. The most obvious of these tokens include the phrase "under God" in the flag salute, the choice of "In God We Trust" as a motto, and the incorporation of Catholic, Protestant, and Jewish clergy into important public ceremonies, like inaugurations, the opening of House and Senate sessions, swearings-in—the list is endless. The civil religion seems to be to most Americans a substratum both underlying particular religions and encompassing America's purpose.

II

While the concept of civil religion has implications at once wider (Sandoz 1972; Strout 1974) and narrower (Novak 1972; Henderson 1972), if the version of the concept offered here is a sound one and has, in some form, been a continuing thread througout American history, its relationship to the First Amendment prohibition that "Congress shall make no law respecting an establishment of religion or prohibiting the free exercise thereof . . ." comes into immediate question. Vocal allegiance to a separation of church and state is a cornerstone of our democracy. Do Americans ignore an inherent incompatability by their adoption of civil religion? I think not because the Founding Fathers built their Republic carefully (see McLaughlin 1973, pp. 197-255). In the first place, this amendment was clearly a prohibition directed against Congress alone; established churches existed in several states, and a variety of religious tests for public office were in use at the time of the adoption of the Bill of Rights. Of course, by employing the doctrine of incorporation, the Court has made the First Amendment applicable to all of the states, presumably limiting them also. (Some states have stronger constitutional prohibitions regarding religious freedom than the federal one.)

The First Amendment's prohibition, taken in its most obvious form, has two components: a requirement (at the national level) that all taxpayers contribute to the support of a particular religious denomination or that all applicants for admission to certain professions or public office join a specific religious denomination, and a prohibition on laws designating or prohibiting particular religious practices. (Both stem from what establishment meant under English law at the time. The Church of England received tax support; the holding of public office, receiving a commission in the army or navy, and taking a degree at Oxford or Cambridge all required that one be a communicant of the Church of England; and Parliament was responsible for any changes made in the Book of Common Prayer.) Indeed, James Madison certainly had both elements in mind in the debate over the Bill of Rights in the First Congress: "Mr. Madison said he apprehended the meaning of the words to be that Congress should not establish a religion and enforce the legal observance of it by law, nor compel men to worship in any manner contrary to their conscience" (*Annals of Congress* 1834, p. 842). In short, the federal government could show no preference to any single religious group. (It might very well be argued that the prohibition of a religious test for office in the Constitution itself already accomplishes this governmental restraint.)

The First Amendment, in its original conception, was consonant with government aid to religion in general. For instance, the Northwest Ordinance of 1787 supported this view: "Religion, morality, and knowledge being necessary to good government and the happiness of mankind, schools and the means of education shall forever be encouraged." Even those religious groups most active in support of disestablishment did not always envision a complete detachment of church and state. Among the various alternatives proposed in the debates in Virginia over disestablishment were maintaining the tax for support of religion with (a) the majority of voters in a parish determining to which denomination the money would go, or (b) the individual taxpayer being able to specify his chosen denomination. In the absence of a religious preference, the state would assign taxes to any educational or charitable purpose (McLaughlin 1973, pp. 223-226).

To be sure, the notion of a "wall of separation" between church and state was present and advocated, but it had its deepest roots and its principal adherents in the small pietist groups who insisted that state support of religion meant state control, thus endangering true religion and especially theirs (see Howe 1965, pp. 5-10). The whole concept of an American civil religion, on the other hand, held that all religions have a common core and that each promotes the same desirable ends, thereby maintaining consistency with a policy of government support for religion as long as it was nonpreferential. These early delineations are brought more clearly into focus when contemporary court cases are considered. The justices of the Supreme Court have been forced to deal with this shadowy presence of civil religion, and in doing so, have produced some distortions in the original images.

III

A discussion of three landmark church-state cases points out certain questions regarding the American civil religion that have had to be decided by the Court. These decisions reflect, in part, the incorporate nature of contemporary interpretation of the First Amendment. But other considerations intrude to complicate the problem. In one case the Court had to deliberate an objection, raised on particular sectarian grounds, to a fundamental ceremony of the civil religion; in another it decided whether the practices of a particular denomination are compatible with the civil religion; and in the last case the Court gave the First Amendment an interpretation that is blatantly incompatible with the proposed concept of civil religion.

In the Flag Salute cases (*Minersville School District* v. *Gobitis; West Virginia State Board of Education* v. *Barnette*), the Supreme Court dealt with the refusal of Jehovah's Witnesses to engage in a required flag salute, a refusal based on their contention that the salute constituted idolatry forbidden by scripture. That the Court reversed itself—first upholding the compulsory flag salute and then deciding, after all, that the requirement did violate "free exercise of religion"—suggests the imprecise nature of an entity that everyone recognizes but that few attempt to define. The ultimate problem lies in the fact that the flag salute is a secular ceremony (similar to the use of a creed in religious observance) and its use is attacked on theological grounds. In this connection, one should note that the Jehovah's Witnesses constitute a particular problem for the American civil religion in that they reject participation in the political process, including voting, because of their belief in the imminence of the end of the world. The conflict is due to the fact that their emphasis on the otherworldly denies entirely the relevance of the political.

In an earlier case (*Pierce* v. *Society of Sisters of the Holy Name*), the Court struck down an Oregon statute outlawing Roman Catholic parochial schools. Here the Court reemphasized the nonsectarian character of American civil religion. But a far more controversial case, the school prayer decision, illustrates the magnitude of the problem when a Court interpretation of the First Amendment falls into obvious conflict with civil religion.

The school prayer at issue in *Engel* v. *Vitale* was as succinct a formulation of the American civil religion as one can find anywhere. It reads: "Almighty God, we acknowledge our dependence upon Thee, and we beg Thy blessings upon us, our parents, our teachers and our country." This prayer included the most prominent features of the American civil religion, that is, a belief in God and a belief that America is responsible to God for her actions. It was deliberately, almost painfully, nonsectarian. In ruling the prayer to be unconstitutional, the Court argued, in effect, that civil religion is incompatible with the establishment clause, thereby placing itself directly athwart a deeply ingrained and widespread idea in American society. It is no wonder, then, that the most substantial attempt to overturn a Supreme Court decision by constitutional amendment which has occurred in response to any recent Supreme Court decision was mounted in opposition to *Engel* v. *Vitale*.

That the Court did, indeed, place itself in a position of opposition to the American civil religion was evident in Justice Stewart's dissent in the case. He placed school prayer in the same category as that of the invocations to God that are used on public occasions, in essence pointing out as acceptable those features of public life that are the visible and outward signs of the existence of the American civil religion. Of note is the fact that both Robert N. Bellah and Justice Stewart point out that every American president has invoked God in his inaugural address.

The most vexing of questions in this area is that of government aid to parochial schools. The place of such aid is not altogether clear within the context of the American civil religion. Monetary aid, although in theory capable of being nondiscriminatory, does in fact favor those religions (Roman Catholic, Lutheran Church—Missouri Synod, and Seventh Day Adventist, for example) whose overall denominational policy includes provision for parochial schools. However, most state-aid plans for aid to parochial schools have been rejected by the Court on First Amendment grounds. This position contrasts sharply with the upholding of certain forms of aid to sectarian colleges (*Tilton* v. *Richardson*), perhaps reflecting the fact that most denominations have colleges and universities.

IV

Established Court policy in church-state relations proves incompatible with actual American practice regarding the upholding of civil religion. A remarkable contrast exists between what is taken to be the definitive reading of the First Amendment in our own era and actual American custom. The latter appears to impose restraints that the Court recognizes in fact but not in theory. In addition, certain inadequacies in the Court's recent reading of the First Amendment have provoked a dichotomy between that amendment and the American civil religion not present at the Founding.

The Supreme Court's definitive reading of the First Amendment occurred in Justice Black's opinion for the Court in *Everson* v. *Board of Education:*

The "establishment of religion" clause of the First Amendment means at least this: Neither a state nor the federal government can set up a church. Neither can pass laws which aid one religion, aid all religions, or prefer one religion over another. Neither can force nor influence a person to attend or to remain away from church against his will, or force him to profess a belief or disbelief in any religion. No person can be punished for entertaining or professing religious belief or disbeliefs, for church attendance or non-attendance. No tax in any amount, large or small, can be levied to support any religious activities or institutions, whatever they may be called, or whatever form they may adopt to teach or practice religion. Neither a state nor the federal government can, openly or secretly, participate in the affairs of any religious organizations or groups and *vice versa*. In the words of Jefferson, the clause against establishment by law was intended to erect "a wall of separation between church and State."

The inadequacy of Justice Black's statement as a basis for public policy is indicated by a brief enumeration of a few of the many ways in which religion is supported by state and federal governments. Tax money pays military chaplains and their staffs, builds and maintains churches on military bases, and supports chaplains in prisons, both federal and state. The tax laws, by allowing one to deduct contributions to a church from his taxable income, provide from 14 percent to 70 percent of that contribution, depending on one's tax bracket. By exempting most church property from taxation, municipalities indirectly support religion by providing free to them city services for which others pay via taxation.

This catalog is partial. However, the Court has refrained, and very

55

likely will continue to refrain, from moving restrictively into these well-established areas of state support of religion precisely because these practices are consistent with the American civil religion even if not with the contemporary reading of the First Amendment. The American civil religion plays a significant, if unrecognized, role in determining Court policy making. Indeed, the manner in which the civil religion constrains the Court may be taken as indicative of its inconsistency.

Cases

Engel v. Vitale, 370 U.S. 421 (1962).

Everson v. Board of Education, 330 U.S. 504 (1947).

Minersville School District v. Gobitis, 310 U.S. 586 (1940).

Pierce v. Society of Sisters of the Holy Name, 268 U.S. 510 (1925).

Tilton v. Richardson, 403 U.S. 672 (1971).

West Virginia State Board of Education v. Barnette, 316 U.S. 624 (1943).

Zorach v. Clauson, 343 U.S. 306 (1952).

References

Annals of Congress. 1834. *The Debates and Proceedings in the Congress of the United States: the First Congress, 1789-1791* (Washington: Gales & Seaton).

Bellah, Robert N. 1967. "Civil Religion in America," *Daedalus,* XCVI (Winter), 1-21. Reprinted in Richey and Jones 1974, pp. 21-44.

_____. 1974. "American Civil Religion in the 1970's," in *American Civil Religion,* ed. Russell E. Richey and Donald G. Jones (New York: Harper and Row), pp. 255-272.

Garret, James Leo, Jr. 1973. "'Civil Religion': Clarifying the Semantic Problem," *Journal of Church and State,* XVI (Spring), 187-195.

Greeley, Andrew M. 1973. "Civil Religion and Ethnic Americans," *Worldview,* XVI (February), 21-27.

Henderson, Charles P., Jr. 1972. *The Nixon Theology* (New York: Harper and Row).

Herberg, Will. 1974. "America's Civil Religion: What It Is and Whence It Comes," in *American Civil Religion,* ed. Russell E. Richey and Donald G. Jones (New York: Harper and Row), pp. 76-88.

Howe, Mark DeWolfe. 1965. *The Garden and the Wilderness: Religion and Government in American Constitutional History* (Chicago: The University of Chicago Press).

Long, Charles H. 1974. "Civil Rights—Civil Religion," in *American Civil Religion*, ed. Russell E. Richey and Donald G. Jones (New York: Harper and Row), pp. 211-221.

McLaughlin, William G. 1973. "The Role of Religion in the Revolution: Liberty of Conscience and Cultural Cohension in the New Nation," *Essays on the American Revolution*, ed. Stephen G. Kurtz and James H. Huston (Chapel Hill: University of North Carolina Press), pp. 197-255.

Marty, Martin E. 1974. "Two Kinds of Two Kinds of Civil Religion." in *American Civil Religion*, ed. Russell E. Richey and Donald G. Jones (New York: Harper and Row), pp. 139-157.

Mead, Sidney E. 1967. "The 'Nation with the Soul of a Church,'" *Church History*, XXXIV (September), 262-283. Reprinted in Richey and Jones 1974, pp. 45-75.

Novak, Michael. 1972. *Choosing Our King: Powerful Symbols in Presidential Politics* (New York: Macmillan).

Richey, Russell E., and Donald G. Jones, eds. 1974. *American Civil Religion* (New York: Harper and Row).

Sandoz, Ellis. 1972. "The Civil Theology of Liberal Democracy: Locke and His Predecessors," *The Journal of Politics*, XXXIV (February), 2-38.

Strout, Cushing. 1974. *The New Heavens and the New Earth: Political Religion in America* (New York: Harper and Row).

Wilson, John R. 1974. "A Historian's Approach to Civil Religion," in *American Civil Religion*, ed. Russell E. Richey and Donald G. Jones (New York: Harper and Row), pp. 115-138.

Additional References

Bellah, Robert N. 1974. *The Broken Covenant: American Civil Religion in Time of Trial* (New York: Seabury Press).

———. 1975. "Rejoinder to Lockwood: 'Bellah and his Critics,'" *Anglican Theological Review*, LVII (October), 416-423.

Lockwood, Joan. 1975. "Bellah and his Critics: An Ambiguity in Bellah's Concept of Civil Religion," *Anglican Theological Review*, LVII (October), 395-416.

Richardson, Herbert W. 1975. "Robert Bellah's 'The Broken Covenant,'" *Anglican Theological Review*, LVII (October), 480-490.

6

The Supreme Court and Church-State Policy

Daryl R. Fair

The popular image of the United States Supreme Court with respect to church-state policy and civil liberties policy in general is that of judges laying out rules and standards for the rest of society to follow. Actually the role of the Court, although by no means unimportant, is somewhat more modest than that. Perhaps the Court can best be viewed as one actor in a cyclical policy-making process.

The Policy Process

Charles O. Jones depicts the policy cycle as consisting of five stages: getting problems to government, formulating proposals, legitimating policy, applying policy, and evaluating policy (Jones 1970, pp. 27-134). The Court's greatest role is in legitimating policy and overseeing its application. In the remaining three stages, policy makers other than the Court loom larger. Because the policy process is cyclical, Court pronouncements made during the legitimating and application stages of one cycle become inputs to the processes of getting problems to government and formulating proposals in subsequent policy cycles.

Getting Problems to Government

Interest groups make an important contribution in getting problems to government. The major religious denominations were instrumental in raising the problems that led to the adoption of released-time religious instruction programs in many public schools following World War I. Groups and individuals perform the function of challenging existing church-state policy. The Jehovah's Witnesses successfully questioned a wide variety of municipal ordinances and state laws as applied to them. The American Civil Liberties Union has been involved in a number of suits challenging state aid to parochial schools, as have the Committee for Public Education and Religious Liberty, Americans United for Separation of Church and State, and the American Jewish Congress. Individuals such as Vashti McCollum (released time) and Madalyn Murray (Bible reading) have also brought suits against existing church-state policies.

The general course of events may also bring out problems not previously perceived. The change of a community from a condition of religious homogeneity to one of religious pluralism may bring to the attention of government a host of issues. Thus, private individuals, the groups with which they are associated, and events in general all serve to get church-state problems to government.

Formulating Proposals

The above-named interest groups are also involved in formulating proposals on church-state policy. Not only do they suggest doctrine to the courts in which they bring cases, but they also propose policies to other decision makers. Church groups have often suggested released-time religious instruction plans to school boards and state parochial school aid to legislatures. Group proposals must be introduced formally by public officials, of course, and these officials sometimes develop proposals substantially or entirely on their own. The Elementary and Secondary Education Act (ESEA) of 1965, for example, was developed almost exclusively by the executive branch of the national government (Eidenberg and Morey 1969, pp. 75-95).

The ESEA has great significance for church-state policy because it provides special programs for educationally disadvantaged students from low-income families; students from both public and parochial schools are eligible for these programs, which are developed and administered by state and local public educational agencies. This arrangement, sometimes called the "church-state settlement," was probably written with an eye to past pronouncements of the Supreme Court, particularly the Court's statement that government financial aid to religious institutions is a violation of the Constitution, but public welfare measures that benefit children are permissible even when the benefits go to parochial school students (*Everson* v. *Board of Education*). The ESEA provisions seem clearly to take *Everson* into account, and show how the Court directly affects policies by providing the rationale by which they are justified.

Legitimating Policy

Legitimating policy is the business of public officials. Legislatures come most readily to mind, but they are not the only legitimators. Bills passed by legislators must typically be signed by chief executives, and, since church-state policy is frequently subjected to constitutional challenge, courts are also often called on to pass judgment upon them.

Boards of education have frequently been the legitimators of church-state policy because a major constitutional issue has been religious observances in public schools. Released-time religious instruction is a policy adopted by boards of education. Such programs were twice challenged before the Supreme Court, which invalidated programs on public school grounds (*McCollum* v. *Board of Education*) but sustained programs held away from school (*Zorach* v. *Clauson*). This shows that the role of courts, particularly the Supreme Court, is quite significant with respect to policy legitimation.

Policy Application

Administrators are the key actors in policy application. One type of issue they face is the application of a secular regulation to persons who object on religious grounds. Thus, the problem facing unemployment compensation officials in *Sherbert* v. *Verner* was whether a Seventh Day Adventist fired for refusal to work on Saturdays was entitled to unemployment compensation benefits. Administrators may also be involved in carrying out a program directly related to church-state issues, as with programs of aid to parochial schools. In the application, they may alter policy. Thus, the U.S. Office of Education, in drafting guidelines for administration of the ESEA, initially omitted many of the central terms of the church-state settlement reached in the bill itself; the final version was an improvement over the first, but probably deviated somewhat in at least two respects from what had been envisioned by Congress (Kelley and LaNoue 1966, pp. 150-155). Such early stages in the administration of a new program involve crucial decisions that parties interested in policy outcomes cannot afford to ignore.

State and local educational agencies engaged in administration of ESEA also have an opportunity to influence church-state policy, as *Wheeler* v. *Barrera* illustrates. While the Supreme Court refused to decide the constitutional issues the parties raised, the justices did affirm the U.S. Court of Appeals' holding that Missouri public educational agencies were violating the act because they were not providing eligible nonpublic school children a meaningful program comparable in size, scope, and opportunity to that provided to eligible public school students.

Policy Evaluation

The final stage of the cycle is policy evaluation. Formal mechanisms for evaluation of church-state policy by governmental agencies have, in general, been lacking. Existing policies may be evaluated when new proposals are being formulated and considered, but regular, systematic appraisals of church-state policy are not made. Scholars provide evaluation of a sort, but most efforts have focused on specific matters such as the doctrinal consistency of the Supreme Court (Morgan 1972), or compliance with Court decisions (Dolbeare and Hammond 1971). A broader view of church-state policy is needed in future attempts at evaluation by scholars. Specifically stated criteria with which to appraise policy are also essential to meaningful evaluation (Fair 1972).

It can be seen, then, that many actors are involved in the church-state policy process. The U.S. Supreme Court is one of the more important of these, but it shares the stage with a strong supporting cast.

Church-State Doctrine

Because of the Supreme Court's importance in church-state matters, a basic knowledge of its decisions is necessary to an understanding of church-state policy. Issues in the field of church-state policy may, for convenience, be divided into two categories corresponding to the First Amendment phrases dealing with religion: nonestablishment of religion and freedom of religion. Neither category was much litigated in the federal courts until the two provisions were "incorporated" into the Fourteenth Amendment's Due Process Clause, making them applicable to the states (*Cantwell* v. *Connecticut; Everson* v. *Board of Education*). Since that time, the Court has been growing more intolerant of government action challenged under the nonestablishment provision, while at the same time becoming more demanding that government, in the name of freedom of religion, make affirmative accommodations with religious belief. The Court has not been entirely consistent about either matter, but the general contours of these positions are clear.

Nonestablishment of Religion

In general, the position of the Court on nonestablishment issues can be characterized as increasingly separationist even though there are some notable exceptions to this tendency. The Court's nonestablishment decisions of the past three decades have dealt with a number of controversial issues. In 1961 the justices upheld Sunday "blue laws" against nonestablishment challenges by concluding that such laws no longer served to advance religion but had become secular public welfare measures designed to provide the population a day of rest (*McGowan* v. *Maryland*). Another accommodation between church and state was sustained in 1970 when the Court approved tax exemptions for church property used for religious purposes (*Walz* v. *Tax Commission*). However, the two most controversial nonestablishment issues handled by the Court have undoubtedly been religion in the public schools and government financial aid to church-related schools.

The issue of religion in the public schools includes such matters as released-time religious instruction (see p. 59), prohibitions on teaching the theory of evolution, and religious observances. With respect to evolution, the Court said that to prohibit the teaching of this theory would be to give preference to a fundamentalist Christian version of truth (*Epperson* v. *Arkansas*). The Court's decision did not entirely settle this issue, for in 1973 Tennessee passed a law, now being challenged in the state courts, requiring textbooks that include the theory of evolution to give equal emphasis to the Creation. The forms of public school religious observances on which the Court has ruled are prayers and Bible reading. In *Engel* v. *Vitale*, the justices halted the use of a nondenominational prayer prepared by the New York Board of Regents, while in *Abington School District* v. *Schempp*, recitation of the Lord's Prayer and reading from the Bible were held to be prohibited religious exercises. It was in the latter case that the Court developed the basic doctrine on which the justices have relied in the parochial school aid cases.

Prior to the school prayer cases, the Court had decided *Everson* v. *Board of Education*, in which public payment for transportation of students attending nonpublic schools was sustained. The Court's justification was on the ground that the law was a public welfare measure providing for safe transportation of children to school, not an aid to religion. In *Schempp*, however, Justice Clark refined and generalized this "child-benefit" approach by stating that to pass muster under the nonestablishment provision, government programs must have a legitimate secular purpose and a primary effect that neither advances nor inhibits religion. Using these tests, the Court five years later sustained state provision of secular textbooks for students attending church-related schools (*Board of Education* v. *Allen*). The real battles over financial aid to church-related schools were yet to come, but before they did the Court added a third element to its nonestablishment test by ruling that there could not be "excessive entanglement" of government and religious institutions in the carrying out of programs (*Walz* v. *Tax Commission*). While administrative entanglement was the original concern, the Court later also mentioned "political entanglement," said to result from contests over increased funding levels (*Lemon* v. *Kurtzman*).

Enrollment growth in, and increasing financial pressures on, parochial schools had been a problem for some time, but they reached alarming proportions during the 1960s. In response to these concerns and the political demands generated from them, several states enacted programs of aid to parochial education. In 1971 the justices relied upon the "excessive entanglement" aspect of the three-pronged *Schempp-Walz* test in striking down state aid for supplementing parochial school teacher salaries, and for purchasing textbooks and instructional materials for use in parochial schools (*Lemon* v. *Kurtzman*).

Both the pressures on the parochial schools and state legislators' attempts to find constitutional forms of parochial school aid continued, producing another round of decisions in 1973. Here the Court voided state aid for parochial school administration of state-mandated attendance requirements, health records, and competency examinations; state payment for maintenance and repair of parochial school facilities and equipment; and state tuition-assistance plans of several sorts (*Levitt* v. *Committee for Public Education*; *Committee for Public Education* v. *Nyquist*; *Sloan* v. *Lemon*). All these forms of aid were held to have failed the "primary-effect" test.

By 1975 parochial school aid was back before the Court again. In *Meek* v. *Pittenger*, the justices reinforced their earlier policy by upholding a textbook-loan program but voiding loans of instructional material and equipment and provision of professional staff to supply auxiliary services such as remedial and accelerated instruction, guidance counseling and testing, and speech and hearing services. The program of instructional material and equipment loans—a $12,000,000-a-year operation—was found to violate the "primary-effect" test, because the Court views parochial schools as institutions pervaded by religion. Thus, any substantial direct state support of parochial schools is viewed as having a primary effect that advances religion. The auxiliary-services program failed to clear the "excessive-entanglement" hurdle, because of the administrative supervision required to ensure religious neutrality by teachers engaged in auxiliary services within the parochial schools. Justice Brennan, in a separate opinion, argued for the elevation of "political entanglement" to the status of a distinct, fourth nonestablishment test, and would have used it to void even the textbook-loan program his colleagues were willing to uphold.

The problem with the political-entanglement doctrine is its inability to prevent that which it purports to guard against. The Court's decisions on parochial school aid have consistently generated renewed struggles in state legislatures over alternative forms of aid that might meet with the Court's approval. Thus, the Court's own decisions have caused the very political entanglement about which the justices have been concerned.

The issue of state aid to parochial schools has not quite run its course. The constitutionality of the Elementary and Secondary Education Act, avoided in *Wheeler* v. *Barrera*, has yet to be decided, but it is likely that the Court's ruling on auxiliary services in *Meek* will cause constitutional problems for those attempting to sustain it. Governmental aid to church-related institutions of higher education also presents some unresolved judicial problems. Aid for construction of secular buildings has been sustained because the secular is more easily separable from the religious at the college level than at elementary and secondary levels, and because college students, being more mature, are less susceptible to religious indoctrination than are younger students (*Tilton* v. *Richardson*; *Hunt* v. *McNair*). These distinctions have enabled higher education to benefit from government aid without running afoul of the "primary-effect" and "excessive-entanglement" tests. However, aid to church-related higher education was back before the Court at the start of its October 1975 Term, in the form of a suit challenging Maryland's noncategorical grants to its church-related higher education institutions (*Roemer* v. *Board of Public Works*).

Freedom of Religion

While becoming increasingly separationist on nonestablishment issues, the Court has developed greater sensitivity to claims based upon the free-exercise provision. Originally the Court had interpreted freedom of religion to extend no religious exemption from the government's legitimate secular regulations. Thus, the bigamy law passed by Congress for the territory of Utah could properly be applied to a polygamous Mormon (*U.S.* v. *Reynolds*). This "secular-regulation rule" remained unchanged until 1940. In that year, however, Justice Roberts wrote that, "In every case the power to regulate must be so exercised as not, in attaining a permissible end, unduly to infringe the protected freedom" (*Cantwell* v. *Connecticut*, at 304). After adoption of this view, the Court began to provide religion-based exemptions when the government could not demonstrate that it had a "compelling interest" in maintaining the integrity of the regulation in question. While this position was not spelled out until 1963 (*Sherbert* v. *Verner*), the Court seems to have used something akin to this test prior to that time.

A number of the early exceptions arose from cases dealing with Jehovah's Witnesses. Their unorthodox religious practices brought them into conflict with municipal tax laws applicable to door-to-door solicitors, ordinances forbidding knocking on doors or ringing doorbells to deliver handbills to occupants without their invitation, and prohibiting distribution of handbills on city streets. The Court held the Witnesss entitled to religious exemptions from all of these regulations (*Jones* v. *Opelika; Mur-*

dock v. *Pennsylvania; Martin* v. *Struthers; Jamison* v. *Texas*). However, the justices held a law forbidding children to sell newspapers on public streets applicable to a Witness who allowed her children to help sell the sect's literature. The state's interest in the health and welfare of children outweighed the individual's interest in religious exercise (*Prince* v. *Massachusetts*).

Similarly, refusals of requests for religious exemptions included the Court's sustaining of the right of Illinois to deny bar admission to an otherwise qualified applicant who was a conscientious objector to war (*In re Summers*). As recently as 1961, the Court refused a request by an Orthodox Jewish merchant for exemption from Pennsylvania's Sunday blue law. In spite of his argument that he suffered discrimination because he chose to close his business on Saturday for religious reasons and then was forced to keep it closed on Sunday by state law, the Court found no violation of the free exercise provision (*Braunfeld* v. *Brown*). Some of these holdings against the individual's free exercise claim seem plainly inconsistent with both earlier and later rulings of the Court, perhaps because they were decided before the Court fully adopted the compelling interest test. Another recent exemption created by the Court involved the Old Order Amish, excepted from Wisconsin's compulsory education laws because the denomination believes in education only up to the eighth grade rather than to age 16 as the state law required (*Wisconsin* v. *Yoder*).

The California Supreme Court also created a notable exemption when it held that a Navajo Indian was not subject to the state's law against the use of peyote because the chewing of this substance was part of the ritual of his church (*People* v. *Woody*). Dr. Timothy Leary fared less well when he attempted to obtain an exemption from the federal marijuana laws on the ground that use of this drug was part of his religious practice. The Court of Appeals for the Fifth Circuit ruled that, because the national government had a compelling interest in maintaining these laws, Leary's religious freedom claim could not be honored (*Leary* v. *U.S.*).

These cases bring us to the difficulty involved in trying to square the Court's position on religious exemptions with its strick separationism in nonestablishment matters. The Court has consistently held that the truth of religious beliefs is not subject to test by government (*Watson* v. *Jones*; *U.S.* v. *Ballard*; *Kedroff* v. *Saint Nicholas Cathedral*; *Presbyterian Church* v. *Mary Elizabeth Blue Hull Memorial Church*). While this view avoids governmental judgments about religious faith, it may lead to the conclusion that every person who seeks an exemption from less fundamental secular regulations that conflict with sincerely held but highly unusual religious beliefs is entitled to the exemption. Such a position has the deficiency of preferring the religious over the secular and therefore violating the strict separationist interpretation that the Court has given the nonestablishment provision. The conscientious objector cases decided during the Vietnam war illustrate this problem well.

The Court has never held that conscientious objectors to war are constitutionally entitled to an exemption from military service. Congress has, however, provided by statute for such an exemption. The 1948 act provided conscientious objector status to persons opposed, because of their religious training and belief, to any participation in war. Religious training and belief was defined as meaning, ". . . an individual's belief in a relation to a Supreme Being involving duties superior to those arising from any human relation, but . . . not . . . essentially political, sociological, or philosophical views, or a merely personal moral code" (62 Stat. 612). In *Seeger* v. *U.S.*, the Court interpreted this act to apply to individuals whose belief in a Supreme Being was not phrased in orthodox terms. The test, said the justices, was whether there was, " . . . a sincere and meaningful belief which occupies in the life of its possessor a place parallel to that filled by the God of those admittedly qualifying for the exemption" (*Seeger* v. *U.S.*, at 176).

Congress reacted by amending the law in 1967 to delete the reference to a Supreme Being, but to retain the language excluding essentially political, sociological, or philosophical views, or a merely personal moral code from the status of religious training and belief (81 Stat. 104). In *Welsh* v. *U.S.*, the Court rendered the efforts of Congress nugatory. While Welsh was convicted of refusing to submit to induction prior to the 1967 amendment, the Court's ruling obviates the congressional attempt to restrict conscientious objector status to the conventionally religious. In *Welsh*, a plurality of the justices wrote that the law ". . . exempts from military service all those whose consciences, spurred by deeply held moral, ethical, or religious beliefs, would give them no rest or peace if they allowed themselves to become a part of an instrument of war" (*Welsh* v. *U.S.*, at 344). Thus, the Court extended conscientious objector status to secular as well as religious pacifists and did so without relying upon the Supreme Being language excised from the law by Congress. It would seem that the plurality gave this rather remarkable construction to the statute in order to avoid the problem highlighted by Justice Harlan in his concurring opinion. Harlan concluded that Congress, by granting conscientious objector status only to persons claiming opposition to war on religious grounds, favored religion over nonreligion and thus violated the nonestablishment provision. Justice Harlan's position can be applied to religious exemptions created by courts as well as to those carved out by legislatures.

For the Court to continue to maintain strict separationism in establishment cases while extending further the availability of religious exemptions from secular regulation in freedom of religion matters is for the justices to prefer religion over nonreligion in a fashion at least arguably in

66

violation of the Court's own nonestablishment rules. There are several options available for dealing with this doctrinal problem. They include alteration of the strict separationist position, return toward the secular regulation rule, creation of a principle to reconcile the conflict that seems apparent at present, and, after the fashion of the *Welsh* plurality opinion, refusal to admit that a problem exists. Resolution of this problem could well be the most important church-state issue facing the Court. The doctrines created in nonestablishment and freedom of religion, when considered apart, are logically sound and, to some, seem desirable policy. When considered together, however, these doctrines produce a dilemma that the Court may not be able to ignore for long. Finding a way out of this situation could therefore be the prime church-state doctrinal task of the Court in the latter half of the 1970s.

Cases

Abington School District v. Schempp, together with Murray v. Curlett, 374 U.S. 203 (1963).
Board of Education v. Allen, 392 U.S. 236 (1968).
Braunfeld v. Brown, 366 U.S. 599 (1961).
Cantwell v. Connecticut, 310 U.S. 296 (1940).
Committee for Public Eduation v. Nyquist, 413 U.S. 756 (1973).
Engle v. Vitale, 370 U.S. 421 (1962).
Epperson v. Arkansas, 393 U.S. 97 (1968).
Everson v. Board of Education, 330 U.S. 1 (1947).
Hunt v. McNair, 413 U.S. 734 (1973).
Jamison v. Texas, 318 U.S. 413 (1943).
Jones v. Opelika, 319 U.S. 103 (1943).
Kedroff v. Saint Nicholas Cathedral, 344 U.S. 94 (1952).
Leary v. U.S., 383 F. 2d 851 (5th Cir. 1967).
Lemon v. Kurtzman, together with Earley v. DiCenso and Robinson v. DiCenso, 403 U.S. 602 (1971).
Levitt v. Committee for Public Education, 413 U.S. 472 (1973).
McCollum v. Board of Education, 333 U.S. 203 (1948).
McGowan v. Maryland, 366 U.S. 420 (1961); Two Guys from Harrison-Allentown v. McGinley, 366 U.S. 582 (1961); Gallagher v. Crown Kosher Market, 366 U.S. 617 (1961).
Martin v. Struthers, 319 U.S. 141 (1943).
Meek v. Pittenger, 421 U.S. 349 (1975).

Murdock v. Pennsylvania, 319 U.S. 105 (1943).

People v. Woody, 40 Cal. Rptr. 69 (1964).

Presbyterian Church v. Mary Elizabeth Blue Hull Memorial Church, 393 U.S. 440 (1969).

Prince v. Massachusetts, 321 U.S. 158 (1944).

Roemer v. Board of Public Works, prob. juris. noted, 420 U.S. 922 (1975).

Seeger v. U.S., 380 U.S. 163 (1965).

Sherbert v. Verner, 374 U.S. 398 (1963).

Sloan v. Lemon, 413 U.S. 825 (1973).

In re Summers, 325 U.S. 561 (1945).

Tilton v. Richardson, 403 U.S. 672 (1971).

U.S. v. Ballard, 322 U.S. 78 (1944).

U.S. v. Reynolds, 98 U.S. 145 (1878).

Walz v. Tax Commission, 397 U.S. 664 (1970).

Watson v. Jones, 13 Wallace 679 (1872).

Welsh v. U.S., 398 U.S. 333 (1970).

Wheeler v. Barrera, 417 U.S. 402 (1974).

Wisconsin v. Yoder, 406 U.S. 205 (1972).

Zorach v. Clauson, 343 U.S. 306 (1952).

References

Dolbeare, Kenneth, and Hammond, Phillip. 1971. *The School Prayer Decisions: From Court Policy to Local Practice* (Chicago: University of Chicago Press).

Eidenberg, Eugene, and Morey, Roy D. 1969. *An Act of Congress: The Legislative Process and the Making of Education Policy* (New York: Norton).

Fair, Daryl R. 1972. "A Framework for Analyzing the Elements of Stability in Judicial Policy-Making," *Rutgers-Camden Law Journal,* 3 (Spring), 395-409.

Jones, Charles O. 1970. *An Introduction to the Study of Public Policy* (Belmont, Calif.: Wadsworth).

Kelley, Dean M., and LaNoue, George R. 1966. "The Church-State Settlement in the Federal Aid to Education Act," *Religion and the Public Order, 1965,* ed. Donald A. Giannella (Chicago: University of Chicago Press), pp. 110-160.

Morgan, Richard E. 1972. *The Supreme Court and Religion* (New York: Free Press).

7

A New Vision of Equality: Testing the Effects of Gatekeeping Criteria

Donald W. Jackson

Albemarle had required applicants for employment in the skilled lines of progression to have a high school diploma and to pass two tests. . . . [one], allegedly a measure of non-verbal intelligence and . . . [the other], allegedly a measure of verbal facility . . . . Albemarle engaged an industrial psychologist to study the "job relatedness" of its testing program. His study compared the test scores of current employees with supervisorial judgments of their competence in ten job groupings selected from the middle or top of the plant's skilled lines of progression.

Albermarle Paper Co. v. *Moody,*
at 410-11.

Are employment tests, degree requirements, and the like demonstrably related to actual job performance? If they are not, they may constitute discriminatory employment practices under Section 703(h), Title VII, of the Civil Rights Act of 1964. The policy supported by such court rulings, if extrapolated to its logical conclusion, can have a dramatic effect on the ways many educational and employment decisions are made. It is also important to note that the policy is not limited to the context of Title VII and Equal Employment Opportunity Commission Guidelines. There is precedent for the requirement of empirical validation under the Equal Protection Clause (*Walston* v. *County School Bd.*, at 925).

Recent questions like these and facts like those in *Albemarle* have required federal judges to deal with complex methodological issues, while most likely they have not even the feeble reed of a single course in research methodology on which to lean. The purpose of this chapter is to point out some implications of this recent public policy interface between social science and the law.

Sources of the Policy

Section 703(h) of Title VII permits an employer "to give and act upon the results of any professionally developed ability test provided that such test, its administration or actions upon the results is not designed, intended or used to discriminate because of race, color, religion, sex or national origin." The Equal Employment Opportunity Commission Guidelines, first issued in 1966, represent that agency's interpretation of the intent of 703(h). Thus, the "use of any test which adversely affects hiring, promotion, transfer or any other employment or membership opportunity of classes protected by Title VII constitutes discrimination unless . . . the *test has been validated* and evidences a *high degree of utility*. . . ." (Guidelines 1974, p. 772; emphasis added) This illustrates a possibly unrivaled promulgation of social science research canons as substantive public law.

The EEOC Guidelines in effect adopted methodological standards of the American Psychological Association (American Psychological Association 1966; 1974), although in certain instances the Guidelines are more specific than the standards of the APA. Like the APA pamphlet, the Guidelines stress *criterion-related* validity, which is "demonstrated by comparing test scores with one or more external variables considered to provide a direct measure of the characteristic or behavior in question." The preferred method for criterion-related validation is *predictive validation*, in which applicants are administered a test, are hired without regard to test scores, and are observed in the actual performance of jobs, after which correlations are finally calculated between initial test scores and rated job performance. The alternate means of criterion-related validation is *concurrent validation*, in which current employees' test scores and job performance ratings are correlated (APA 1974, p. 26).

Where a showing can be made that criterion-related validation is not feasible, *content validity*, "demonstrated by showing how well the content of the test samples the class situations or subject matter about which conclusions are to be drawn," or *construct validity*, "evaluated by investigating what qualities a test measures, that is, by determining the degree to which certain explanatory concepts or constructs account for performance on the test," may be used (Guidelines 1974, p. 773).

The use of criterion-related validity requires not only that employment tests in fact measure what they purport to measure, but also that tests and other screening devices have demonstrable relationships to job performance. Such a position obviously required the EEOC to propose standards for demonstrating relationships.

Significance Levels

The Guidelines in effect adopt the conventional 0.05 level of statistical significance. However, the APA duly notes that statistical significance is partly a function of sample size and recommends that confidence intervals for reported parameters be used, rather than simply reporting that the null hypothesis can or cannot be rejected. The Guidelines also require that the relationship between tests or other criteria and job performance have "practical significance" (Guidelines 1974, p. 774). The strength of association sufficient for "practical significance" is not specified in the Guidelines, which instead note that "practical significance" is affected by situational factors. One commentary, presumably addressed to the business community, notes that:

Validity coefficients in personnel selection measures have generally not been very high. Average usable coefficients are in the vicinity of .30 to .40 and only occasionally as high as .50. Although much higher correlations would be desirable, those in the range of .30 to .40 or higher *are large enough to be practically meaningful.* (Bassford 1974, p. 42; emphasis added)

Knowledgeable observers can readily discern the methodological and epistemological problems that lurk in the Guidelines. First, should not Type I and Type II error *both* be taken into account in deciding whether an employment test is acceptable? In the context of employment tests, the two decision errors are as follows:

Type I Error (alpha): Rejecting the null hypothesis when it is true, that is, incorrectly deciding that there is a significant relationship between an employment test and job performance.

Type II Error (beta): Accepting the null hypothesis when it is false, that is, incorrectly deciding that there is no significant relationship between an employment test and job performance.

These two decision errors and two correct decisions can best be illustrated in the familiar two-by-two table (see Figure 7-1):

		True Condition	
		H_0 = No relation	H_1 = Significant relation
Decision	No relation	Correct	Type II Error
	Significant relation	Type I Error	Correct

Figure 7-1. Statistical Decision Making Relative to Employment Tests.

The Guidelines suggest a 5 percent risk of error as an acceptable one for Type I error, but do not mention Type II error. It is well known that .01 and .05 are significance levels conventionally used in reporting social science research. While those conventions are probably often used unthinkingly, they presumably are founded on the kind of risk that is viewed as unacceptable to researchers, that is, the risk of Type I error in misleading other researchers in the same field. Type II error, which involves the risk of not reporting results that are in fact meaningful, apparently is not as important in a research community. Yet, research conventions may be inappropriate in the context of validating employment tests. The risks we are willing to take depend on the consequences of the decisions to be made (Palumbo 1969, p. 120).

The second major difficulty with the Guidelines is in determining "practical significance." Assuming that correlation coefficients in employment tests are computed for continuous variables, then the squares of the coefficients tell us how much of the variance in job performance can be accounted for through the scores on employment tests. Thus, coefficients ranging from .30 to .50 only account for 9 percent to 25 percent of the variance in actual job performance. Such correlations may be acceptable in exploratory social science research, but they hardly seem sufficient to sustain the usage of employment tests that otherwise are shown to discriminate against certain classes of job applicants.

Administering the Policy

In 1971 in *Griggs* v. *Duke Power Co.*, a unanimous U.S. Supreme Court, interpreting Title VII and EEOC Guidelines, held that diplomas and employment tests are discriminatory when: (a) they are not shown to be significantly related to successful job performance; (b) they operate to exclude minority applicants at a significantly higher rate than white applicants; and (c) the jobs in question had formerly been filled preferentially by whites. The *Griggs* ruling disposed of the relatively easy situation in which an employer had adopted diploma and testing requirements "without meaningful study of their relationship to job-performance ability." In such an instance, applicants had only to show that the criteria used by the employer excluded blacks at a rate significantly higher than whites. Having shown that, the burden shifted to the employer to demonstrate that its criteria served the legitimate interest of the business in choosing between qualified and unqualified applicants. Since the employer in *Griggs* had not undertaken any program of validation, it obviously failed to meet its burden of proof. Absent such validation, the Court noted that:

The facts of this case demonstrate the inadequacy of broad and general testing devices as well as the infirmity of using diplomas or degrees as fixed measures of capability. History is filled with examples of men and women who rendered highly effective performance without the conventional badges of accomplishment in terms of certificates, diplomas or degrees. (at 433)

But how can courts appraise tests and other criteria when an employer makes a validation study and claims that its criteria have a demonstrable relationship to job performance? At that point, the courts must interpret EEOC Guidelines and, indirectly, the APA standards. It is apparent that the necessity of evaluating the validity, statistical significance, and strength of association of employment tests and other selection criteria places judges in the somewhat novel position of having to rely on social scientists (most often industrial psychologists or psychometricians) in the practical application of legal standards. Shall the courts defer to expert witnesses so as to cope with these cases? Witnesses are usually partisans, but perhaps one answer is for the courts to appoint their own experts, as they already do in other technical areas.

A great many cases have been reported since *Griggs*. Several involve judicial discussions of content, construct and criterion-related validity—most of them apparently "cribbed" from the Guidelines or from the APA pamphlet. Two cases should suffice to illustrate how the federal courts have dealt so far with questions of validation. They reveal judges either perceptibly groping for a way through strange territory or accepting and reciting by rote Guideline or APA standards.

In *U.S.* v. *Georgia Power Co.*, the Fifth Circuit addressed the chief question left open by *Griggs*: "What comprises an adequate demonstration that a company's testing program satisfies the proviso of Section 703(h) of Title VII?" Citing a law review article, the court noted that criterion-related validation is the "most accurate way to validate an employment test." Georgia Power had employed an expert to conduct a validation study. The company's expert testified that his analysis "did a pretty good job" of demonstrating a "positive relationship between job performance and test scores"(at 913). However, he admitted on cross-examination that under EEOC and APA standards only one of 13 job classifications was validly test related.

The Fifth Circuit did not conclude that *Griggs* required literal compliance with EEOC Guidelines, but nonetheless found that the Guidelines provided a "suitable framework" for validation and agreed that the Guidelines should be followed "absent a showing that some cogent reason exists for noncompliance" (at 913). The court dwelt on the Guidelines' .05 significance standard, which was achieved for only two of the studied job classifications. For six other classifications the relationship between test and job performance had significance levels approaching .50. Given that disparity between study results and the Guidelines, the court held that the company failed to show a demonstrable relationship, while noting that the .05 level set "a desirable goal and not a prerequisite"(at 915).

Issues like those of *Georgia Power* reached the U.S. Supreme Court in *Albemarle Paper Co.* v. *Moody*, decided June 25, 1975. As in *Georgia*

Power, the company employed an industrial psychologist to validate its testing program. He correlated test scores with subjective supervisorial rankings of employees, applied the conventional .05 level of significance, and reported phi coefficients for the relationships studied. Writing for the majority, Justice Stewart noted that:

> The study showed significant correlations for the Beta Exam in only three of eight lines. Though the Wonderlic Tests's Form A and B are in theory identical and interchangeable measures of verbal facility, significant correlations for one Form but not for the other were observed in four job groupings. In two job groupings neither Form showed a significant correlation. Within some of the lines of progression, one Form was found acceptable for some job groupings but not for others. Even if the study were otherwise reliable, this odd patchwork of results would not entitle Albemarle to impose its testing program under the Guidelines. (at 431-32)

The Supreme Court thus applied the Guideline standard for statistical significance, although it still had to determine the *proportion* of statistically significant results that would be sufficient to validate a test. Broadly construed, Justice Stewart's opinion can be read as an endorsement of the Guidelines which it said are "entitled to great deference."

Chief Justice Burger (the author of *Griggs*) and Justice Blackmun each separately noted his concern that the Court's application of the EEOC Guidelines made them the sine qua non of test validation. Both would have allowed greater flexibility, and Chief Justice Burger would have deferred to the district judge's findings of fact in favor of Albemarle's experts.

Implications of Policy Administration

It is important to remember that, before an employment test or other screening device can be questioned as to its validity, there must be a showing that the test or device operates to exclude applicants who fit within the categories protected by civil rights legislation at a rate significantly higher than other applicants. When that burden is met—when it is shown that a test is in fact discriminatory—the burden shifts to the employer, who must show that a legitimate business purpose of choosing "qualified applicants" is served by the test. Statistical significance and strength of association should be assessed in that context. What, then, are the consequences of Type I error in validating tests? Making a Type I error would mean that invalid tests would continue to be used, in spite of their demonstrated discriminatory effect. That being the case, only a minimal risk seems acceptable. Perhaps that risk should be even less than the conventional 5 percent. What of the consequences of Type II error?

Making a Type II error would mean that an employment test would be rejected in spite of its actual validity. Thus, the discriminatory effect of the test would be avoided, but the legitimate business purpose of selecting "qualified applicants" would be frustrated. Given the goal of civil rights legislation and ensuing Guidelines of ending job discrimination, a risk of Type II error higher than that of Type I seems justified. Accepting relatively high Type II error simply places the burden of justifying employment tests on the employer, as the statutes and Guidelines already do.

The "practical significance" of correlations between tests and actual job performance also requires careful evaluation. Remembering again the discriminatory effects of tests that have been successfully challenged, it seems proper to require that such correlations be quite strong before test use is sustained. Correlations of .30 ($r^2 = 9\%$) do not seem justified under such an argument. Here the suggestion of the APA seems appropriate. Instead of simply reporting the probability of Type I error, why not report confidence intervals around a reported coefficient, and let the courts decide whether the range of variance possibly accounted for is sufficient to justify the use of an employment test?

It is worth noting that the interests of applicants and employers in practice coincide if statistically significant and substantially valid tests are used. The applicants would then be ensured that their employment is founded on tests that validly measure their prospect of succesful job performance. Employers would serve their legitimate business interests by selecting the best qualified applicants.

Other Policy Consequences

This chapter has dwelt mostly on employment tests, but the policy and its ramifications apply equally to diplomas and other educational criteria for employment. In fact, the case against diplomas is even stronger, for rarely do we even attempt to measure the relationship between educational credentials and successful job performance. Education has long been such an article of faith in our society that we simply assume that such credentials represent valid employment criteria. This dogma has been appropriately called "credentialism" (Francis 1975, p. 1377). At least where "credentialism" has a discriminatory effect, it is clearly illegal under the *Griggs* ruling, if it is not shown that there is a demonstrable relationship between educational criteria and successful job performance (Francis 1975, pp. 1382-92). High school degree requirements for employment may be the first to go, but the principles of empirical validation apply equally to other educational criteria. Another potential subject for empirical validation is the admission criteria for higher education. The *DeFunis* case, particulary Justice Douglas' dissent (at 340), illustrates the prospects for future contests there.

One can also speculate about still greater extrapolation of the requirement of empirical validation. What if all educational and employment criteria were required to survive empirical validation, even absent showings of discrimination under prohibited statutory or constitutional categories? What if anyone could challenge educational or employment criteria? The bastions of racism, sexism *and credentialism* might then fall. Instead of criteria predicated on *status*— black, white, brown, male, female, high school or college graduate—educational and employment criteria would have to be founded on *qualities* derived from empirical validation—on the talents, knowledge, experience, and skills (however acquired) that have demonstrable relationships with actual academic or job performance. Under such a policy many criteria that now are only assumed to be valid or that "have always been that way" would be suspect.

Of course, some serious questions can be raised concerning the administration and outcomes of such a policy. For one thing, the cases here reviewed suggest that courts, absent training or reliance on impartial experts, are not very well qualified to oversee empirical validation. A more troublesome problem is that the requirement of empirical validation ultimately might mean that only criteria subject to rigorously reliable and valid measurement can be used. While everyone might welcome the demise of arbitrary and discriminatory subjectivism in educational and employment decisions, there are nonetheless likely to be some important criteria that are not capable of rigorous measurement and validation. If that proves to be the case, a policy like that suggested here might involve the identification of those criteria that *can* be measured rigorously and those that *cannot*. Those criteria that are incapable of rigorous measurement, but that nevertheless seem worth retaining, can best be administered by people who warrant our confidence that their decisions will accord with the values and preferences of society. Presumably their discretion would be subject to review, as we review judicial discretion today, but it would be even better if we were able to develop valid criteria for selecting them.

Cases

Albemarle Paper Co. v. Moody, 422 U.S. 405 (1975).

DeFunis v. Odegaard, 416 U.S. 312 (1974).

Griggs v. Duke Power Co., 401 U.S. 424 (1971).

U.S. v. Georgia Power Co., 474 F.2d 906 (5th Cir. 1973).

Walston v. County School Bd., 492 F.2d 919 (4th Cir. 1974).

Regulations

"Guidelines on Employment Selection Procedures" (EEOC Guidelines) 29 C.F.R. 1607 (rev. July, 1974).

References

American Psychological Association (APA).1966. *Standards for Educational and Psychological Tests and Manuals*.

_____.1974. *Standards for Educational and Psychological Tests,* rev. ed.

Bassford, Gerald L. 1974. "Job Testing—Alternative to Employment Quotas," *Business Horizons*, XVII (February), 37-47.

Francis, Richard L. 1975. "Diplomas, Degrees and Discrimination," *The Hastings Law Journal*, 26 (May) 1377-1402.

Palumbo, Dennis J. 1969. *Statistics in Political and Behavioral Science* (New York: Appleton-Century-Crofts).

Additional References

For more extended treatment of this subject, three articles are especially noteworthy. They are Alfred W. Blumrosen, 1972, "Strangers in Paradise: *Griggs* v. *Duke Power Co.* and the Concept of Employment Discrimination," *Michigan Law Review*, 71 (November), 59-110; Peter Koenig, 1974, "'They Just Changed the Rules on How to Get Ahead' (Field Report on Psychological Testing of Job Applicants)," *Psychology Today* (June), 87-103; and Willo P. White, 1975, "Testing and Equal Opportunity: Getting a Fair Chance," *Civil Rights Digest* (Spring), 42-51.

8

Patterns of Differential Treatment of Minorities

Werner F. Grunbaum

A general expansion of civil liberties has resulted in reducing differential patterns of treatment for various groups. This chapter describes the various types of groups, the treatment patterns they receive, and suggests why certain groups receive such treatment.

Differential treatment patterns depend upon numerous factors, such as the severity of the crime (Ares 1963), the nature of the victim (Bullock 1961; Nagel 1972), the attitudes of judicial decision makers (Nagel 1962), the backgrounds of judicial decision makers (Cook 1973), attitudes of police administrators, legislative activity, pressure group activity (Haft 1974), and economic conditions of society in general. Table 8-1 contains an outline of the patterns of treatment of disadvantaged, paternalized, and quasi-legitimate groups. The general pattern here has been one of differential treatment resulting from numerous factors.

Table 8-1
Patterns of Differential Treatment of Minorities

Examples	Characteristics	Differential Treatment Pattern
Disadvantaged Groups: American Indians Blacks Chicanos	Requiring societal intervention because these group members have less education and less wealth	Disadvantaged Pattern: Denial of rights granted the criminally accused
Paternalized Groups: Women Juveniles Mentally ill Prison inmates	Requiring societal protection because these groups traditionally are not considered to be equal	Paternalized Pattern: Denial of procedural rights granted to members of other groups
Quasi-legitimate Groups: Homosexuals Prostitutes	Requiring societal control because these groups traditionally are not considered worthy of equality	Quasi-legitimate Pattern: Double standard applied to members of these groups in legislation and enforcement of laws

Disadvantaged Pattern

Disadvantaged groups have less education and less wealth than the dominant groups in American society (Nagel 1972). These groups include American Indians, blacks, and Chicanos. These groups are subjected to a more unfavorable treatment pattern than are nonindigents and whites in the area of rights usually granted to the criminally accused. Although some unfavorable treatment results from the inability of many members of these groups to pay for superior legal counsel, their inability to post bonds, and other problems arising from being poor, their treatment cannot be explained solely by their lack of wealth. Attitudes of police administrators and judges, for example, also contribute to their differential treatment.

An example of differential treatment of Chicanos by police administrators is found in the Rio Grande Valley in the activities of the modern Texas Rangers. Amid frequent charges of brutality, violation of the civil rights of farm workers, favoritism toward growers, and of strike-breaking, the Rangers enforced the law through physical coercion, leading to their characterization as the "Mexican Americans' Ku-Klux-Klan" (Proctor 1970).

Similar attitudes are found in the remarks of judges who tell Chicanos that "we ought to send you out of the country— send you back to Mexico" and that they are "lower than animals and haven't the right to live in organized society—just miserable, lousy, rotten people" (Wagner and Haug 1971). Such views also affect minority group lawyers, who have considerable difficulty protecting their clients' rights.

In the administration of justice in the South, judges engage in a pattern of sentence disparity between blacks and whites. Controlling for such factors as the type of offense, type of plea, previous record, and presence or lack of counsel, one study found blacks receiving sentences that were on the average 4.7 years longer than sentences received by whites while the average white sentence was 72 percent of the average black sentence (Southern Regional Council 1969).

An example of differential treatment of American Indians by legislators is found in Title 18, Section 1153 of the United States Code, which provides that any Indian who commits rape within Indian country shall be subject to the same laws and penalties as all other persons within the exclusive jurisdiction of the United States while any Indian who commits rape upon any female Indian within Indian country shall be imprisoned at the discretion of the Court. Thus, the maximum punishment for raping a non-Indian is theoretically execution while the maximum penalty for raping an Indian is life imprisonment. This practice was upheld by the courts in *Gray* v. *U.S.* in 1968 on the grounds that American Indians may be governed by a set of laws distinct from that applicable to the rest of the nation (MacMeekin 1969).

Paternalized Pattern

Paternalized groups are subjected to a more unfavorable treatment pattern than the general male adult population in terms of being granted procedural rights. The paternalized pattern of differential treatment segregates those thought not to be equal (Nagel 1972). Children are often denied constitutional rights granted to others accused of crime. Women have been denied certain rights traditionally granted to men while the mentally ill are often imprisoned with fewer procedural safeguards than given to the criminally accused.

Differential treatment of women, juveniles, the mentally ill, and prison inmates is justified on the grounds that these groups require societal protection. Because such differential treatment may lead to ill-defined and potentially oppressive state power, the general trend has been to give women, juveniles, the mentally ill, and prison inmates the power to resist arbitrary state authority, and an expansion of civil liberties for these groups has taken place in recent years.

The courts have continued to expand the legal and political rights of women. In *Roe* v. *Wade*, the Supreme Court upheld the rights of women to make decisions related to child bearing. In several cases, the Supreme Court has struck down instances of differential treatment of women. For example, in *Frontiero* v. *Richardson*, the Supreme Court eliminated differential treatment of women as related to obtaining dependent's benefits while in the armed services. Another example is found in *Taylor* v. *Louisiana*. In this case the Supreme Court held that women may not systematically be excluded from jury panels.

While women's rights have expanded rapidly, the rights of juveniles have not. In general our differential laws concerning juveniles do not properly distinguish those situations in which children require protection and those situations in which they must be ensured autonomy.

The Supreme Court's landmark *Gault* decision provided that juvenile courts give children many of the same constitutional rights previously decreed for adult criminal defendants, such as sufficient notice to permit defense to charges, assigned counsel, and the privilege against self-incrimination and the rights of confrontation and cross-examination. However, New York laws governing the voluntary placement of children in state institutions, which are indicative of statutes in other states, are illustrative of the way in which children are treated (Chase and Weiss 1973). The welfare agency may withhold the child without any evidentiary hearing unless it is of the opinion that by returning the child to its parents "the interest of such child will be promoted thereby and that such parent is fit, competent and able to duly maintain support and educate such child." This entire process may take place even without prior notice to the mother at the time of the voluntary placement that she may lose the child forever.

Underlying the failure to treat juveniles fairly is the fact that most juveniles who come in contact with our legal system are poor, black, or Chicanos. The American legal system uses its paternal powers based upon the dependency of children as a weapon against children rather than using this dependency in a constructive way (Uviller 1973).

Among the most disadvantaged people in America are involuntarily institutionalized mentally ill persons (Morris 1970). They are also socially disadvantaged because society considers them as outcasts. Mentally ill patients are legally disadvantaged because they are often committed as "dangerous" on ill-defined grounds and medically disadvantaged as well because no medical consensus exists as to the appropriate mode of treatment and because mental institutions are often severely understaffed. Economically disadvantaged mental patients are often required to attend state institutions with limited facilities, thus compounding differential treatment, while the economically privileged have the choice of superior private facilities for their treatment. Some legal improvements may be in sight, as the Supreme Court has held that a state may not involuntarily confine persons who are mentally ill unless they are dangerous either to themselves or others (*O'Connor* v. *Donaldson*) and the Court of Appeals for the District of Columbia has asserted the principle of "a right to treatment" (*Rouse* v. *Cameron*). Chief Judge David L. Bazelon recognized that the purpose of involuntary hospitalization is treatment, not punishment, and that without treatment a hospital assumes the role of penitentiary where one may be held indefinitely without being convicted for a specific offense.

The Joann Little trial in 1975 and a number of current federal court actions around the country attacking conditions in various local jails amply attest to the crowded and often inhumane conditions under which prison inmates must live. There has been some expansion of civil liberties for prison inmates but inadequate attention has been given to the fact that most prisoners come from poor backgrounds and that racial and ethnic minorities are overrepresented. Some prisons contain primarily Chicanos, some hold many whites, most have large proportions of blacks, but all contain mostly those of impoverished backgrounds (Smith and Fried 1974). Accordingly, many problems in prisons mirror greater societal problems generally. Correcting internal abuses and focusing upon individual rehabilitation of prisoners will not solve this problem. However, the formation of prisoner unions and newsletters are at least hopeful signs that changes of any kind are possible (Smith and Fried 1974).

Quasi-legitimate Pattern

The basic pattern here is that of a double standard applied to members of quasi-legitimate groups but not to others. This pattern is applied to groups not thought *worthy* of equality. Accordingly, society treats as outcasts such groups as homosexuals and prostitutes through criminal sanctions on the basis that the state has a compelling interest to do so.

Differential treatment in enforcing prostitution laws is based on a double sexual standard: While the prostitute is prosecuted, her "respectable" male customers rarely are brought into court except to testify against her although prostitution is illegal for both. Such differential treatment also applies to homosexuals because they are often in danger of being arrested for solicitation (Young 1972). While in many states solicitation is illegal for any male proposing sex to any female, almost all arrests for solicitation involve prostitutes, transvestites, and gay males. Since solicitation arrests are next to impossible without the use of police decoys, selective patterns of differential enforcement result.

It is generally thought that the state has a compelling interest in outlawing prostitution because it is linked with organized crime, because it is allegedly responsible for ancillary crime, and because it is often thought responsible for the transmission of venereal disease. However, an increasing number feel that such grounds for a compelling state interest do not exist (Haft 1974). The President's Commission on Law Enforcement stated that prostitution plays a small and declining role in organized crime. Field research in Seattle also found few traces of organized crime (James 1972). In fact, organized crime has turned to more profitable ventures associated with fewer risks such as politics, business, the stock market, and labor unions. As far as venereal disease is concerned, less than 5 percent may be attributed to prostitutes (Winick 1971).

It has also been argued that prostitution and homosexuality should be outlawed on the grounds that the state has an obligation to protect the moral fiber of the country and that these activities are immoral and therefore should be outlawed. Such a point of view cannot be taken lightly because it is an attitude characterizing many judges, legislators, and opinion makers.

Factors Affecting Differential Treatment

The general pattern for the treatment of disadvantaged, paternalized, and quasi-legitimate groups is one of differential treatment resulting from numerous factors. The severity of the crime helps to explain the differential treatment of individuals. For example, suspects are less likely to be released on bail for more severe crimes than for less serious ones (Ares

1963). Persons out on bail will have an easier time accumulating evidence and preparing their defense than persons who are not released on bail. Furthermore, defendants who arrive in court in the same manner as court spectators are more likely to make a better impression on juries than defendants brought to their trial in handcuffs and escorted by police officers.

However, the nature of the offense is not the only factor affecting differential treatment. Differential treatment of certain groups can also be explained by the nature of the victim (Nagel 1972). Blacks receive relatively more favorable treatment when charged with crimes against persons of their own race than they tend to receive in crimes dealing with property owned by whites (Bullock 1961; Nagel 1967). The arrest and prosecution of prostitutes, while their male customers are usually not arrested, constitutes another example of such treatment (Haft 1974).

Some differential treatment of groups can also be explained by the attitudes of judicial decision makers. For example, judges with attitudes favoring the poor in American society tend to favor less privileged defendants in appellate criminal proceedings more than do other judges (Nagel 1962). Also, some judges tend to ridicule certain minority group members and minority group lawyers (Wagner and Haug 1971).

Backgrounds of judges may have comparable effects to the attitudinal factor. Judges who come from small towns, who do not have previous military experience, and who live in communities with strong American Legion influence, tend to impose stricter sentences upon persons accused of Selective Service Act violations than do federal judges who serve in larger communities, have previous military experience, and are Democrats serving in localities with strong American Civil Liberties Union branches (Cook 1973). Judges in the South tend to discriminate against blacks in their sentencing behavior (Southern Regional Council 1969).

Another aspect of differential treatment results from selective enforcement of laws by police and other local administrators. For example, the Texas Rangers interfered in efforts to unionize Chicano workers in Texas while they did not interfere generally in labor disputes (Servín 1970). Laws enforced by police decoy squads against homosexuals and prostitutes are selective because of the nature of the enforcement device. The activities of local and national legislators also influence differential treatment patterns. Numerous examples exist of local legislators who have rewritten municipal penal codes dealing with prostitution to enable the police more effectively to arrest male customers. National legislators have also influenced differential patterns through such legislation as the Civil Rights Act of 1964.

Interest group activity also helps to explain the differential treatment of various groups. Litigation initiated by the National Association for the

Advancement of Colored People (NAACP) helped to produce increased civil rights for blacks in the South during the past years (Vose 1959). Also, the activities of COYOTE (Call Off Your Tired Old Ethics), a prostitutes' organization, and work of gay liberation groups, especially Gay Liberation churches, publicized the plight of their constituents and won several court battles (Haft 1974; Young 1972).

Societal conditions are important as factors underlying differential treatment of groups generally. Patterns of economic affluence have aided the women's rights movement. Also, high crime rates characterizing crimes against persons have led some critics to conclude that victimless crimes such as those dealing with consenting adults and certain sex crimes waste large amounts of police manpower, which might better be used against more serious crime.

Factors such as these help to explain some of the patterns of treatment of disadvantaged, paternalized, and quasi-legitimate groups. The general pattern results in differential treatment for these minorities.

Conclusion

The disadvantaged pattern subjects disadvantaged groups to more unfavorable treatment than nonindigents and whites in the area of rights usually accorded to the criminally accused. The paternalized pattern subjects paternalized groups to more unfavorable treatment than the general adult male population in terms of being given procedural rights usually granted to other groups. The quasi-legitimate pattern subjects quasi-legitimate groups to a double standard used in legislation and law enforcement that is usually not applied to other minority groups. However, improved economic conditions and the general expansion of the equal protection clause and due process have helped end some patterns of differential treatment.

Cases

In re Gault, 387 U.S. 1 (1967).
Frontiero v. Richardson, 411 U.S. 677 (1973).
Gray v. U.S., 394 F. 2d 96 (9th Cir., 1968).
O'Connor v. Donaldson, 422 U.S. 563 (1975).
Roe v. Wade, 410 U.S. 113 (1973).
Rouse v. Cameron, 373 F. 2d 451 (D.C. Cir., 1966).
Taylor v. Louisiana, 419 U.S. 522, (1975).

References

Ares, C. 1963. "The Manhattan bail project: an interim report on the use of pretrial parole," *New York University Law Review*, 38 (January), 67-95.

Bullock, H. 1961. "Significance of the racial factor in the length of prison sentences," *Journal of Criminal Law, Criminology, and Police Science*, 52 (November-December), 411-417.

Chase, Oscar, and Jonathan Weiss. 1973. "The case for the repeal of Section 383 of the New York Social Services Law," *Legal Rights of Children: Status, Progress and Proposals*, ed. Rena K. Uviller (Fair Lawn, N.J.: R. E. Burdick), pp. 37-47.

Cook, Beverly Blair. 1974. "Sentencing behavior of judges: draft cases—1972," *University of Cincinnati Law Review*, 42, 597-633.

Haft, Marilyn G. 1974. "Hustling for rights," *Civil Liberties Review*, 2 (Winter-Spring), 8-26.

James, Jennifer. 1972. "A Formal Analysis of Prostitution in Seattle." Doctoral thesis, University of Washington.

MacMeekin, Daniel H. 1969. "Red, white and gray: equal protection and the American Indian," *Stanford Law Review*, 21 (May), 1236-1248.

Morris, Grant H. 1970. *The Mentally Ill and the Right to Treatment* (Springfield, Illinois: Charles C. Thomas).

Nagel, Stuart. 1972. *Rights of the Accused* (Beverly Hills, Calif.: Sage Publications), 19-23.

_____. 1967. "Disparities in criminal procedures," *UCLA Law Review*, 14 (August), 1272-1305.

_____. 1962, "Judicial backgrounds and criminal cases," *Journal of Criminal Law, Criminology, and Police Science*, 53 (September), 333-339.

Proctor, Ben H. 1970. "The modern Texas Rangers: a law-enforcement dilemma in the Rio Grande Valley," *The Mexican-Americans: An Awakening Minority*, ed. Manuel P. Servín (Beverly Hills, Calif.: Glencoe Press), pp. 212-227.

Servín, Manuel P. 1970. *The Mexican-Americans: An Awakening Minority* (Beverly Hills, Calif.: Glencoe Press).

Smith, Joan, and William Fried. 1974. *The Uses of the American Prison: Political Theory and Penal Practices* (Lexington, Mass.: D. C. Heath).

Southern Regional Council. 1969. *Race Makes the Difference: An Analysis of Sentence Disparity among Black and White Offenders in Southern Prisons* (Atlanta, Ga: Southern Regional Council).

Uviller, Rena K. ed. 1973. *Legal Rights of Children: Status, Progress and Proposals* (Fair Lawn, N.J.: R. E. Burdick).

Vose, Clement. 1959. *Caucasians Only* (Berkeley: University of California Press).

Wagner, Nathaniel N., and Marsha J. Haug. 1971. *Chicanos: Social and Psychological Perspectives* (St. Louis, Missouri: C. V. Mosby Company).

Winick, Charles, and Paul Kinsie. 1971. *The Lively Commerce* (Chicago: Quadrangle Books).

Young, Allen. 1972. "Out of the closets and into the streets," *Out of the Closets: Voices of Gay Liberation*, eds. Karla Jay and Allen Young (Douglas Books), pp. 6-31.

**Part II
New Areas of Civil Liberties
Policy**

9

A New Bill of Rights: Novel Dimensions of Liberty and Property

Stanley H. Friedelbaum

Traditional Freedoms and Their Safeguards

The advent of the bicentennial year offers an opportunity for a reassessment of a constitutional plan that has endured and flourished as one of the few testaments to American "exceptionalism" (Bell 1975, p. 223). In the past, as now, the status of human liberties provides an index of the system's ability to adapt to profound changes without the sacrifice of historic values. Yet, the preservation of traditional liberties, however desirable, will not suffice to meet the needs of a society that has altered course dramatically since the Bill of Rights was framed; in the wake of Watergate, Vietnam, and kindred events, human liberties must·be both resilient and novel. Development cannot proceed in a spirit that venerates the past by way of a literal and unbending adherence to the "fundamental truths" envisioned by the First Congress or, for that matter, by the framers of the Fourteenth Amendment. Instead, there must be recognition of the urgency for change that can take account of a plethora of compelling and, at times, conflicting demands arising from a tangled skein of events and phenomena: a complex and ever-changing technology; vast economic expansion offset by intermittent recession; shrinking sources of energy and raw materials; shifting demographic patterns; a pervasive communications revolution; growing urban crises; burgeoning bureaucracies and a proliferation of administrative law and regulations; and rising expectations of groups formerly denied access to the centers of power.

The Supreme Court failed to engage in a consistently activist role in the safeguarding of fundamental rights until the era of the late 1950s and 1960s when judicial leadership evidenced itself in a number of areas. At the same time, Congress has reassumed an historic posture of guardianship (Commager 1943, p. 422) by approving such measures as the Equal Rights Amendment, the Civil Rights Act of 1964, the Voting Rights Act of 1965, and the Speedy Trial and Privacy Acts of 1974. Nor have the state appellate courts been wanting in their contributions as guarantors of the public interest. The New Jersey Supreme Court decided the apportionment cases before the United States Supreme Court held the issue justiciable and, more recently, has ruled expansively with respect to school funding, restrictive zoning, and like practices that encourage inequality (Friedelbaum 1975, pp. 206-42). Other state courts, especially those in California and New York, have demonstrated a similar initiative.

If the United States Supreme Court's work is not exclusive, its contemporary case law has at least contributed a broad range of opinions advancing libertarian and humanitarian interests while echoing older values. The resulting end product is based in part on the *substantive* due process (determination of the "reasonableness" of a statute) used earlier to defend property interests, although there is still considerable reticence to concede that anything but *procedural* due process serves as the basis for judicial decision. While the Court no longer substitutes its own values as it did at the height of its invalidation of attempts at economic regulation, major incursions upon the prevailing doctrine of deference to legislative acts have occurred in the area of civil liberties.

The New Bill of Rights

Definitions and Judicial Techniques

A series of cases, marked by inventive briefs subsequently translated into the judicial idiom, have created a galaxy of rights—often limited and at times unpredictable. In the aggregate, these rights complement and, at points, rival the traditional freedoms preserved by the first eight amendments. The new bill of rights consists of safeguards for public employees whose positions are in jeopardy; for students in danger of suspension or expulsion from school; for consumer-debtors threatened with repossession of goods purchased under conditional sales agreements; for welfare recipients faced with the imminent prospect of a termination of public assistance benefits; and for persons who assert a right of privacy both within and outside the marital relationship.

Substantive due process ranks foremost among the judicial techniques resorted to in the creation of the new bill of rights. For the first time since the Court's retreat from its much condemned pre-1937 role as a "censor" of legislation and as a protector of private property interests, the opinions of the late 1960s and early 1970s signaled a return to a substantive predicate. New meanings, varying according to context, have attached to liberty and property. Since, as Justice Frankfurter once explained, due process is "compounded of history, reason, the past course of decisions, and stout confidence in the strength of the democratic faith which we profess" (*Joint Anti-Fascist Committee* v. *McGrath*, at 161-63), it retains the accommodative characteristics that invite the exercise of judgment and defy mechanical constraints or rigid guidelines. The phrase "due process" has always provided flexibility for judges willing to write their views into the Constitution, whether in the area of economic regulation or, more recently, in the field of civil liberties.

A doctrine of irrebuttable presumptions has also served in the protection of substantive liberties. Within a rapidly developing framework, the indispensability of an individualized finding is being insisted upon whenever the legislative presumption is not " necessarily or universally true in fact, and when the State has reasonable alternative means of making the crucial determination" (*Vlandis* v. *Kline* at 452). Thus, the Court has condemned as violative of due process a state's generalized assumption that unwed fathers are unfit to raise their children. "The private interest here," a majority held, "that of a man in the children he has sired and raised, undeniably warrants deference and, absent a powerful countervailing interest, protection" (*Stanley* v. *Illinois* at 651). In effect, the Court has adopted an exacting standard for judging legislation by shifting to the state the burden of sustaining its actions by way of particularized determinations. Justice Rehnquist, sharply critical of this line of reasoning, has referred to the irrebuttable presumption doctrine as a "highly theoretical analysis that relies heavily on notions of substantive due process" (*Vlandis* v. *Kline* at 463).

A Developing Catalog of Rights

The notion of occupational freedom and the rights of public employees, students, and related groups have emerged from the right-privilege dichotomy in which they had previously been enmeshed. The "tough-minded distinction between constitutionally protected rights of private citizens and unprotected governmental privileges . . . [that had] . . . been applied to defeat a great variety of claims associated with government employment or other forms of largess" (Van Alstyne 1968, p. 1440) was gradually eroded. As early as the mid-1950s, a right to work was being attributed to liberty and property interests by Justice Douglas, who described the right as the "most precious liberty that man possessed" (*Barsky* v. *Board of Regents* at 472). During succeeding years, constitutional protection was extended to guard against impermissible deprivations of professional status affecting admissions to the bar. The Fourteenth Amendment, by absorbing the self-incrimination clause of the Fifth Amendment, served as a standard to ensure that licensees were not denied "first-class citizenship" (*Spevack* v. *Klein* at 516).

As the McCarthy era yielded to the less restrictive influences of the 1960s, decisions in public employee cases, in particular, shifted ground dramatically—from a limited focus, reflective of the times, to a more generalized restriction on state action. No longer did the Court emphasize distinctions intended to narrow the scope of loyalty oaths and inquiries into subversion. Instead, there was a reelaboration of property and liberty interests under the Fourteenth Amendment. The property interests of public employees were held to include not only explicit contractual provisions but also implicit agreements or circumstances of service that might establish the basis of entitlement to continued employment. Thus, there existed the possibility of de facto tenure, an idea that hitherto would have been rejected. Liberty was no longer confined to the absence of bodily restraint or to the role of a catalytic agent in the absorption of segments of the Bill of Rights. Instead, it encompassed such notions as the imposition of personal stigma or other reputational disability on the public employee and, more generally, the possible foreclosure of the individual's opportunity to pursue his or her chosen career (*Board of Regents* v. *Roth*, at 572-78; *Perry* v. *Sindermann*, at 596-603). The assertion and discovery of these property or liberty interests do not ensure reinstatement or prevent dismissal for cause, but they do trigger the requirement of a hearing and other due process safeguards. Although the Court remains divided over the need for a pretermination hearing, the constitutional basis of the employee's right to due process is no longer in doubt (*Arnett* v. *Kennedy*, at 164-67). There are even faint hints, thus far found in dissenting opinions, that public employment is a right and that the onus of justification for nonappointment lies with the employing agency.

An explicit emphasis on "basic" and "protected" liberty, within a public employee context, also appears in a case assessing the validity of termination-return stipulations in relation to pregnant public school teachers. The Court has taken exception to the irrebuttable presumption established by boards of education that female teachers must leave their employment several months before the birth of a child and cannot return to the classroom before a specified period of time has elapsed, and a majority has warned that rules must not "needlessly, arbitrarily, or capriciously impinge upon this vital area of a teacher's constitutional liberty" (*Cleveland Board of Education* v. *La Fleur*, at 640). A like reproof has been visited upon state practices denying unemployment compensation benefits to women during the last trimester of pregnancy and the first six weeks following the birth of a child on the ground, held untenable by the Court, that an inability to accept employment must be presumed (*Turner* v. *Department of Employment Security*).

A burgeoning concept of professional or vocational self-direction necessarily presupposes adequate access to the educational system, still the principal channel of career preparation, if not always the sole gateway to upward social mobility. Student interests in property and in liberty closely parallel those set out in the public employee cases. With respect to property, claims of entitlement to public education arise from state constitutional and statutory grants; in relation to liberty, efforts to suspend or to exclude adversely restrict the options of those who seek to pursue higher education or to secure positions in the job market. Although the Court has required only elemental due process when short-term suspensions have occurred, there are indications that full-scale evidentiary hearings may be mandatory should more serious steps to exclude be challenged (*Goss* v. *Lopez*). A recent decision, affirming summarily the validity of a state law empowering teachers and school officials to use "reasonable force" to maintain order, seems to have been premised upon a prior requirement of minimal procedural guarantees (*Baker* v. *Owen*).

A correlative right of conjugal privacy derives from the same source as the interest identified in relation to vocational and educational pursuits. Only a decade ago, the Court evidenced a marked reluctance to link a fledgling right of privacy to a substantive predicate in the Fourteenth Amendment. A majority achieved the desired result of invalidating a state's anticontraception laws (and establishing a right of marital privacy) by the discovery of penumbras and emanations deriving from specified clauses in the Bill of Rights (*Griswold* v. *Connecticut*). What has come to prevail in succeeding years is a reasonably coherent body of law that reveals components of a right of conjugal privacy: a broadly stated personal discretion in matters of marriage and family living; the "right of the *individual*, married or single, to be free from unwarranted government intrusion into matters so fundamentally affecting a person as the decision whether to bear or beget a child" (*Eisenstadt* v. *Baird*, at 453); and, with qualifications, the freedom of a woman to decide whether to terminate her pregnancy (*Roe* v. *Wade*). In effect, constitutional safeguards have been created to shield the most intimate aspects of personal life arising from sexual intercourse and its consequences.

As the state interest has been found wanting when individual conjugal interests are advanced, so skepticism attaches to governmentally favored economic interests that formerly prevailed over the rights of consumers and the underprivileged. Oft-repudiated notions of economic due process have been revitalized although the process has been a highly selective one. But there is little danger of a return to a judicially inspired laissez-faire. The object is to reform parts of a traditional commercial code that has brought hardship to those least able to challenge or to endure the proceedings instituted against them. Contrary to the teachings of Social Darwinism, contemporary judicial pronouncements reflect compassion for the weak and the helpless, not the idealization of an unrelenting and destructive competition in the marketplace.

The application of safeguards in the economic area has been uneven.

State efforts to terminate welfare benefits, considered substantial property interests, have been subjected to strict procedural requirements (*Goldberg* v. *Kelly*). Challenges to the adequacy of such practices as garnishment and replevin, however, have been met by varying decisions narrowly limited to specific factual settings (compare *Fuentes* v. *Shevin, Mitchell* v. *W.T. Grant Co.*, and *North Georgia Finishing, Inc.* v. *Di-Chem, Inc.*). It is plain that constitutionally impermissible deprivations of the property interests of debtors have not been defined with any degree of certainty. Yet, the Court's judgments have resulted in a moderate revision of significant aspects of consumer and poverty law. A rudimentary due process envelops what has long been left to local devices. Although the precise form of an evidentiary hearing has not been uniformly prescribed, the states no longer remain free of nationally imposed strictures where "no more than private gain is directly at stake . . ." (*Fuentes* v. *Shevin*, at 92-93). Justice Black's comments concerning an "emotional rhetoric" (*Sniadach* v. *Family Finance Corp.*, at 344-45) and his references to an "ambulatory power" to set aside legislative judgments (*Goldberg* v. *Kelly*, at 276-77) have not been persuasive. Clearly, the Court has decided to re-enter some of the areas of economic and social policy that it had previously renounced with a remarkable degree of finality.

Liberalizing Causes of Action

Apart from due process considerations, a compelling method of redress for deprivations of federally guaranteed rights has been facilitated by way of expansive interpretations of the civil rights acts. Pleas of immunity on the part of public officials have been discounted with resulting awards of monetary damages to those whose personal interests in liberty have been invaded "under color" of law. The Court has rejected the argument that the relationship between a citizen and a federal agent, acting in violation of Fourth Amendment rights, is akin to that existing between private individuals. To the contrary, a majority declared, an officer exercising his authority unconstitutionally "possesses a far greater capacity for harm than an individual trespasser exercising no authority other than his own" (*Bivens* v. *Six Unknown Federal Narcotics Agents*, at 391-92).

A unanimous Court reaffirmed the absence of an absolute immunity for public officials when, in the wake of the Kent State University student fatalities that had occurred during the anti-Cambodian demonstrations of the spring of 1970, damage actions were filed against state officers. The Eleventh Amendment was said to provide no shelter for officials charged with violations of federal rights under color of state law (*Scheuer* v. *Rhodes*, at 237). Although municipalities cannot be sued under the civil rights statutes (*City of Kenosha* v. *Bruno*, at 513), actions against offending officials as individuals clearly are not barred. The Court recently ruled that school board members are personally liable in monetary damages for deprivations of the substantive and procedural rights of students. As a majority put it, each member "must be held to a standard of conduct based not only on permissible intentions, but also on knowledge of the basic, unquestioned constitutional rights of his charges." Justice Powell, in dissent, observed that this standard left little substance to the doctrine of qualified immunity (*Wood* v. *Strickland*).

Outlook for the Future

Will the Court of the late 1970s continue to expand the profile of a new bill of rights? Justice Rehnquist never ceases to remind his colleagues of the dangers implicit in a wanton return to substantive due process. There are signs of realignments in a Court that persists in reaffirming, at least for the record, a broad commitment to a comprehensive state police power. But deference itself has become a varying, selective standard that at times serves to promote particular results and to reflect changing economic attitudes. How else can recent decisions hostile to a vigorous enforcement of the antitrust laws (*United States* v. *General Dynamics Corp.*; *United States* v. *Marine Bancorporation*; *United States* v. *Connecticut National Bank*) be explained? Similarly, a narrow statutory construction, tied to restrictive definitions of such terms of art as "in commerce" and "affecting commerce" (*Gulf Oil Corp.* v. *Copp Paving Co.*), has diminished the regulatory authority of Congress and of the administrative agencies.

Is creative growth predictable or even probable in the light of past judicial responses? That an interdependence exists between property and liberty is undeniable (*Lynch* v. *Household Finance Corp.*, at 552). However, if current indicators serve, it is liberty that appears likely to be expanded. There is little likelihood that the property interests of public employees will build further in an era of governmental uncertainty and financial stringency. And the new property of the consumer-debtor-welfare cases, judged by the treatment accorded it in recent years, seems to have lost some of the fervor that first imparted meaning to it. Although ground may not be yielded, there are no prospects of major thrusts along the road to a more emphatically defined social justice. The abortion decisions and the sexual privacy opinions are distinguishable from these cases and, for that matter, from the older Social Darwinist pronouncements where major questions of economic policy had been resolved. If, in fact, the libertarian philosophy of John Stuart Mill has been substituted for the ungenerous dogmas of Herbert Spencer, it follows that an individually oriented personal autonomy is being exalted rather than the exemplary results that may be expected to flow from the free play of uncontrolled economic forces. The overall direction of public policy is less conspicuously involved, for the new right of privacy has been compelled to give way when a traditional exercise of the state's police power, as in zoning cases, is juxtaposed (*Belle Terre* v. *Boraas*). Thus, recent additions to personal rights have remained much in the seclusive tradition of the original Bill of Rights. Future advances, fashioned along similar lines, ought not to impair the regulatory power of government in meeting the challenges of an advanced industrial society.

Cases

Arnett v. Kennedy, 416 U.S. 134 (1974).

Baker v. Owen, 96 S. Ct. 210 (1975).

Barsky v. Board of Regents, 347 U.S. 442 (1954).

Belle Terre v. Boraas, 416 U.S. 1 (1974).

Bivens v. Six Unknown Federal Narcotics Agents, 403 U.S. 388 (1971).

Board of Regents v. Roth, 408 U.S. 564 (1972).

Cleveland Board of Education v. LaFleur, 414 U.S. 632 (1974).

Eisenstadt v. Baird, 405 U.S. 438 (1972).

Fuentes v. Shevin, 407 U.S. 67 (1972).

Goldberg v. Kelly, 397 U.S. 254 (1970).

Goss v. Lopez, 419 U.S. 565 (1975).

Griswold v. Connecticut, 381 U.S. 479 (1965).

Gulf Oil Corp. v. Copp Paving Co., 419 U.S. 186 (1974).

Joint Anti-Fascist Committee v. McGrath, 341 U.S. 123 (1951).

Kenosha v. Bruno, 412 U.S. 507 (1973).

Lynch v. Household Finance Corp., 405 U.S. 538 (1972).

Mitchell v. W.T. Grant Co., 416 U.S. 600 (1974)

North Georgia Finishing, Inc. v. Di-Chem, Inc., 419 U.S. 601 (1975).

Perry v. Sindermann, 408 U.S. 593 (1972).

Roe v. Wade, 410 U.S. 113 (1973).

Scheuer v. Rhodes, 416 U.S. 232 (1974).

Sniadach v. Family Finance Corp., 395 U.S. 337 (1969).

Spevack v. Klein, 385 U.S. 511 (1967).

Stanley v. Illinois, 405 U.S. 645 (1972).

Turner v. Department of Employment Security, 96 S. Ct. 249 (1975).

United States v. Connecticut National Bank, 418 U.S. 656 (1974).
United States v. General Dynamics Corp., 415 U.S. 486 (1974).
United States v. Marine Bancorporation, 418 U.S. 602 (1974).
Vlandis v. Kline, 412 U.S. 441 (1973).
Wood v. Strickland, 420 U.S. 308 (1975).

References

Bell, Daniel. 1975. "The End of American Exceptionalism," *The Public Interest* (Fall), 193-224.

Commager, Henry Steele. 1943. "Judicial Review and Democracy," *The Virginia Quarterly*, 19, 417-428.

Friedelbaum, Stanley H. 1975. "Constitutional Law and Judicial Policy-Making," *Politics in New Jersey,* eds. A. Rosenthal and J. Blydenburgh (New Brunswick, N.J.: Eagleton Institute of Politics), pp. 206-242.

Van Alstyne, William W. 1968. "The Demise of the Right-Privilege Distinction in Constitutional Law," *Harvard Law Review*, 81, 1439-1464.

10 The Constitutional Right to Terminate a Pregnancy

Marilyn Falik

On January 22, 1973 the Supreme Court declared restrictive abortion laws unconstitutional. In companion cases, *Roe* v. *Wade* and *Doe* v. *Bolton*, the Court held that states may not categorically proscribe abortions by making their performance a crime *nor* prescribe elaborate procedural guidelines that make abortions unnecessarily difficult to obtain. In spite of the Court's mandate, women continue to be frustrated in the exercise of their constitutional right to privacy and personal liberty, specifically the right to terminate pregnancy.

Rather than settling the abortion question conclusively, the Supreme Court decision kindled a national protest movement. Antiabortion advocates have been relatively unsuccessful in generating congressional support for a Human Life Amendment, but these forces have demonstrated consummate skill in lobbying for restrictive procedural requirements that limit the availability and accessibility of abortions. Principal impediments that have been enacted are (1) conscience clause provisions, which permit hospitals—public, private, and denominational—to refuse to perform abortions; (2) consent clause provisions, which require spousal consent or, in the case of a minor, parental consent; and (3) special limitations or total bans on Medicaid reimbursements for elective abortions performed on welfare recipients. Advocates of abortion rights continue to challenge the constitutionality of each of these provisions, and often have been successful. (For examples of unsuccessful attempts, see *Greco* v. *Orange Memorial Hospital Corp.*; *Taylor* v. *St. Vincent's Hospital.*)

Salient Aspects of the 1973 Abortion Ruling

The constitutional basis for invalidating restrictive abortion laws rests primarily on the Court's interpretation of the Fourteenth Amendment. In *Roe* v. *Wade*, the Court rejected the "right-to-life" contention that Constitutional references to "person" include the fetus and concluded that the word "person" as used in the Fourteenth Amendment "does not include the unborn." With respect to the woman's right to obtain an abortion, the Court held that the right of privacy, "whether it be founded in the Fourteenth Amendment's concept of personal liberty and restrictions upon State action, as we feel it is, or . . . in the Ninth Amendment's reservation of rights to the people, is broad enough to encompass a woman's decision whether or not to terminate her pregnancy" (*Roe* v. *Wade*, at 153). Endorsing a Fourteenth Amendment Due Process position, the Court cautioned that state action "may be justified only by a compelling state interest" (at 155).

Repeatedly throughout both opinions, the Court emphasized that medical considerations—primarily those related to the health and well-being of the pregnant woman—are paramount in determining what constitutes permissible state action. Progress in the medical sciences now permits the performance of abortions with minimal danger to the life and health of the pregnant woman. Applying the principle of lapsed constitutionality, the Court sought to demonstrate that its abortion ruling was consistent with the underlying purpose and legal rationale for restrictive abortion statutes in observing that state courts, which had earlier interpreted abortion laws, had focused primarily on the state's interest in the woman's health.

Since it is an established medical fact that, until the end of the first trimester, the maternal mortality rate is greater than in abortion, *Roe* prohibited any state restrictions on the performance of abortions during the first three months of pregnancy. Prior to the second trimester, the formula requires that the decision and its effectuation be left to the medical judgment of the pregnant woman's attending physician. During the second trimester, a state may, if it chooses, regulate the performance of abortions *only in ways that are reasonably related to maternal health*. For the stage subsequent to viability, a state may proscribe abortions, but the Court held that the state's interest in protecting potential life is subordinate to the physician's obligation to preserve the life and health of the pregnant woman. Equally important in its ruling was the Court's concern for the patient-physician relationship, encompassing both the physician's right to practice medicine and maternal health: ". . . medical judgment may be exercised in the light of all factors—physical, emotional, psychological, familial, and the woman's age—relevant to the well-being of the patient. This allows the attending physician the room he needs to make his best medical judgment. And it is room that operates for the benefit, not disadvantage, of the pregnant woman." (*Doe* v. *Bolton*, at 192)

In the case of *Doe* v. *Bolton*, the Court further delineated its position on what constitutes permissible state action. Several provisions of Georgia's "liberalized" abortion statute were declared unconstitutional because they were considered "unduly restrictive of patient's rights and needs" (at 198). A requirement that hospitals performing abortions be accredited was declared invalid; the Court did not discern the existence of a reasonable relationship between the statute's requirement that hospitals performing abortions be accredited by the Joint Commission on Accreditation of Hospitals and the state's compelling interest in maternal health. Statutory provisions requiring that a hospital review committee screen and approve applications for abortions and that two additional practicing physicians concur with the treating physician's recommendation were considered to be an unnecessary constraint on the woman's right to obtain an abortion and the physician's right to practice medicine. The Court concluded that "the Statute's emphasis . . . on the attending physician's best clinical judgment . . . should be sufficient" (at 199). A residency requirement for the person seeking abortions was also declared invalid because it violated the equal protection and privileges and immunities clauses of the Constitution.

Unresolved Issues

While setting forth the trimester formula for state action, the Supreme Court left unanswered certain key questions. Is a public hospital required to perform abortions, or make its facilities available to physicians who perform abortions? What is the proper role, if any, of the prospective father, husband, or parents of the pregnant woman? Must public assistance programs pay for "elective" abortions desired by Medicaid recipients? If a state may not categorically prohibit abortions, may a state endorse a policy that may ultimately have the same impact? May states delegate authority to "interested" parties who claim a fundamental interest in the abortion decision? What obligation, if any, do public authorities have in implementing the abortion ruling? Whether pregnant women seeking abortions are accorded equal treatment shall be determined by the Supreme Court's answers to each of these questions.

Recent federal court rulings support the contention that conscience clause provisions, prior consent requirements, and restrictions on Medicaid reimbursements for "elective" abortions are unconstitutional. (On conscience clauses with respect to public hospitals: *Doe* v. *Hale Hospital; Nyberg* v. *City of Virginia, Minnesota; Orr* v. *Koefoot; Hathaway* v. *Worcester City Hospital.* Consent requirements: *Murray* v. *Vandevander; Jones* v. *Smith; In re P.J.; Doe* v. *Doe; Coe* v. *Gerstein.* Medicaid restrictions: *Doe* v. *Rampton; Coe* v. *Westby; Klein* v. *Nassau County Medical Center; Doe* v. *Rose; Doe* v. *Wohlgemuth.*) Powers that the state does not possess under *Roe* and *Doe* cannot be delegated by statute to other public authorities or otherwise recognized "interested" parties. With regard to the conscience clause as it pertains to public hospitals, the Eighth Circuit Court of Appeals held: "It would be a nonsequitur to say that the abortion decision and its effectuation is an election to be made by the physician and his patient and then allow the state, through its public hospitals, to effectively bar the physician from using state facilities to perform the operation." (*Nyberg* v. *City of Virginia, Minnesota*, at 1346)

Similarly, with respect to prior consent requirements, another court ruled that

> the state has no authority to interfere with a woman's right of privacy in the first trimester . . . nor can it interfere with the right before the fetus becomes viable in order to protect potential life. It follows inescapably that the state may not statutorily delegate to husbands and parents an authority the state does not possess . . . a state which has no power to regulate abortions in certain areas simply cannot constitutionally grant power to husbands and parents to regulate in those areas. (*Coe* v. *Gerstein,* at 698-99)

Certainly, the logic of this argument applies to statutory restrictions affecting indigent women's right of privacy and personal liberty in the abortion decision. To deny poor women access to abortions under Medicaid would thus be violative of the equal protection and due process clauses of the Constitution. A federal district court recognized this attempt to discriminate against the poor as an illegal interference with reproductive freedom. "Under traditional Equal Protection standards, once the State chooses to pay for medical services rendered in connection with the pregnancies of women, it cannot refuse to pay for the medical services rendered in connection with other indigent women electing abortion, unless the disparate treatment supports a legitimate State interest" (*Doe* v. *Wohlgemuth*, at 186). However, it is inconceivable that the state would have a legitimate interest that would coerce indigent women to bear children.

Prior consent is the most complex and emotionally laden unresolved issue. Husbands and parents of minors claim a personally compelling interest in the decision to terminate a pregnancy. It is recognized that their interests may be substantially different from that of the state. Nonetheless, a strict interpretation of *Roe* v. *Wade* and *Eisenstadt* v. *Baird* suggests that the imposition of consent requirements at the behest of "interested" parties constitutes an abrogation of a woman's right of privacy in the abortion decision. *Roe* clearly states that "the right of privacy is broad enough to encompass a woman's decision whether or not to terminate her pregnancy" (at 153). In *Eisenstadt* v. *Baird*, the right to limit child bearing is defined as an individual right to reproductive freedom: "The marital couple is not an independent entity with a mind and heart of its own, but an association of two individuals with separate intellectual and emotional makeup. If the right of privacy means anything, it is the right of the *individual* . . . to be free from unwarranted governmental intrusion into matters so fundamentally affecting a person as the decision whether or not to bear or beget a child.'' (at 453)

When familial disagreement arises concerning procreation decisions, the situation is clearly a zero-sum game, because the right to obtain an abortion or the right to limit child-bearing is an indivisible right. To recognize the interests of potential fathers and grandparents as being equal to the interests of the pregnant woman results in an untenable situation. If prospective fathers and grandparents refuse to give consent, a woman is compelled to bear a child. Compulsory child-bearing may be characterized as involuntary servitude banned by the Thirteenth Amendment. One court asked: If a husband has a right to prohibit his wife from obtaining an abortion, does he also have a right to compel her to have an to abortion, or a right to compel her to take contraceptives to prevent pregnancy? This would seem ludicrous; therefore, the Florida Court of Appeals concluded: "It is unquestioned that a woman has a fundamental right to determine whether or not *to bear a child* . . . and it would be beyond the province of logic and reason to suggest that she could be *compelled* to procreate." (*Jones* v. *Smith*, at 344; emphasis added) Thus, the decision to terminate a pregnancy as well as the decision to carry a pregnancy to term is not amenable to participatory democracy.

Although parental power is independent of that wielded by the state, parents should not have an unlimited right to frustrate the fundamental rights of their minor children. In those instances where a minor seeks an abortion, the *In re Gault* ruling applies: "Neither the Fourteenth Amendment nor the Bill of Rights is for adults alone." (at 13) In spite of the liberal abortion ruling, a recent study indicates that out-of-wedlock births continue to increase. Illegitimacy rates among 15-19 year olds have increased most sharply and births among teenagers are becoming an ever-increasing proportion of all births. Since the right to obtain an abortion has been deemed a fundamental right of privacy and personal liberty, parental consent requirements constitute an infringement of a young woman's right to reproductive freedom.

Conclusion

As landmark decisions, *Roe* v. *Wade* and *Doe* v. *Bolton* mark a turning point in the Court's interpretation of the Constitution with respect to fundamental individual rights in general and women's rights in particular. In spite of its affirmative ruling, women—young and old, married and single—experience frustration as they attempt to exercise a constitutional right of privacy. Where fundamental rights are involved, the Supreme

Court is bound to take an active role in delimiting the areas in which the state may regulate the abortion procedure.

Cases

Coe v. Gerstein, 376 F. Supp. 695 (S.D. Fla. 1973), cert. denied, 417 U.S. 279 (1974).

Coe v. Westby, 43 U.S.L.W. 2142 (D. S. Dak., 1974).

Doe v. Bolton, 410 U.S. 179 (1973).

Doe v. Doe, 314 N.E. 2d 128 (Mass. 1974).

Doe v. Hale Hospital, 500 F. 2d 144 (lst Cir. 1974).

Doe v. Rampton, 366 F. Supp. 189 (D. Utah), vacated on other grounds, 410 U.S. 950 (1973).

Doe v. Rose, 499 F. 2d 1112 (10th Cir. 1974).

Doe v. Wohlgemuth, 376 F. Supp. 173 (W.D. Pa. 1974).

Eisenstadt v. Baird, 405 U.S. 438 (1972).

In re Gault, 387 U.S. 1 (1967).

Greco v. Orange Memorial Hospital, 374 F. Supp. 277 (E.D. Texas 1974), cert. denied, 96 S. Ct. 433 (1975).

Hathaway v. Worcester City Hospital, 475 F. 2d 701 (1st Cir. 1973).

Jones v. Smith, 278 So. 2d 339 (Fla. Ct. App. 1973), cert. denied, 415 U.S. 958 (1974).

Klein v. Nassau County Medical Center, 347 F. Supp. 296 (E.D. N.Y. 1972).

Murray v. Vandevander, 522 P. 2d 302 (Okla. Ct. App. 1974).

Nyberg v. City of Virginia, Minnesota, 495 F. 2d 1342 (8th Cir. 1974).

Orr v. Koefoot, 377 F. Supp. 673 (D. Neb. 1974).

In re P.J., 12 Crim. L. Rep. 2549 (D.C. Super. Ct. 1973).

Roe v. Wade, 410 U.S. 113 (1973).

Taylor v. St. Vincent's Hospital, 369 F. Supp. 948 (D. Mont. 1973).

11 The Eighth Amendment: A New Frontier of Creative Constitutional Law

Larry C. Berkson

The editor has quite appropriately chosen to place this chapter on cruel and unusual punishment in Part II: New Areas of Civil Liberties Policy. Traditional scholars may object to such a classification. After all, the concept has been traced to the Laws of King Alfred (900 A.D.), to Edward the Confessor (1042), to the Magna Carta (1215), and to the English Bill of Rights (1689) (Granucci 1969). On the American continent, the inhibition was written into the Massachusetts Body of Liberties as early as 1641. Later it was adopted as part of the Virginia Declaration of Rights. When the Continental Congress prepared plans for the government of the Northwest Territory, it included a bill of rights containing the inhibition. With little discussion or debate, the concept became part of the Eighth Amendment to the United States Constitution in 1791. The inhibition also restricts the states, as it has been incorporated by court decision into the due process clause of the Fourteenth Amendment. Today only the Vermont and Connecticut constitutions do not contain provisions specifically dealing with the concept. In the former, however, the state supreme court has ruled that it is a part of the common law (*State* v. *O'Brien*). Connecticut merely provides that excessive fines shall not be imposed.

In spite of this lengthy history, the concept of cruel and unusual punishment has, until very recently, remained an obscure, if important, part of the Bill of Rights. For example, after an exhaustive search of opinions reported prior to 1870, only 20 cases were found that dealt with the prohibition. Beginning with that date, however, larger numbers of cases raising the issue did begin appearing before state and federal courts. The total by 1916 was slightly over 200 cases. The number of cases reported during each subsequent ten-year period rose in rather even increments until the 1956-66 era. At that time, litigation of the inhibition nearly doubled (253 cases).

It is clear that the inhibition has truly emerged from obscurity since 1966. Although the ten-year period is yet to be completed, litigation has increased nearly five-fold over the previous era. In part, this rise is due to the revolution that has taken place in judicial attitudes toward court supervision of internal prison practices and regulations. Traditionally courts followed the policy of nonintervention (the "hands-off doctrine") (Friend 1967). However, the failure of state legislators and prison administrators to correct barbaric and deplorable conditions and practices increasingly has drawn the judiciary into consideration of the internal administration of certain penal institutions (Goldfarb and Singer 1970). Thus, while prior to 1966 only 16 cases concerning the administration of prisons were brought before the courts, 233 have been litigated since that time.

Oddly enough, the United States Supreme Court has never accepted or ruled on an administrative action case argued on cruel and unusual punishment grounds. Indeed, the Court has confronted the inhibition itself in a substantial manner only ten times in its history. The fact that six of the ten cases have appeared within the past 28 years is a further indication that the concept has emerged from relative obscurity.

Policy on Cruel and Unusual Punishment

Cruel and unusual punishment may be inflicted by legislators (statutes), judges (sentences), or administrators (institutional rules and regulations). These groups may inflict one of two types of punishment: corporeal or incorporeal. The former punishments are of the variety that inflict some degree of physical bodily harm while the latter are of the type that inflict almost no physical bodily harm.

Corporeal Punishments

Historically, a large number of corporeal punishments have been regarded as cruel and unusual. Dicta in decisions of the 1800s suggest that the punishments of quartering, disembowelling, gibbeting, burning, crucifixion, breaking on the wheel, strangling, burying, boiling, or blowing from a cannon's mouth, were thought to be prohibited by the inhibition. Such mutilations as dismemberment of limbs, ears and nose, slittings and castration were also thought to be prohibited, as were the less harsh punishments of pillorying and ducking.

One of the most often litigated corporeal punishments has been whipping. In spite of the fact that early state courts specifically declared its imposition valid, the punishment has come under constant attack. The result has been a gradual reduction of its use, until presently the penalty has almost entirely disappeared. The only jurisdiction in the United States that allows its imposition by statute is Delaware. Even there the whipping post has fallen into absolute disuse. Nonetheless, the punishment has never been declared cruel and unusual by the United States Supreme Court, and thus prison administrators are allowed to use it under certain conditions. This practice has also become greatly suspect, and by court decision is not allowed in certain districts.

A punishment that continues to be practiced, however, is the paddling of students. It is permitted by statute in every state but New Jersey. Recently, four separate federal district courts in New Mexico, Pennsylvania, Texas, and Vermont have upheld its imposition under controlled conditions, and the Supreme Court has now affirmed its use.

Another practice that has been challenged is that of sterilization. Subsequent to Indiana's enactment of the world's first such statute (1907), 13 states adopted provisions for the sterilization of criminals, and 28 for the sterilization of insane and feeble-minded persons (O'Hara and Sanks 1956). Today there is little question that the sterilization of individuals in the latter category is permissible. As early as 1927, for example, Justice Holmes noted: "The principle that sustains compulsory vaccination is broad enough to cover cutting the Fallopian tubes." (*Buck* v. *Bell*, at 207) Yet, there remains some question as to whether the sterilization of criminals is constitutionally permissible. State decisions on the subject are about equally divided. However, the actual number of sterilizations performed has declined during the past two decades and now appears to be contrary to general public policy (Paul 1968).

Foremost among the corporeal punishments to be actually challenged in the courts has been the death penalty. Abolitionists first attacked certain modes of inflicting it, among them hanging, shooting, electrocution, and gaseous asphyxiation. Hanging was continually upheld by the courts because of its long usage and wide acceptance. Likewise, shooting was viewed as permissible because it had long been used by the military and because it was often the method chosen by individuals who were to be executed. Neither electrocution nor gaseous asphyxiation, however, could be justified on such grounds. Indeed, both were "modern" scientific inventions unknown at the common law. Nonetheless, courts had little difficulty in upholding the new methods. Primary reliance was based on the fact that in each instance, the legislature had introduced the new procedure as a humanitarian advancement to ease the pain and suffering of the unfortunate subject. As such, the courts simply could not equate these methods with torture and thus there was no violation of the Eighth Amendment.

Unsuccessful in attempts to limit new modes of inflicting the death penalty, abolitionists launched another attack against the punishment, arguing that it was excessive when imposed for certain crimes, such as robbery, arson, kidnapping, espionage, assault, and rape. In nearly every instance, however, the punishment was not considered cruel and unusual when taking into consideration the circumstances actually surrounding the offense, the dastardly nature of the offense and the background of the defendant. One major exception exists. In *Ralph* v. *Warden*, the Fourth Circuit Court of Appeals noted that the victim of a rape was not of a tender age and that the attending physician had found no outward evidence of injury or violence, or any unusual psychological trauma. The court also noted that the trend was clearly toward abolishing capital punishment for the offense. Thus, it was concluded that when life is neither taken nor endangered, the Eighth Amendment forbids the imposition of the death penalty.

Finally, the death penalty has been attacked as cruel and unusual per se. In 1972, for the first and only time to date, these advocates were successful. In *People* v. *Anderson*, the California Supreme Court held that the inhibition in its state constitution prohibited imposition of death under any circumstances. The court recognized the facts that 41 states provided for the penalty, that juries were willing to impose it, and that public opinion polls suggested that a majority of people favored its retention. However, the court distinguished between those persons "far removed" from the actual experience of capital punishment and those persons constituting the "informed public." It was with the latter group that the court was primarily concerned. The people closest to the actual application of the penalty, noted the court, were rejecting it with increasing frequency. For example, it was noted that the punishment was rarely, if ever, carried out. There had been a steady decrease in the number of executions throughout the nation. Furthermore, lengthy terms of imprisonment while awaiting execution were thought to have dehumanizing effects and often to be so degrading and brutalizing that they constituted psychological torture. Moreover, the court noted, the prisoner could be isolated from society by far less onerous means.

Four months later, the United States Supreme Court issued its long-awaited opinion on the subject in *Furman* v. *Georgia*. Neither abolitionists nor antiabolitionists, however, gained a clear victory. The decision itself consolidated three cases. Two involved the rape of white females by black males. In neither case was the woman hospitalized. The third case involved a mentally deficient black who had unknowingly murdered a white householder while committing a felony. The Court held in its brief *per curiam* opinion that as presently applied, the death penalty constituted cruel and unusual punishment. Only two justices of the five-man majority, however, thought it was unconstitutional per se. Nonetheless, the five did agree that it was being imposed in an arbitrary manner by judges and juries alike, and thus was unconstitutional. Justice Douglas perhaps best summarized this point of view when he stated: "People live or die, dependent on the whim of one man or of 12."

The dissenters relied primarily on the rationale of judicial self-re-

straint. To them, the legislatures rather than the courts should set the parameters of punishment. For example, Justice Blackmun went so far as to
indicate that were he a legislator, he would vote for abolition. However,
in his role as a judicial officer, he simply could not make such policy.

Subsequent to *Furman*, no less than 32 states reenacted death penalty
statutes. The Court has recently set for reargument the *Fowler* case involving the North Carolina mandatory death sentence. Again, the Court is
being asked to declare the death penalty per se cruel and unusual. However, in light of the *Furman* decision, greatest emphasis has been placed on
the fact that the punishment is still imposed arbitrarily. It is argued that
juries still have the authority to determine such facts as premeditation and
malice, and may do so in an arbitrary manner. Moreover, prosecutors
may exercise their uncontrolled discretion to reduce charges for certain
defendants. Likewise, it is claimed, the governor may grant executive
clemency to certain persons or groups in an arbitrary fashion. It is with
these intractable issues that the Court has yet to deal.

Certain types of confinement have been attacked as cruel and unusual.
The long-imposed punishment of solitary confinement has been held constitutional whether imposed by legislative statute or administrative order.
Nonetheless, literally dozens of courts have ordered its discontinuance
when such personal accessories as soap, toilet paper, towels, tooth brush,
comb and clothing have not been provided during such incarceration.
Moreover, the room must be heated and ventilated properly. A mattress
must be supplied during sleeping hours and the duration of incarceration
must be strictly limited to a short number of days.

Other types of incarceration that restrict the activities of inmates have
been challenged. These are variously referred to as segregated confinement, maximum security confinement, control confinement, and isolated
confinement. Restrictions in these units are clearly less severe than those
found in solitary confinement. It is the unanimous conclusion of appeals
courts that this mode of punishment does not inflict cruel and unusual
punishment per se (Stevens 1971). Generally, as long as prison officials
have reasonable justification for placing an inmate in such a unit, the incarceration will be upheld. Among the reasons approved are that an inmate is constantly in violation of prison rules, that an inmate is a particularly intractable prisoner, and that an inmate needs to be protected from
his fellow prisoners.

Perhaps one of the most extreme instances of restricting a prisoner's
activities occurred in *Fulwood* v. *Clemmer*. A Black Muslim had been
placed in a control cell for allegedly preaching a sermon tending to incite
a breach of the peace. The cell was 8 feet by 12 feet with no windows,
natural light, bed, wash basin, or furniture. He was allowed no exercise,
visitors, mail, or reading matter. The light switch and mechanism for

flushing the toilet were beyond his reach. He was allowed only 2,000 calories a day, and only occasionally a shower and shave. After 13 days he was removed to the Special Treatment Unit where he remained for 18 days. He was then returned to the control cell where he spent 15 more days before being again released to the Special Treatment Unit, where he remained for 6 months. While in the Special Treatment Unit, he was required to eat in his cell; consequently, his food was always cold. He was not permitted to work, see movies, watch television, have visitors, or participate in rehabilitative programs. In all, he spent over 2 years in solitary and restricted confinement. The District Court for the District of Columbia held that the punishment was "not reasonably related" to the rule infraction, was disproportionate and, in sum, constituted cruel and unusual punishment.

Restricted diets have also been declared constitutional. Several statutes imposing the punishment have historically been upheld. Likewise, restrictions by officials on the quantity of food to be served convicts who have violated prison rules have generally been held constitutional (Hirschkop and Millemann 1969). Nonetheless, the trend has been against using such punishment, and presently, the Federal Bureau of Prisons prohibits its use. Further, Federal Judge Merhige of the Eastern District of Virginia recently found that the penalty is rarely used today and is generally disapproved of as obsolete. To him, it amounts to "an unnecessary infliction of pain" and is "inconsistent with current minimum standards of respect for human dignity." As such, he had no difficulty in determining in *Landman* v. *Royster* that the punishment, imposed in the prisons of Virginia, was in violation of the Eighth Amendment.

Among the most recent controversial decisions dealing with corporeal punishment have been those that have declared entire penal systems or specific facilities within such systems unconstitutional. Many of the penal institutions found in the various states are extremely antiquated (Singer 1971). In 1961, for example, more than 100 prisons in use had been built before the Civil War. By 1967 a minimum of 11 percent of all prisons were over 80 years old. As a result, many jails are totally inadequate for the functions they are to perform. Sporadic challenges have been made to these environments since 1904. Yet, it was not until 1970 that prisoners incarcerated in a jail or penitentiary were first successful in obtaining a declaration that their environment inflicted cruel and unusual punishment. In *Curley* v. *Gonzales,* a New Mexico court held that conditions in a local jail were so intolerable that they were unconstitutional.

The following week the first of several decisions involving the Arkansas state penitentiary system was handed down by a federal court. In *Holt* v. *Sarver,* Chief District Judge Henley found conditions throughout the system "shocking to the conscience of reasonable civilized people."

Upon investigation, he found that the system used few employees, used armed trustees to guard the rank and file, confined convicts when they were not working, required inmates to sleep at night in overcrowded, open, dormitory-type barracks, and provided few, if any, programs of meaningful rehabilitation. Moreover, the cells were characterized as filthy, unsanitary, cold, wet, and sometimes rat-infested.

In 1972 a second statewide penitentiary system was declared unconstitutional (*Gates* v. *Collier*). Parchman Prison in Mississippi had been built in 1903, and the physical facilities were in extreme disrepair. They were found to be "subhuman" and "unfit for human habitation under any modern concept of decency." The electrical wiring was in a poor state of repair and presented safety hazards. There was a general lack of firefighting equipment. The windows were stuffed with rags for insulation against the elements. Bathroom facilities were lacking and those that existed were poorly maintained. Waste disposal systems were deemed "shockingly inadequate" and a "health hazard." As in Arkansas, the trustee system was used and was replete with payoffs, favoritism, extortion, and participation in illegal activities. For these reasons and others, Federal Judge Keady declared the entire environment constitutionally impermissible and ordered rectification of the deficiencies.

During the same period a number of jails were declared in violation of the Eighth Amendment. In 1970 Judge Christenberry found that conditions in the Orleans Parish Prison in New Orleans "so shocked the conscience as a matter of elemental decency" and were "so much more cruel than . . . necessary" that confinement there constituted cruel and unusual punishment (*Hamilton* v. *Shiro*). Subsequently, the Pulaski County Jail in Arkansas, the Lucas County Jail in Ohio, Holmesburg Prison in Pennsylvania, and the Greystone section of Santa Rita Rehabilitation Center in California have been held violative of the Eighth Amendment. In each instance there were exacerbated problems with heating, ventilation, plumbing, and sanitation facilities. Food, bedding, clothing, and bathing facilities were entirely inadequate. The cells were generally dim, shabbily painted, and greatly overcrowded. Often pretrial detainees were incarcerated with convicted prisoners. There was an almost total lack of recreation, exercise, and vocational guidance for these prisoners. Similarly, the conditions surrounding incarceration in several juvenile detention facilities have recently been found to be impermissible.

Incorporeal Punishments

Not only may physical and psychological punishments be cruel and unusual, but incorporeal ones may be as well. Foremost among these are excessive sentences. In no less than five cases issued before 1910 were such sentences declared unconstitutional. Nonetheless, in 1892 the United States Supreme Court, in *O'Neil* v. *Vermont,* refused to hold that the Eighth Amendment applied to "all punishments which by their excessive length or severity are greatly disproportionate to the offenses charged." Involved was a conviction on 307 separate offenses of selling intoxicating liquor unlawfully. A justice of the peace fined John O'Neil $20 on each count plus costs of prosecution and commitment. The total came to $6,638.72, and, if not paid, he was to be imprisoned three days for each dollar, a total of 19,914 days, or more than 54 years.

In 1910, however, the dissenters in *O'Neil* were victorious. A disbursing officer for the Philippine Branch of the Coast Guard had misappropriated a small sum of money. He was found guilty under a statute providing for the minimum punishment of 12 years and 1 day of *cadena temporal* (imprisonment in chains at "hard and painful" labor, which meant carrying a chain from wrist to ankle at all times), civil interdiction (deprivation of rights of parental authority, guardianship and marriage), perpetual and absolute disqualification to vote, debarment from holding public office or receiving retirement pay or honors, and subjection to official surveillance during life. On appeal, the United State Supreme Court held that it was the intent of the founding fathers to restrict excessively severe punishments. Such penalties, wrote Justice McKenna, "amaze those who . . . believe that it is a precept of justice that punishment for crime should be graduated and proportioned to [the] offense." (*Weems* v. *U.S.,* at 366-67) Thus, the Court found that the sentence came under the condemnation of the Bill of Rights, both on account of its degree and kind.

Since the *Weems* decision, no fewer than 19 opinions have declared certain punishments or statutes in violation of various cruel and unusual punishment inhibitions. One of the most recent cases involved a youth who had been convicted of making an unlawful sale of marijuana. The statute under which he was to be sentenced provided a mandatory minimum of 20 years imprisonment. The Michigan Supreme Court in the *Lorentzen* case noted that the statute was equally applicable to a first offender high school student as to a "wholesaling racketeer." It was further noted that the penalties for other harmful substances were much less harsh. Thus, the court held that the statute failed to meet the test of proportionality and therefore was cruel and unusual.

Besides excessive sentences, a number of other incorporeal punishments have been challenged as inflicting cruel and unusual punishment, most of them quite unsuccessfully. For example, in spite of concerted efforts, habitual offender statutes have never been declared unconstitutional (Katkin 1971). Likewise, multiple sentences in single prosecutions (one act may result in the violation of several statutes) have been continually upheld, as have indeterminate sentences and unequal sentences imposed on co-defendants charged with the same offense (Alperin 1970; Kaminski 1959; Note 1958).

Other incorporeal punishments that have been challenged as inflicting cruel and unusual punishment are deportation, banishment, and expatriation. It is clear that deportation is perfectly constitutional. There is, however, some question about banishment. Certainly it has never been in accord with general public policy in the United States. No state provides for it statutorily. As a punishment for crime, the few cases on the subject would indicate that it is impermissible. For example, in 1962 the Ninth Circuit Court of Appeals held in *Dear Wing Jung* that it was either cruel and unusual punishment or a violation of due process. Equally suspect is the practice, occasionally used by judges, of releasing convicts on condition that they leave the state. To date, many such sentences have been vacated on the ground that the trial judge, when imposing such a sentence, exceeded his authority, because banishment is not provided for by law. Nonetheless, it appears that governors have the authority to grant pardons attaching a condition of banishment.

One of the United States Supreme Court's most important Eighth Amendment cases, *Trop* v. *Dulles*, involved the issue of expatriation. Albert Trop, a 20-year-old private, was stationed in French Morocco during World War II. For a breach of discipline he was confined to the stockade. He escaped, but turned himself in the next day, never having made contact with the enemy. For his conduct, he was convicted of desertion and sentenced to three years at hard labor, forfeiture of all pay and allowances, and was issued a dishonorable discharge. In 1952 he applied for a passport, but was denied on the ground that he had lost his citizenship by reason of desertion. In 1955 he sought declaratory judgment that he was a citizen, but was denied. The Supreme Court granted certiorari. Chief Justice Warren reasoned that by Trop's "conduct," he had not lost his citizenship, because desertion in wartime "does not necessarily signify allegiance to a foreign state." He noted that unlike an earlier case, denationalization was not claimed to be a means of solving international problems. He noted of the punishment that there might not be "physical mistreatment" or "primitive torture," but instead there was a "total destruction of the individual's status in organized society. It is a form of punishment more primitive than torture, for it destroys for the individual the political existence that was centuries in the development. . ." (at 101)

Another type of incorporeal punishment that has been challenged involves status statutes. Traditionally crimes have been defined in terms of acts or failures to act. However, there are a few offenses that are defined in terms of *being* rather than *acting*. These statutes first came to the attention of the United States Supreme Court in 1962. Lawrence Robinson had been convicted of violating a statute that stated: "No person shall use, or be under the influence of narcotics. . . ." The jury had made no distinction as to which aspect of the statute had been violated, the "use" or being "under the influence." In *Robinson* v. *California,* Justice Stewart noted that the second part of the statute made the "status" of narcotic addiction a criminal offense for which the offender might be prosecuted at any time before he reforms. Thus, he considered it to be in the same category as making it a criminal offense to be mentally ill, to be a leper, or to be afflicted with a venereal disease. "We hold," he concluded, "that a state law which imprisons a person thus afflicted as a criminal, even though he has never touched any narcotic drug within the State or been guilty of any irregular behavior there, inflicts cruel and unusual punishments in violation of the Fourteenth Amendment." (at 667) Subsequently several state courts declared similar statutes unconstitutional.

The second category of status crimes regularly considered by the courts has been that of drunkenness. Two circuit courts of appeal in 1966 declared statutes dealing with the subject unconstitutional, relying upon *Robinson.* In 1968, however, the United States Supreme Court had occasion to review a similar case, *Powell* v. *Texas.* Leroy Powell had been arrested and charged with violation of a Texas statute, which provided: "Whoever shall get drunk or be found in a state of intoxication in any public house except his own, shall be fined not exceeding one hundred dollars." Justice Marshall noted that on its face the statute did not fall within the *Robinson* holding. Powell was convicted not for being a chronic alcoholic, but for being in public while drunk. Thus, the Texas statute was not punishing mere status, but overt behavior. It is this distinction that has generally been used to uphold statutes involving not only drugs and alcoholic usage, but acts of prostitution and homosexuality as well. Some successful litigation has taken place when vagrancy statutes are involved. For example, two recent Nevada decisions have declared such provisions unconstitutional on their face because their effect was to make status a crime.

Conclusion

From the foregoing discussion, it should be clear that with a few minor exceptions, Americans may not be excessively punished, expatriated, whipped, sterilized, banished, or punished merely because of their status in society. On the other hand, in contrast with most industrialized societies of the world, they may be sentenced to death. Nonetheless, there have been no executions in the United States since 1967. The *Furman* decision prohibited infliction of capital punishment on those under sentence of death at the time. Presently, numerous courts have stayed executions until the United States Supreme Court again has a chance to consider the issue in *Fowler*.

It should be equally clear that the Eighth Amendment is no longer an obscure and forgotten part of the Constitution. Litigation based on the cruel and unusual punishment concept has increased nearly five-fold during the past decade. Moreover, the parameters of the inhibition have been considerably broadened.

Perhaps the most important development in this respect has been the extention of the concept to protect inmates incarcerated in jails and penitentiaries. In spite of the fact that these citizens leave many of their civil rights at the prison gates, the Eighth Amendment protects them from many questionable practices used by dispassionate administrators in the past. Further, the facilities in which they are incarcerated may be attacked as unconstitutional unless they meet certain minimum standards. The Eighth Amendment has indeed become one of the new frontiers of creative constitutional law.

Cases

Buck v. Bell, 274 U.S. 200 (1927).

Curley v. Gonzales, Civil No. 8372 (D. N.M., February 12, 1970).

Dear Wing Jung v. United States, 312 F.2d 73 (9th Cir. 1962).

Fowler v. North Carolina, 43 L.W. 3577 (1975).

Fulwood v. Clemmer, 206 F. Supp. 370 (D. D.C. 1962).

Furman v. Georgia, 408 U.S. 238 (1972).

Gates v. Collier, 349 F. Supp. 881 (N.D. Miss. 1972).

Hamilton v. Shiro, 338 F. Supp. 1016 (E.D. La. 1970).

Holt v. Sarver, 309 F. Supp. 362 (E.D. Ark. 1970).

Landman v. Royster, 333 F. Supp. 621 (E.D. Va. 1971).

O'Neil v. Vermont, 144 U.S. 323 (1892).

People v. Anderson, 493 P.2d 880 (Cal. 1972).

People v. Lorentzen, 194 N.W.2d 827 (Mich. 1972).

Powell v. Texas, 392 U.S. 514 (1968).

Ralph v. Warden, 438 F.2d 786 (4th Cir. 1970).

Robinson v. California, 370 U.S. 660 (1962).

State v. O'Brien, 106 Vt. 97, 170 A. 98 (1934).

Trop v. Dulles, 356 U.S. 86 (1958).

Weems v. United States, 214 U.S. 349 (1910).

118

References

Alperin, Howard J. 1970. "Length of Sentence As Violation of Constitutional Provisions Prohibiting Cruel and Unusual Punishment," *ALR3d*, XXXIII, 335-86.

Friend, Charles E. 1967. "Judicial Intervention in Prison Administration," *William and Mary Law Review*, IX (Fall), 178-92.

Goldfarb, Ronald, and Linda Singer. 1970. "Redressing Prisoners' Grievances," *George Washington Law Review*, XXXIX (December), 175-320.

Granucci, Anthony. 1969. " 'Nor Cruel and Unusual Punishments Inflicted': The Original Meaning," *California Law Review*, LVII (October), 839-65.

Hirschkop, Philip, and Michael A. Millemann. 1969. "The Unconstitutionality of Prison Life," *Virginia Law Review*, LV (June), 795-839.

Kaminski, Edward C. 1959. "Indeterminate Sentencing—Half Step Toward Science in Law," *Western Reserve Law Review*, X (September), 574-85.

Katkin, Daniel. 1971. "Habitual Offender Laws: A Reconsideration," *Buffalo Law Review*, XXI, 99-120.

Note. 1958. "Consecutive Sentences in Single Prosecutions: Judicial Multiplication of Statutory Penalties," *Yale Law Journal*, LXVII (April), 916-31.

O'Hara, James V., and Howland Sanks. 1956. "Eugenic Sterilization," *Georgetown Law Journal*, XLV (Fall), 20-44.

Paul, Julius. 1968. "The Return of Punitive Sterilization Proposals," *Law and Society Review*, III (August), 77-106.

Singer, Richard G. 1971. "Prison Conditions: An Unconstitutional Roadblock to Rehabilitation," *Catholic University Law Review*, XX (Spring), 365-93.

Stevens, Correale F. 1971. "Punitive Segregation in State Prisons," *Dickinson Law Review*, LXXVI (Fall), 125-43.

12 Informational Privacy

Jerome J. Hanus

An arrest record precludes government employment although charges
have been dropped; an applicant for a mortgage is inexplicably refused; a
teacher's caustic comment follows a pupil into adult life. Such incidents
illustrate an individual's loss of control over information about himself
maintained in records. Whether one views this loss with alarm or considers it merely an inevitable irritant of modern life depends upon the degree
to which one values the underlying right of privacy.

Definition

Privacy may be usefully defined as "the claim of individuals, groups, or
institutions to determine for themselves when, how, and to what extent
information about them is communicated to others." (Westin 1967, p. 7)
The concept also is best understood if qualified in some way, for example,
as associational privacy, marital privacy, or informational privacy. (See
comments by Fried 1968; Lusky 1972; Miller 1971; Parker 1974.)

Privacy is one of the few new concepts in law and political philosophy
that is almost certain to take its place among such classical ones as justice, equality, freedom, property, and representation. Like these familiar
concepts, which influence and are affected by public policies, privacy is
rich in metaphor and mythology and is sufficiently opaque to offer opportunity for endless commentary. Here, after a brief introduction, we focus
primarily on only one facet of the topic: the legislative development of
the right of informational privacy.

Development

Privacy had its legal and political genesis in 1890, when Samuel D. Warren and Louis D. Brandeis, elaborating upon Judge Thomas Cooley's
Treatise on the Law of Torts, urged recognition of a right of privacy in tort
law, defined as a "right to be let alone." Their understanding of the right
was quite straightforward: people engaged in activities of nonpublic im-
port should be left alone by the press and by government. More important
than their policy recommendation, however, was the rationale for recog-

nizing such a right. While the basis of their argument rested on human dignity, they also recognized the invention of new technologies, which, in the hands of unscrupulous men, could pose a threat to personal freedom. Some 37 years later, in his eloquent *Olmstead* dissent, Justice Brandeis reemphasized his earlier sentiments but gave much greater emphasis to the threat posed by technology, of which wiretapping, the issue in the case, was but one example.

Another 40 years passed before Brandeis' dissent prevailed (*Berger* v. *New York; Katz* v. *United States*). In the intervening period, the nation experienced its transition to the modern industrial state, donned the panoply of military might, and assumed responsibility for individual welfare. Among the institutional results of the changes were the Veterans' Administration, whose files on veterans, their relatives, and beneficiaries now include material on 50 percent of the population, and the Social Security Administration, whose files touch almost the entire population. Such organizations were also the basis for fears about the invasion of privacy, as computer technology made the exchange of data on a person, and the compilation of a comprehensive record on him, an intimidating reality. The accumulation of massive record systems at the local, state, and federal levels resulting from rapidly increasing criminal activity has made the matter even more worrisome as the large numbers of suspects, combined with their mobility, have encouraged intergovernmental centralization of criminal justice information.

These developments, reinforced by the adoption of selected aspects of libertarian individualism by influential public opinion leaders, have resulted in a perception of these information-gathering activities significantly different from that of the post-World War II period, when the liberalism of the time led many to consider them purely beneficial. In addition, House and Senate investigations have kept people attuned to abuses of government information practices. From these hearings flowed a number of federal statutes, which now provide significant protection in this newly emerging area of civil liberties. We now look specifically at those affecting credit records, criminal justice records, school records, and government record-keeping in general.

Credit Records

With over 80 percent of the buying public now relying on credit and with over 170 million consumer reports furnished in 1973 alone, the United States is clearly a "credit" society. In 1969, 2,200 credit bureaus held records on over 100 million people in the United States. The bureaus collect and disseminate reports to over 400,000 creditors. Included in many of these credit files is information on eating and drinking habits, marital relationships, other behavioral traits, religious and political preferences, and general reputations. This information, received from friends, acquaintances, and employers of the individual, is usually included in *investigative consumer reports*, and used by prospective employers, insurers, and landlords for determining the extension of credit. Information about a person's credit standing, credit capacity, status of bank accounts, outstanding liabilities, and bill-paying habits is supplied by department stores, banks, and businesses with which one already has an account and is referred to as a *consumer report*.

Without the extension of credit in timely fashion, not only would persons on limited incomes be deprived of the advantages of a modern industrialized economy (e.g., buying TV sets and cars "on time") but the overall economy would probably suffer a decline. The high mobility rate of Americans requires that a lender have quick and accurate access to such records. A family moving from one section of the country to another may well find itself short on cash, in need of a house and furnishings, and even a loan to cover outstanding credit payments. A consumer report allows the borrower to benefit by having credit available when needed, and the lender benefits by not suffering large credit losses.

This transformation in financial relationships from a monetary to a credit economy has brought in its train a host of new difficulties, only now being resolved, which extract a high social price. The existence of a credit bureau industry in which information on a variety of disparate activities can be swiftly assembled in an automated file and disseminated to businesses and government agencies requesting them carries the obvious potential for infringment on individual rights. What to do about this problem, and what costs to sustain in making changes, is much less obvious.

The policy issue is how to improve the welfare of the individual without inadvertently crippling important credit services. The dangers to the individual are (1) the loss of a benefit because of false or misleading information in the record, and (2) the "chilling" effect on a person resulting from knowledge that records exist on his personal activities.

The first danger may arise from several sources. In the case of an investigative consumer report, a vindictive source may be making or reporting untrue statements, or the report may include "public record" information (e.g., tax liens, bankruptcies, arrests) that is outdated or incomplete. Finally, the context of information—such as when one delayed paying a bill because of shoddy or damaged merchandise—may not be reported.

The second danger, which relates directly to the exercise of civil liberties, is one with which it is difficult to come to grips. No one has a "right" to a job, to a good credit rating, or to credit. If one wants credit, so the argument goes, then one has to be willing to surrender certain amenities, in this case, informational privacy. And requiring such trade-offs is not unprecedented. What remains unresolved is the problem of how much "chilling" may be permitted as well as the logically prior questions of when it occurs and with what subsequent damage.

If credit records are not to be prohibited altogether, a rule of reasonableness and fairness must be followed. This is the approach used in the Fair Credit Reporting Act of 1970, Congress' first attempt to balance the competing interests. The act regulates investigative reports and consumer reports and imposes obligations on both collectors and users of the reports. An investigative consumer report may not be prepared without the consumer being notified within three days that the request has been made. The consumer may then request from the creditor a complete and accurate disclosure of the nature and scope of the investigation requested. The consumer is also given the right to know the nature and sources of the information contained in the files of the reporting agency. However, medical information and the sources used solely in an investigative file may be exempted from the disclosure requirement.

The act also provides procedures for correcting or disputing material in the report held by the reporting agency. Information relating to arrests, convictions, suits, and judgments that occurred more than 7 years earlier, and bankruptcies adjudicated more than 14 years earlier, may not be included. Recipients of the reports must have a "legitimate business need," and the credit bureau is supposed to ensure that the assertion is valid. Noncompliance is a basis for a civil suit by the consumer and is also an unfair trade practice within the jurisdiction of the Federal Trade Commission.

The act has been criticized because of the restrictions on a subject's access to his credit report, the looseness of provisions governing the dissemination of the report, the lack of any prohibitions on the collection of certain types of information, and the difficulty in proving an invasion of privacy under its provisions. The statute's strength and importance lie in the specific rights that it gives consumers in asserting control over information about themselves.

Criminal Justice Records

Criminal justice record keeping raises two distinguishable privacy situations: (1) where probable cause of a suspect's criminal activity has not been established, and (2) where a person arrested but not convicted continues to be tracked via his arrest records. The first situation, although raising questions under the First, Fourth, and Fifth Amendments relating to surveillance, wiretapping, and use of informers, does not raise informational privacy questions in the sense of "maintaining some control over information which has been collected." Rather, the question is whether the collection should have been made in the first place and reflects the facet of privacy defined as the "right to be let alone."

The second situation, dealing with information storage and dissemination, raises complex informational privacy questions compounded by the large number of law enforcement records in existence and the ease with which they can be, and are, disseminated among all levels of government. More specific issues as to the records themselves include the lack of disposition information in the records, the erroneous information kept, the length of time over which records are maintained, and the transfer of record information to private employers.

A centralized computer center in the FBI-National Crime Information Center in Washington, D.C., is connected with terminals in police stations throughout the country. NCIC files contain information relating to stolen securities, motor vehicles, boats, guns, licence plates, and wanted persons. Currently, however, only four states participate in the FBI's computerized criminal history system (containing data on identification, arrest, court disposition, appeals, and custody status), also included in the NCIC.

Congress began to deal with criminal justice records in the Crime Control Act of 1973, although regulations were not issued until early 1975. The act limits the use of information in the records, permits individuals to have access to their records and to correct erroneous information, and specifies that disposition as well as arrest data must be included. However, the act deals only with criminal history, not investigatory files. Thus, a person has access only to files that contain descriptions and notations of completed actions, but not to the unevaluated information. For the individual, the primary benefit of the act is a right to ensure the accuracy and completeness of records but, because investigatory records are used to make adverse determinations about individuals, controls on the records are needed if protection is to be more meaningful.

Unanswered questions relating to policy on regulation of investigatory files are how useful such files are to law enforcement agencies and how pervasive are abuses of the information they contain. Too stringent restrictions might impair legitimate agency activities. Nor is it clear whether the allegedly illegal use of information systems by the FBI and CIA results from agency policies or work imperatives or are only ad hoc in nature. Legislation can respond to the former by prohibiting the disputed policies and establishing an effective oversight mechanism, but ad hoc abuses appear almost impossible to prevent. At a minimum, however, some form of citizen access to "sanitized" investigatory files would increase confidence in the agencies and act as a pressure against misuse of files by government officials.

School Records

The earliest record compiled on an American is his school file. Begun when the student is in kindergarden, a record is created and added to by teachers and counselors describing the pupil's progress through the school system. For many, the system does not end until one's admission to a profession. This record keeping is caused in large part by our society's reliance upon its schools to test, label, and categorize its children as a means for identifying the proficient and the dependable.

Informational privacy questions are raised by the contents of the files, particularly their inclusiveness, and by the numbers of people with access to the file, with respect to both of which abuses occur. Among the items included in a school record are grades and class standing; IQ, aptitude, and achievement scores; interest inventory results and personality test profiles; health information; and race, nationality, religion, and other family background information. Most records also contain written comments or evaluations made by teachers, counselors, and administrators, which may be of the following sort: "A real sickie—absent, truant, stubborn, and very dull. Is verbal only about irrelevant facts. Can barely read (which was a huge accomplishment to get this far). Have fun." (Divoky 1974) In a tightly competitive market for admission to a professional school or a job after graduation, nonderogatory letters of recommendation are often a necessity; yet a casual comment by the appraiser, included in a file, might be understood to be negative and lead to nonselection.

Concerning the second question, some school systems have computerized their school records in central data banks to which law enforcement agencies, federal agencies such as the Selective Service Board, and, depending upon local regulations, credit and insurance companies might have access. In addition, there is constant pressure for release of information from researchers and federal civil rights agencies. For example, in 1974 the U.S. Office of Education threatened to cut off over 5 million dollars in federal funds if the Washington, D.C., school system did not administer a battery of tests, some of which requested large amounts of personal and family information.

Governmental responses to the dangers and inequities in the handling of school records have occurred at both the federal and state levels. Most important is the Family Educational Rights and Privacy Act of 1974, popularly known as the Buckley Amendment, which applies the principles of informational privacy to all educational institutions receiving federal funds. Under the act, parents are given the right to see the information collected on their child and have a right to challenge its accuracy and its dissemination. When a student reaches age 18 or enters a postsecondary educational institution, the rights accorded the parents are transferred to the student alone. Kept from the parents' or students' reach are administrative records that are not disseminated, law enforcement files, and medical records. "Directory information" (e.g., names and addresses, date of birth, telephone numbers, height and weight of athletic team members) may be routinely released unless the parent objects within a short time after receiving notice of the intended use. All instructional material used in connection with any research or experimentation program must be available for inspection by the parents or student. However, federal audits of federally supported education programs are authorized so long as the data collected is not personally identifiable. The Secretary of Health, Education and Welfare may deny funds to any institution that has a policy of releasing student information without the written consent of the parents or student.

The act seems to be making an impact on school record keeping. Although early reports indicate that few people are taking advantage of the opportunity to inspect their files, such inspection could bring some peace of mind when it is discovered that nothing derogatory is included. One result might be greater confidence in teachers and schools. Newspaper accounts also indicate that school files are becoming slimmer as confidential evaluations and recommendations are destroyed. Fewer remarks about family background situations are being made and more care is being taken to obtain parental permission before making a written evaluation of a student.

These consequences however may be double-edged when considered as benefits or costs. Probably fewer letters of recommendation are being written and those written are likely to be more noncommital. This will mean increased reliance on grades and qualifying examinations, thus narrowing the criteria for selection of students. Also discouraged may be written observations by teachers of behavior patterns of pupils not doing well in class. Since almost all studies of school achievement conclude that the condition of home life is a critical learning variable, the usefulness of psychological counseling could be reduced. If this occurs, schools emphasizing individualized instruction and personal attention to pupils will be most affected. Finally, there may be a reduction in the number of research studies of pupils and thus the loss of some insight into student behavior.

Government Record Keeping

The rapid proliferation of automated data banks in the federal government in the 1960s and 1970s—containing in excess of one and one-quarter billion separate records on American residents—stimulated worries by many citizens that the nation's tradition of limited government was in jeopardy. Lending substance to this concern were the proposal for a National Data Center that would centralize all federal records, disclosures of military surveillance of citizens, the maintenance of "blacklists" by federal agencies, and the increasing use of the Social Security number as a standard universal identifier. Legislation enacted in 1974 sought to respond to these concerns by creating a statutory right of individuals to exercise a measure of control over information about themselves which they have voluntarily or involuntarily provided the federal government. The Privacy Act of 1974 has received surprisingly little publicity but nevertheless is causing considerable consternation among information system specialists. Along with the amended Freedom of Information Act, the Privacy Act requires a shift in perceptions and attitudes by administrators as well as a major change in information-handling procedures. Like the three statutes discussed earlier, the act places a legal tool in the hands of the individual, which can be used to enhance his political and economic powers.

The act imposes minimum regulations on all executive agencies but fewer responsibilities on units with especially distinctive or sensitive records, for example, the CIA and law enforcement agencies. Some types of records are also exempted from access. These include statistical records, testing materials, investigatory files compiled for determining suitability for federal employment and federal contracts, and classified information containing confidential sources. However, all agencies must publish notices of the character and existence of their personal record keeping systems; there are to be no secret record systems. Agencies may maintain only such personal information as is "relevant and necessary" to their purposes and they are restricted in the maintenance of information on religious and political activities and beliefs; except for "routine uses," they may not disclose information (even within the agency) without the consent of the individual; the sale or rental of mailing lists is prohibited; and the use of the Social Security number as a personal identifier is restricted.

The act establishes the Privacy Protection Study Commission to recommend ways for ensuring informational privacy. The Office of Management and Budget has oversight responsibility as do the appropriate congressional committees. However, the most effective enforcement is expected to come from affected individuals, supported by public interest groups, because they have motivation, a legal right to go to court if necessary, and may receive attorney fees and court costs if they substantially prevail.

Among the benefits expected from the legislation are a reduction in government collection of information, more complete and accurate records, reduced dissemination of records without the knowledge of the record subject, increased citizen confidence in government, and disclosure of governmental errors and improper practices. However, possible costs must also be expected. The act's sanctions are likely incentives for agencies to centralize their information systems, thereby establishing a number of federal data centers. And the intent of the act may be counterproductive in at least one respect. One agency information officer has commented that a new record must be created for each record accessed by the subject. If this is indeed the case generally, an amendment of the act to resolve this unanticipated result will be necessary.

Summary

A right of informational privacy is now recognized in federal legislation. The four statutes discussed here suggest that a consensus is emerging on the substantive principles of informational privacy. A person has a right to have his record accurate, up-to-date, and fair. Procedures for implementing the right include notification to the subject of the existence of the record, a right of access to the record, specific time periods within which the record holder must acknowledge the request, opportunity to challenge information in the record, and provision for administrative or judicial review.

Deficiencies in these statutes can be remedied by amendment, and experience gained under them can be the basis for extending the right to other governmental sectors. The cautious governmental approach in this complex area encourages respect for the right of informational privacy and manifests responsible concern for the individual and social welfare of the citizenry. However, despite the increased support given the right, it is unlikely to be recognized as "fundamental" because of the important position that information collection and dissemination has assumed in our society.

Cases

Berger v. New York, 388 U.S. 41 (1967).
Katz v. United States, 389 U.S. 347 (1968).
Olmstead v. United States, 277 U.S. 438 (1927).

Statutes

Crime Control Act of 1973, 42 U.S.C. 3771.

Fair Credit Reporting Act of 1970, 15 U.S.C. 1681 et seq.

Family Educational Rights and Privacy Act of 1974, 20 U.S.C. 1232a.

Freedom of Information Act, 5 U.S.C. 552.

Privacy Act of 1974, 5 U.S.C. 552a.

References

Cooley, Thomas M. 1888. *Treatise on the Law of Torts* (Chicago: Callaghan).

Divoky, Diane. 1974. "How Secret School Records Can Hurt Your Child." *Parade Magazine* (March 31), 4-5.

Fried, Charles. 1968. "Privacy," *Yale Law Journal,* 77 (January), 475-93.

Lusky, Louis. 1972. "Invasion of Privacy: A Clarification of Concepts," *Political Science Quarterly,* 87 (June), 192-209.

Miller, Arthur R. 1971. *The Assault on Privacy* (Ann Arbor: University of Michigan Press).

Parker, Richard B. 1974. "A Definition of Privacy," *Rutgers Law Review,* 27 (Winter), 275-96.

Warren, Samuel D., and Brandeis, Louis D. 1890. "The Right to Privacy," *Harvard Law Review,* 4 (December), 193-220.

Westin, Alan F. 1967. *Privacy and Freedom* (New York: Atheneum).

13 The Right to Know

Richard E. Morgan

Dramatic events of the late 1960s and early 1970s, grouped roughly under the rubrics "Vietnam" and "Watergate," have focused national attention sharply on the question of what government may properly keep secret. This has occurred simultaneously with heightening sensitivity (at least among liberal elites) to the value of personal privacy—privacy defined as control of information about oneself (Westin 1967). New public law concerning information seeking is developing, and there is wide concern these days with "the right to know."

To speak of the right to know, however, is not at all the same thing as to speak, say, of the right to free exercise of religion or of the privilege against self-incrimination. The right to know has no certain lodging within the constitutional text. The American political tradition is rich in rhetoric concerning the importance of "the people" having "the facts" on which to base electoral judgments, but legal definitions—the ones that count—have been late in coming. Even now the content of the right to know is not subject to very precise description. The piecemeal response of the legal system to a variety of information problems has resulted in an incomplete and disjointed statutory edifice resting on a shallow constitutional foundation.

In 1953 Harold Cross published *The People's Right to Know,* for two decades the most frequently cited work in the field. The book was almost completely filled with a catalog of state laws on access to public records and with criticism of the restrictive access provisions of federal law (5 U.S.C. 22, the 1789 "Housekeeping Act," and 5 U.S.C. 1001, part of the Administrative Procedure Act of 1946). There was only a thin chapter on the First Amendment because litigation to that time had been premised, characteristically, on a right to speak or publish, not on a right to hear or seek information. However, by the mid-1960s, things were beginning to change from the picture Cross had painted. There has been some constitutional development, considerable innovation in federal statutory law, and some improving and refining of state law.

A Constitutional Right to Know

The Supreme Court has now recognized that the First Amendment's protection of speech carries with it some basic public right to information and

129

confers some degree of protection on journalists seeking news. However, these judicial references have been tantalizingly oblique and elliptical, and the dimensions of the constitutional right and protection have hardly been suggested. Here are the highlights.

The special libel standard for public officials and public figures created by *New York Times* v. *Sullivan* (1964) really rests on a right-to-know basis. The First Amendment value being protected is not so much the interest of someone in expressing himself as the interest of the public in benefitting from unfettered discussion of the activities of public officials and figures. However, no well-articulated statement of that interest appears in principal case or its progeny.

In May 1965 Chief Justice Warren wrote for the Court in *Zemel* v. *Rusk* denying a claim of a First Amendment right to travel abroad and inform oneself. Later that month, however, in *Lamont* v. *Postmaster General,* the Court, speaking through Justice Douglas, upheld a First Amendment right to receive "communist propaganda" through the mails. The right to know was not specifically mentioned. Rather, Douglas asserted a First Amendment interest in "uninhibited, robust, and wide-open debate" that echoed *New York Times* v. *Sullivan.*

In the famous *Red Lion* case (1969) upholding the FCC's "fairness doctrine," Justice White spoke approvingly of "the right of the public to receive suitable access to social, political, esthetic, moral, and other ideas. . . ." Yet, this interest was insufficient to sustain the claim of a paying advertiser for "access to the media" in *Columbia Broadcasting System* v. *Democratic National Committee* (1973), or the constitutionality of a state "right to reply" statute in the *Miami Herald* case (1974). In both of these cases, contrary to the access theory advocated by Jerome Barron, Chief Justice Burger wrote that the primary First Amendment prohibition of governmental controls on the press outweighed the public interest in information flow.

In *Branzburg* v. *Hayes* (1972) the Court rejected a First Amendment claim, bottomed on a public right to know, of a qualified testimentory immunity for reporters before grand juries. Justice White reasoned that "the First Amendment does not invalidate every incidental burdening of the press that may result from the enforcement of civil or criminal statutes of general applicability" (at 682). Yet, in passing, White remarked that news gathering was not without First Amendment protection, and the Court said that Congress could provide either an absolute or qualified statutory immunity, although it has not yet done so.

There are other cases (*Stanley* v. *Georgia; Kleindienst* v. *Mandel*) in which the Court has referred to a "now well-established" constitutional right "to receive information and ideas." Thus, the phrase may be well-established, but its meaning is anything but clear. The best that can be said of the constitutional status of the right to know after such cases is that there have been repeated references to a right to hear and receive and seek information. However, these rights, of a substantially lower order of First Amendment magnitude than the right to speak, must usually yield to "ordinary legal rules of general applicability."

The Freedom of Information Act

In the recent rapid development of federal statutory law, the restrictive provisions of the "Housekeeping Act" and of the Administrative Procedure Act have been swept away. In their place is the Freedom of Information Act (FOIA) of 1966. Until 1966 a statutory presumption had operated in favor of confidentiality of government documents; that presumption has now been reversed. At the heart of the FOIA (5 U.S.C. 552) is a commitment to a policy of executive, although not legislative or judicial, disclosure. The act has three major dimensions. First, it requires publication of certain executive branch documents such as agency rules and procedural norms; second, it requires that "final opinions" and "statements of policy" must be made available to the public; and third, it provides for public access, on request, to other executive branch documents, *unless they fall into one of nine exempted categories*.

In the first years after the act's adoption, its publication requirements seemed to work well, as did its subsections dealing with release of final opinions and statements of policy. If a document contains such materials, it cannot be exempted. The Supreme Court, in cases such as *Sears, Roebuck* v. *NLRB* and *Grumman Aircraft* v. *Renegotiation Board* (1975), has been careful to specify that it is the *function* of the document in the administrative process (not what the agency *calls* it) that determines whether it is final or is policy, or whether it is ordinary working material and might fall within one of the exemptions.

Trouble developed, however, with respect to the access provisions. Cumbersome procedures for gaining access and the breadth and ambiguity of several exemptions afforded reluctant officials almost endless opportunity for engaging in dilatory tactics (Katz 1970; Davis 1967). To deal with these problems, the act was amended in late 1974 over presidential veto (P.L. 93-502). It appears that the procedural difficulties that originally frustrated access have been largely overcome, but major ambiguities remain within several of the exemptions.

The first exemption originally allowed the withholding of information deemed by the "executive" to affect national defense or foreign policy adversely. This was altered to exempt only materials "specifically authorized under criteria established by an Executive order to be kept secret in the interest of national defense or foreign policy." The exemption was tied to the classification system in an apparent attempt to narrow the exemption, but the existing guidelines for classification are no less ambiguous than the language of the original exemption. The current Executive Order (#11652) embodies a "national security" criterion, the metes and bounds of which have never been established (Note 1973).

Furthermore, in *EPA* v. *Mink* (1973), the Supreme Court held that an agency was not required to submit for *in camera* inspection documents that, although classified as a whole, might contain unclassified, and thus disclosable, portions. The 1974 amendments provided that exempted material must be "properly classified." This seems at least an invitation to the Supreme Court to reconsider *EPA* v. *Mink*, and could be read as authorizing review of the propriety of basic classification. Such review could breed major confusion. While there are a number of good reasons for reforming the security classification system (Futterman 1974), reform is especially important if the classification system is to be an adjunct of the FOIA and is to be interpreted by courts as if it were part of the statute.

Another difficulty with the FOIA, unremedied by the 1974 amendments, involves the fifth exemption for "intraagency memorandums or letters." Congress provided this exemption to allow some limited sphere of bureaucratic privacy for frank internal discussions in the preliminary stages of policy making. However, in implementing the provision, the courts have adopted a test not rationally related to the competing interests that must be adjusted. In a series of decisions, the fifth exemption has been interpreted as protecting documents containing "recommendations" and "opinions" as to policy, but not those containing essentially factual material (Note 1973). Such a test is unsatisfactory because the distinction is artificial—in the world of bureaucratic politics fact and opinions are inextricably intertwined—and because premature disclosure of supposedly "factual material" may be just as disruptive of early policy making as the disclosure of "opinion." Disclosure of incomplete empirical test results may have a more chilling effect on internal discussion than the leaking of some tentative recommendation concerning a minor aspect of a projected program.

A final shortcoming of the FOIA, troubling at least to civil libertarians, is the imperfect protection that the sixth exemption affords to personal privacy. The exemption protects from disclosure "personal, medical, and similar files," but operates only if disclosure would constitute a "clearly unwarranted invasion of personal privacy." (These tests are conjunctive: material must be in a certain class of files *and* its disclosure must seriously invade privacy *and* that invasion must be unwarranted by some disclosure interests.) The inadequacy of the provision can best be seen by contrasting it with the sixth exemption of the Privacy Act of 1974 (P.L. 93-579).

That act seeks to avoid disclosures "which could result in substantial shame, embarrassment, inconvenience, or unfairness to any individual." Because the two statutes are in tension, if not in actual conflict, congressional tightening and clarification are needed.

Information Crimes

Also related to the legislative development of the right to know is the problem of reforming the espionage laws (Edgar and Schmidt 1973). At present, it is unclear whether, for instance, a good faith publication of improperly disclosed defense information is punishable. The abortive prosecution of Daniel Ellsberg highlighted the especial ambiguities of the provisions of 18 U.S.C. 793 and 794. While §794 and certain subsections of §793 require a specific intent to harm the United States, other subsections of §793 (involving authorized possession and retention of material) do not require such an intent as an element of the crime. To add to the confusion, not all classified information is protected by criminal sanctions, but only the presumably narrower category of "defense information."

In late 1975 Congress began consideration of Senate Bill 1, a complete revision of the federal criminal code. Included in this package is a newly defined crime of espionage, and several new information crimes including unauthorized disclosure of defense information and unauthorized disclosure of classified information.

Elements of the redefined crime of espionage (Sec. 1121) would be knowledge that the national defense information disclosed might be used to prejudice the safety or interest of the United States and that the disclosure be made intentionally to a foreign power. In the case of the proposed crime of unauthorized disclosure of national defense information (Sec. 1122), there must also be knowledge that the material might be used to prejudice the safety or interest of the United States, but the proscribed communication is to any person whom the holder knows is not authorized to receive. Both crimes may be committed by anyone who has possession, authorized or unauthorized, of national defense information and communicates it with the requisite knowledge. There is also proposed to be created in Sec. 1123 (2)(B) a lesser crime of failing to return to proper authority national defense information of which one is in unauthorized possession.

The crime of disclosing classified information (Sec. 1124) is differently framed. It can be committed only by persons who are or were themselves authorized to be in possession of classified material. The unauthorized "outsider" who receives the information is immunized from prosecution as an accomplice or conspirator. Furthermore, no criminal liability at all would exist under Sec. 1124 unless and until a new government agency is set up to monitor the classification system and review procedures established by which those curious about the propriety of specific classifications may test them. A defense to the crime would also be created whereby a person who has exhausted his administrative remedies under the review procedure and who did not disclose to a foreign power, and who did not disclose for gain, could argue that the material had not been properly classified when disclosed. The material need not, of course, be defense information, only properly classified according to the standard provided by the prevailing executive order.

The S.1 information crimes are troubling in several respects. First, journalists and other communicators could be subject to prosecution for disclosing defense information (Sec. 1123) if the government could demonstrate that they knew material in which they trafficked might be used to prejudice the safety or interest of the United States—a phrase that could be interpreted to cover a lot of ground. Second, a person publishing in good faith, with no knowledge or interest to harm the United States, could certainly be subject to prosecution for failing to deliver materials of which he has unauthorized possession—and it is hard to publish without possessing. Third, while the crime of disclosing classified information would apply only to past and present public servants and government contractors, it is still troubling that any criminal liability be created by reference to the present classification system. Even with the monitoring agency and review procedures called for by the bill, the ambiguity of the "national security" guidelines for classification remains. While our present information crimes are poorly framed, it may be doubted that those contained in S.1 are much of an improvement.

The Sunshine Act

Mention should be made of another piece of pending federal legislation that would affect the right to know. In late 1975 the Senate passed an open meeting statute ("Sunshine Law"). While the House has yet to act, several points should be made about the measure as approved by the Senate.

Title I applies to procedures of committees and submmcommittees of the Congress and Title II to federal agency (board and commission) procedures; the provisions for both are similar. All meetings, including hearings, are to be open to the public unless a majority of the committee or agency members vote to close the session on one of five grounds. Appeals from such votes run to the respective houses of Congress in the case of their committees and subcommittees, and to the federal district courts in the case of the agencies. However, two of the five statutory grounds for closing a meeting suffer from weaknesses similar to those of the FOIA.

The first ground for closing a meeting is that to open it would "disclose matters necessary to be kept secret in the interests of national defense or the necessarily confidential conduct of the foreign policy of the United States." This employs the same vague terms as the classification system, but does not rely on it as does the first exemption of the FOIA. While escaping the formal limitation of the classification label, nothing is gained in clarity. The third ground is also troubling. This allows a vote to close in the event an open meeting will represent a clearly unwarranted invasion of the privacy of any individual. This is the same phrase ("clearly unwarranted") employed in the sixth exemption of the FOIA, and is, as we noted above, inadequate and in tension with the language of the Privacy Act.

The State Level

The states and some municipalities were well ahead of the federal government in legislating rights to know (Cross 1953), and the question now arises whether a few might not be too far ahead. By the 1940s states were beginning to define what were "public records" and to provide for some sorts of public access to them. By the 1950s, open meeting laws were being adopted, and 25 had been adopted by 1962 and 35 by 1973.

The open meeting laws vary widely in their provisions (Wickham 1973). Some include generous provisions for executive sessions, and some open only meetings at which final actions are to be taken. The trend, however, has been toward greater openness. For instance, California's famous Brown Act allows closing only on narrowly specified privacy grounds, some parole hearings, and, inevitably, national security grounds. Florida has experimented with "complete sunshine," although its courts have been forced to allow some exceptions. Public record laws have also moved in the direction of more access and fewer restrictions. Finally, at the state level, there has been significant progress in legislating testimonial immunity for journalists. Most state shield laws provide qualified immunity, but again, California seems to have opted for an absolutist approach (Whalen 1973).

While it is undoubtedly true that most state meeting and record statutes still allow too much to be concealed, it is worth considering the practicality of those few but apparently fashionable ones that do not provide, as Congress has attempted to provide at the national level, some protection of governmental and personal privacy. It is interesting to note (Stein 1974) that so many disputes over access to records involve the local press and police departments, and that what is sought often has to do with on-going investigations, involving the names and other potentially damaging information about people not charged with any crime.

Looking Ahead

Debate over secrecy *versus* disclosure is going to be a major feature of our political landscape for years to come. As we listen and participate, it will be well to remember that secrecy and disclosure are not indepen-dent values. Degrees of insistence on one or the other must be justified by arguments suggesting how they produce desirable qualities of poli-tics and governance. What is needed in each instance of reexamination of the problems noted earlier is delicate balancing of interests based on practical knowledge of the institutions and sensitivity to the competing values involved. "Open government" is all very well as a slogan, but to paraphrase Charles Schultz's Linus, "There is a difference between a bumper sticker and a policy, Charlie Brown."

Cases

Branzburg v. Hayes, 408 U.S. 665 (1972).

Columbia Broadcasting System v. Democratic National Committee, 412 U.S. 94 (1973).

EPA v. Mink, 401 U.S. 73 (1973).

Grumman Aircraft v. Renegotiation Board, 421 U.S. 57 (1975).

Kleindienst v. Mandel, 408 U.S. 753 (1972).

Lamont v. Postmaster General, 381 U.S. 301 (1965).

Miami Herald Publishing Co. v. Tornillo, 418 U.S. 241 (1974).

New York Times v. Sullivan, 376 U.S. 254 (1964).

Red Lion Broadcasting Co. v. FCC, 395 U.S. 367 (1969).

Sears, Roebuck v. NLRB, 421 U.S. 29 (1975).

Stanley v. Georgia, 394 U.S. 557 (1969).

Zemel v. Rusk, 381 U.S. 1 (1965).

References

Barron, Jerome A. 1973. *Freedom of the Press for Whom? The Right of Access to Mass Media* (Bloomington, Indiana: Indiana University Press).

137

Cross, Harold L. 1953. *The People's Right to Know* (New York: Columbia University Press).

Davis, Kenneth Culp. 1967. "The Information Act: A Preliminary Analysis," *University of Chicago Law Review,* 34, 761-816.

Edgar, Harold, and Schmidt, Benno C., Jr. 1973. "The Espionage Statutes and Publication of Defense Information," *Columbia Law Review,* 73, 929-1087.

Futterman, Stanley. 1974. "What is the Real Problem with the Classification System?" *None of Your Business: Government Secrecy in America,* eds. Norman Dorsen and Stephen Gillers (New York: Viking), pp. 93-104.

Katz, Joan M. 1970. "The Games Bureaucrats Play: Hide and Seek Under the Freedom of Information Act," *Texas Law Review,* 43, 1261-1284.

Note. 1972. "The National Security Interest and Civil Liberties," *Harvard Law Review,* 85, 1130-1326.

Note. 1973. "The Freedom of Information Act and the Exemption for Inter-Agency Memoranda," *Harvard Law Review,* 85, 1047-1067.

Stein, M.L. 1974. "The Secrets of Local Government," *None of Your Business: Government Secrecy in America,* eds. Dorsen and Gillers (New York: Viking), pp. 151-179.

Westin, Alan F. 1967. *Privacy and Freedom* (New York: Atheneum).

Whalen, Charles W., Jr. 1973. *Your Right to Know* (New York: Random House).

Wickham, Donald Q. 1973. "Let the Sunshine In!" *Northwestern University Law Review,* 69, 480-501.

14 Freedom to Travel Abroad

Emmet V. Mittlebeeler

Freedom to travel outside one's own country has been enshrined as a constitutional right in the United States only in the recent past, although its background is almost as old as recorded history. Travel to strange lands and places, for whatever the purpose, has been a major factor in the spread of civilization, whether in meanderings of individuals or in the collective form of migrations and invasions. The Old Testament refers to a passport given by the Persian king to Nehemiah; graffiti of Roman tourists are still inscribed on Egyptian ruins; and for ages the devout have made pilgrimages to places like Mecca, Jerusalem, Rome, and Benares. The importance of travel today is shown by the fact that in 1974 the United States Passport Office issued 2,665,003 passports.

Constitutional Aspects of Travel

This chapter discusses the constitutional right of American citizens, principally travelers like tourists, students, and scholars, and those engaged in commercial ventures, to travel voluntarily out of the United States with the intention of returning. Expatriation, immigration, emigration, exile, and flight therefore are not discussed.

Freedom of foreign travel has been considered by some to be a constitutional right. This development has had a respectable prologue in both philosophy and practice; the first edition of Magna Carta guaranteed the right to leave the realm, and traces of expressions of the right can be found in Locke, Vattel, and Pufendorf. The French revolutionary Constitution of 1791 guaranteed the right to leave the country temporarily (although the right was shortly withdrawn), and constitutions of other states, for example, Venezuela, Argentina, and Korea, have declared the right from time to time. The Constitutional Court of Austria, speaking through Hans Kelsen, reaffirmed the right of Austrian union representatives in the interwar period to leave the country to attend a meeting in the Soviet Union (Parker 1954, p. 853).

Internationally, the Universal Declaration of Human Rights, voted by the United Nations General Assembly on December 10, 1948, declared the right of any person to leave any country, including his own, and return to it, and similar rights are confirmed by the as yet unratified Covenant of

139

Human Rights and the International Covenant on Civil and Political Rights. The Helsinki Conference on International Security and Cooperation in Europe of 1975, the Soviet Union joining, restated the right.

Freedom of travel within the United States has long been recognized. Although no specific clause in the Constitution guarantees such freedom, courts have declared the right to travel freely to the national capital, to offices of the government located elsewhere, and to ports; this was extended in 1868 to the right to pass and repass freely through any part of the United States without interruption, as freely as within one's own state (*Crandall* v. *Nevada*). A more modern application of the principle is the 1969 pronouncement that states may not deny welfare benefits to residents of less than a year (*Shapiro* v. *Thompson*).

The right to foreign travel is likewise within the American constitutional framework. Although the right is not stated in the Constitution, the Supreme Court has included it in the liberty guaranteed in the Fifth Amendment—liberty of which one cannot be deprived without due process of law (*Kent* v. *Dulles*). In 1965 the Court, when it refused to approve validation of a passport for a visit to Cuba—declared off-limits to American travelers by the State Department in 1961—declined to rule that foreign travel rights were protected by the First Amendment; Justice Douglas, dissenting, admitted that the right of travel was at the "periphery" of that amendment, not at the core (*Zemel* v. *Rusk*).

Travel rights, in addition to being given constitutional recognition through pronouncements like that in *Kent* v. *Dulles* and dicta elsewhere, have been reinforced by the policy of the executive branch—going back at least to the days of Secretary of State John Quincy Adams—to foster citizens' travel abroad.

In 1952 President Truman pointed out that we should never be able "to remove suspicion and fear as potential causes of war until communication is permitted to flow . . . across international barriers," and three years later (January 10, 1951), President Eisenhower said to Congress, "The United States remains committed to the objective of freedom of travel throughout the world. Encouragement given to travel abroad is extremely important, both for its cultural and social importance in the free world and for its economic benefits."

The United States delegation, with informal congressional support, voted for Article 13 of the Universal Declaration of Rights in the General Assembly, leading to President Kennedy's call five years later for implementation "through travel and communication, and through increased exchange of people. . . ." And numerous other high officials have often set an example by traveling to distant parts of the globe.

However, in spite of judicial and executive endorsement, freedom of travel has become an area for conflicting policy considerations, reflected in travel restrictions. Because the freedom, like other constitutional freedoms, is not absolute, the State Department's official position has been that travel restrictions *are* legitimate.

Restrictions

Just as encouragement of the right to travel can serve national ends, so, it has been thought, can limitation of the right. Limitations can be classified under three general headings, each one presenting serious civil liberties problems: (1) limitation on travel as an instrument of policy; (2) restrictions as a device for internal security; and (3) travel curtailment as a remedy for economic ills.

In the foreign policy sphere, the president and secretary of state, in discharge of the duty to carry on the nation's foreign affairs, have prohibited travel to specified areas without special permission. Their rationale has been that the national interest supersedes any individual's right to travel. The areas proscribed—announced in the *Department of State Bulletin* and the *Code of Federal Regulations*—vary from time to time, according to the international climate, but as of mid-1975 three areas were under the ban: North Vietnam, North Korea, and Cuba. In the past, mainland China, the Soviet Union, Albania, Hungary, Israel, Libya, and numerous others have been on the prohibited list.

A frequently stated reason for a country ban is the need to indicate official disapproval of a country's behavior, apparently on the theory that if American tourists are no longer to visit the country and spend dollars there, the country might give serious thoughts to mending its ways. A specific reason in the case of North Korea was its provocation of incidents along the military demarcation line with South Korea, and in the case of mainland China, the regime's refusal to renounce the use of force was one reason for the ban. The Castro regime's practice of fomenting revolutionary activity elsewhere in the Western Hemisphere has been given as a reason in the case of Cuba. Restrictions are also employed for bargaining purposes, often to extricate an American citizen from difficulty. Thus, after the newsman William Oatis was imprisoned in Czechoslovakia in 1951, travel to that country was banned. The State Department appears to have felt that the ban was a significant factor in effecting his release. However, evidence that foreign governments have changed disliked policies in less convincing. There is no proof that the Communist Chinese, the Soviets in the early 1920s, the Albanians, or the North Koreans were influenced by bans on travel to their countries; apparently the only sufferers were those adventurous Americans who wished to travel there.

Travel is also often restricted to countries our government has not recognized and in which no diplomatic or consular representatives are stationed, so that citizens cannot be accorded the protection that travelers elsewhere can properly expect. Mainland China, North Vietnam, and North Korea fall into this category, as well as the one noted above. Here, the question arises whether a persistent traveler may waive the protection of the government and assume the risks that many visitors to Far Eastern countries have definitely taken upon themselves.

In support of the restrictions, it can be argued that even an unprotected traveler is in a position to complicate his country's international relations and that in international law the right of protection is that of the traveler's government as against other governments, rather than the right of the citizen as against his own government. However, in the light of the manner in which these bans have been imposed, these reasons seem weak. Not every unrecognized country has been placed on the proscribed list, nor has there always been effective protection for travelers in recognized countries. Some observers have wondered why Rhodesia and the German Democratic Republic were not on the lists, while recognized countries like some in the Middle East were out of bounds. Nor has another rationale for restriction, that countries may be in a state of such disorder that travel there would be hazardous, been applied consistently; for example, no travel restrictions were imposed on the war-torn regions of Nigeria during the Biafra revolt.

Restrictions applying to travel of Americans generally to specified geographical areas are intended to prevent adverse backwash from overseas travel. A second class of restrictions embraces denial of the rights of particular individuals, wherever they wish to go. In the interests of national security, American policy in the 1950s was to restrict the travel rights of persons affiliated with the "international Communist conspiracy." It was felt that members of the Communist Party and sympathizers would seek to travel from the United States in order to make contact with fellow conspirators abroad, and would work mischief upon their return to the United States. As State Department spokesmen explained, a conspiracy can be better implemented as the result of face-to-face contacts than through correspondence across national boundaries. Thus, in the interest of national security, persons who might engage in seditious activity were to be prohibited from leaving the country in the first place. The practice of restricting egress by denying passports to would-be travelers merely because of their political affiliations was halted by the Supreme Court in 1964 (*Aptheker* v. *Secretary of State*). However, the power of the government to restrict if it could be shown travel would result in particular dangerous acts was not denied. Thus, because of the implications for freedom of association, absent criminal charges or a conviction, a passport may not be denied one who is merely a member of a "subversive" or a revolutionary group.

In spite of this ruling, agitation to restrict in other ways the travel of persons whose behavior is deemed detrimental to American security interests—like those who made widely publicized visits to North Vietnam during the recent Indo-Chinese war—still surfaces occasionally. Official interest in restricting travel freedom of individuals is now at a relatively low point, because of the end of hostilities in Indo-China and the cessation of travel by antiwar activists to North Vietnam, but in 1973, in the wake of visits by Ramsey Clark and Jane Fonda, the State Department (unsuccessfully) advocated strengthening statutory prohibitions against such travel.

Considerations similar to those relative to national security apply to restrictions on certain classes of citizens like fugitives from justice or mental incompetents. At the present time, passports are denied (or revoked) when a person is on probation or parole, is under a federal warrant of arrest for a felony, has received a federal grand jury summons in a criminal case, is indebted to the United States, or has been declared mentally incompetent. In such situations the bans are comparable to restraints on liberty on the domestic scene; the state has a policy of keeping lawbreakers within the jurisdiction of the court, while mental incompetents are subjected to restraints for their own protection.

There is still another category of restrictions, occasionally employed abroad but not often used by the United States. For economic policy reasons, and as an indirect discouragement rather than as a direct prohibition, individuals are limited in the amount of money they may take when traveling out of the country. The Johnson administration, alarmed by exchange imbalances, proposed a travel tax with the avowed purpose of keeping Americans at home and thus damning up the outward flow of dollars. The infringement on civil rights from the advocated restriction might have been only incidental but it would have seriously affected international movement.

Policy Making

To understand restrictions on foreign travel it is necessary to acquaint oneself with relevant policy making processes and the mechanics of passport issuance. We know but little as to policy making, and further research is needed to analyze formulation of travel, or passport policy. Because of the close relationship of the freedom to travel and the execution of foreign policy, determinations of passport policy—as distinguished from the issuance of passports to individuals—have been made at a very high level. Complaints have been advanced that the Passport Office does not enjoy sufficient participation in positive policy deliberation, and one study has advocated the elevation of the Office to a Service, so that its voice can be more clearly heard (Staff Report 1960).

In light of the uses to which the travel proclivities of the American public might be directed, it might be supposed that policy respecting travel restrictions is but one facet of policy toward particular countries. An example is provided by the People's Republic of China. It seems clear that just as there was debate in the State Department for years over normalization of relations with that country, there was debate over relaxation of travel bans. Indeed, in the case of China there is evidence that travel restrictions were discussed at a higher level than the top echelons of the State Department.

In November 1970, following a majority vote in the General Assembly in favor of seating the People's Republic, President Nixon ordered the National Security Council to undertake a review of China policy; in accordance with practice, position papers were presented by various agencies, collected and condensed by the National Security Council staff, and then submitted to the president and his chief advisors. Analysis was undertaken by the Senior Review Group, a committee composed of departmental undersecretaries, and chaired by the President's Special Advisor for National Security Affairs, Dr. Henry Kissinger. Travel restrictions were discussed. Because current bans on China travel were soon to expire, a decision on travel had to be made at an early date, and in March 1971 China was taken off the prohibited list—in reality, the last in a series of relaxations, since the practice had long been to validate for mainland China the passport of anyone who could show a legitimate reason for traveling there.

Passport Issuance and Use

In peacetime America prior to 1941, one needed no travel documents to leave the country. From an early date, passports were issued—until 1856 even state and local officials and notaries public might issue them—but they were not required. A person wishing to travel simply traveled, although a passport might be convenient as an identification document or a certificate of nationality (Staff Report 1960; *Freedom to Travel* 1958).Those days of free and easy travel passed with the advent of world wars, and the mechanics of passport issuance became linked with constitutional rights.

Congress in 1918 and 1952 enacted laws under which it would be unlawful for any citizen to leave the United States without a passport, in time of war or during a period of national emergency as declared by the president [8 USC 1185 (b)], and a penal statute prohibits the use of a passport in violation of its provisions, that is, in areas where it is not valid, like North Vietnam (18 USC 1544). The national emergency proclaimed by President Truman on December 16, 1950 (Proclamation #2914, 3 C.F.R. 99), followed by a January 17, 1953 proclamation (#3004, 3 C.F.R. 180) subjecting citizen entry and departure to regulation, is still in effect; and since there is little prospect for rescission of the proclamation, passports will be required for the foreseeable future.

While requirements of passports for travel are within congressional competence, passports that contain a statement of those areas for which the State Department has declared they are invalid are now issued under regulations of the Secretary of State (E.O. 11294); by virtue of those regulations, passports have been made unnecessary for travel to countries in the Western Hemisphere except Cuba (22 C.F.R. 53.2). Passports are issued by the Passport Office, an agency in the Bureau of Security and Consular Affairs. The office is headed by Frances G. Knight, a civil servant with a remarkable capacity for survival; although now past the mandatory retirement age of 70, she remains because of Secretary Kissinger's certification that her retention is "in the best interests of the United States." Like her predecessor, she appears to have exercised much independence of action, although she has clashed with her immediate superior, the Administrator of the Bureau.

Even if a person by some means could gain exit from the United States without a valid passport, his freedom to travel could be seriously limited by not having one. Most countries will admit no one without a passport issued by *some* government; a survey conducted in 1952 revealed that of 37 countries studied, only 5 would admit a traveler without a passport (Note 1952, p. 171n), and of those 5, at least 1 has imposed the requirement since. Even those western European countries most friendly to the United States examine passports presented by American citizens, if only in a cursory fashion, and in most places it is impossible to cash a traveler's check without a passport. Even if the United States were to relax passport requirements immediately, an American traveler would meet difficulties abroad without one.

In short, possession of a passport is connected with the constitutional freedom of travel, and denial or deprivation of this document is a blow. As a result, American courts, faced with legal problems arising from visits of passport holders to countries for which passports are not valid, have had to confront a number of questions, some of them novel. Noting that a passport, issued by the government, is the property of the government, they have concluded that its use can be regulated by the government

(*Lynd* v. *Rusk*). Thus, the government can prohibit its transportation into, say, North Korea. Travel of the individual, however, without his passport, is an entirely different matter. The Supreme Court in 1967 pointed to the absence of any criminal statute prohibiting a citizen from traveling to a country for which he had no valid passport (*U.S.* v. *Laub*). Once outside the United States, the traveler's freedom of movement is unrestricted but, practically speaking, he must find a government that will admit him without a passport.

The earlier noted visits of antiwar activists like Ramsey Clark and Jane Fonda to proscribed North Vietnam produced no prosecution because their passports bore no stamp indicative of North Vietnamese entry; thus, it could not be proven that the documents themselves were actually carried across the North Vietnamese border (Olson 1972).

Conclusions

The ideal situation for travel abroad, from the perspective of civil liberties, is peace time travel for normal, noncriminal citizens without any restrictions whatever. However, in an imperfect world, interests of foreign policy and national security cannot be overlooked. Because it is conceivable that a citizen might wish to make an overseas journey with the proven intention of impairing national security or compromising foreign policy, as by killing a leader like Fidel Castro, Indira Gandhi, or the Shah of Iran, restriction of travel is justified in some cases.

But such situations are infrequent. Furthermore, banning travel in such extreme instances should be done with the greatest of care and every possible guarantee of due process. Otherwise, limitations would be imposed on persons suspect only because of unpopular political views. In any event, new legislation would be required, spelling out in detail the substantive reasons for such action as well as the procedure.

A real danger to civil liberties might come if this country were again involved in an unpopular undeclared war, say in the Middle East, and antiwar citizens turned up in the war zones or close to them. Congressional bills could then be expected, aimed at prohibitions on travel itself (not passports) to areas that the executive department might blacklist. If enacted, such bills would raise serious constitutional questions, the outcome of which one can hardly at this point predict.

Cases

Aptheker v. Secretary of State, 378 U.S. 500 (1964).
Crandall v. Nevada, 6 Wall. 35 (1868).

Kent v. Dulles, 357 U.S. 116 (1958).
Lynd v. Rusk, 389 F. 2d 940 (D.C. Cir., 1967).
Shapiro v. Thompson, 394 U.S. 618 (1969).
U.S. v. Laub, 385 U.S. 475 (1967).
Zemel v. Rusk, 381 U.S. 1 (1965).

References

Freedom to Travel. 1958. Report of the Special Committee to Study Passport Procedures of the Association of the Bar of the City of New York (New York: Dodd, Mead).

Note. 1952. "Passport Refusals for Political Reasons: Constitutional Issues and Judicial Review," *Yale Law Journal,* 61 (February) 171-203.

Olson, A. William (Assistant Attorney General, Internal Security Division). 1972. Statement, *Hearings Regarding H.R. 16742: Restraints on Travel to Hostile Areas,* Committee on Internal Security, House of Representatives (92nd Cong., 2d sess.), (September 19).

Parker, Reginald. 1954. "The Right to Go Abroad: To Have And To Hold A Passport," *Virginia Law Review,* 40 (November), 853-873.

Staff Report. 1960. *Reorganization of the Passport Functions of the Department of State,* Committee on Government Operations, U.S. Senate (86th Cong., 2d sess.).

**Part III
Civil Liberties Policy
Making**

15

The Legal Profession and the Supreme Court's Sexual Equality Decisions

Philippa Strum

During the years 1971-75, the Supreme Court heard more sexual equality cases than during its entire preceding history, and came close to pronouncing the existence of a new constitutional right. This chapter summarizes the decisions and briefly examines the most important causes for the Court's rapid spate of somewhat contradictory rulings. In the area of sexual equality, the judicial system was forced to respond with unusual rapidity to an underlying social problem that had hitherto received almost no judicial notice and for which applicable precedents were therefore almost entirely lacking. The legal profession constituted both a major element in the pressure upon the Court and a source of suggested judicial decrees.

The Decisions

In 1971 the Court ruled that the Martin Marietta Corporation's refusal to accept a job application from a woman with preschool-age children, although it did accept such applications from men, was a violation of §703 (a) of the Civil Rights Act of 1964 (*Phillips* v. *Martin Marietta Corp.*). Ten months later, the Court made the equal protection clause the basis of a unanimous ruling declaring unconstitutional the Idaho statute that made automatic the designation of a male over a potentially equally qualified female as administrator of an estate (*Reed* v. *Reed*). In 1972 the Court overturned an Illinois law based on the assumption that unwed fathers but not unwed mothers are invariably unfit parents (*Stanley* v. *Illinois*). A year later, the Court found a violation of due process in the Air Force's rule that a servicewoman requesting fringe benefits for her dependent husband had to demonstrate that her husband was dependent on her for more than one-half his support, although no such proof was required when a serviceman claimed similar benefits for an allegedly dependent wife (*Frontiero* v. *Richardson*). In *Cleveland Board of Education* v. *LaFleur*, the Court struck down two school boards' mandatory employment termination for pregnant teachers. However, Florida's tax exemption for widows but not widowers was found valid as embodying a substantial relation to the legitimate purpose of cushioning the financial impact of spousal loss upon those for whom the loss imposes a disproportionately heavy burden (*Kahn* v. *Shevin*). Two months later, the justices also upheld the exclusion of pregnancy from coverage by a California disability insurance system designed for those in private employment (*Geduldig* v. *Aiello*). A due process argument that differential tenure treatment of male and female naval officers relied on an unconstitutional classification was similarly rejected by the Court (*Schlesinger* v. *Ballard*). At the same time, however, the Court found a Sixth Amendment violation in Louisiana's statute excluding women from jury panels in the absence of a woman's written request to serve (*Taylor* v. *Louisiana*). The Social Security Act's gender-based distinction that granted survivor's benefits to a widow caring for a child but not to a widower in the same situation was invalidated (*Weinberger* v. *Wiesenfeld*). Utah's sex-differentiated statutory recognition of adulthood for child support purposes was similarly struck down (*Stanton* v. *Stanton*). Finally, in *Turner* v. *Department of Employment Security*, the justices rejected the presumption that women are unemployable during their last three months of pregnancy and first six weeks following delivery, and overturned Utah's denial of employment benefits during that period.

Within five years, although the majority of justices had refused to label gender differentiation a suspect category under the Fourteenth Amendment, the Court had found sex-related categorization constitutionally suspicious unless it was used as a remedial measure in areas where opportunity for women had been limited. The question arises of why the Court so suddenly and rapidly struck out on a course that resulted in obvious doctrinal inconsistency.

Input: "The Movement"

The 1960s brought a dramatic increase in the pace at which the role of American women was changing. The percentage of working women in the American population had approximately doubled since the 1920s. By 1972 women constituted 38 percent of the work force. Approximately 44 percent of all American women aged 16 and over were employed. Roughly 66 percent of the working women were married and living with their husbands, belying the canard that women had to choose between career and femininity. 32,000,000 American women were employed, many learning at first hand about economic discrimination (Ginsburg 1973). Other factors in the changing social reality included the 1963 publication of *The Feminine Mystique,* which was to articulate and validate the complaints of both working and nonworking women; the invention and wide-scale use of the birth control pill; changing demographic patterns; and the general middle-class value placed on higher education and the unhappiness of college-educated women subsequently confined to their homes. Women began to insist upon entry into a host of previously all-male or male-dominated preserves, and within a decade they were to be found at almost all levels of the armed forces, in medical schools, in the priesthood, in elective and appointed office, and, as will be indicated below, in law schools.

Policy Response: President and Congress

The first president to respond to the movement was President Kennedy, who in 1961 established the Commission on the Status of Women. Its 1963 report led in turn to the formation of 50 state commissions. The unhappiness of these commissions with the Equal Employment Opportunity Commission's unwillingness to enforce the 1964 Civil Rights Act's prohibition against sex discrimination impelled some of their members to create the National Organization for Women (NOW) in 1966. President Kennedy's seemingly innocuous act had culminated in the coalescing within five years of a thoroughly "respectable" middle-class women's organization that could focus and legitimate the complaints of women and fight for remediation. At the same time, the civil rights and antiwar movements brought together younger, more radical women. By 1966 there were two well-organized groups of women that understood how ubiquitous and harmful sexism was and had sufficient experience in political activities to begin using the political process for remediation (Freeman 1973; Bernard 1971).

The president was not the only policy maker to respond to the movement. When a segment of society comes together to make new demands on the policy-formation process, it usually does not concentrate on one institution alone. As in the case of the women's liberation movement, demands are made almost simultaneously upon a variety of public and private institutions. The response of each policy making institution to the pressure both legitimizes it and creates a secondary pressure on other policy making institutions to respond similarly. The pressure can thus be viewed as both vertical, or leading from the affected segment of the electorate upwards to the institutions, and horizontal, or flowing among the institutions of policy. In this way the output of one institution becomes an input for another. The Court, for example, both influences and is influenced by lower federal courts and by state courts. Before *Reed* was decided, the Court had a multiplicity of lower court decisions from which to draw (Ginsburg 1971). It also had the example of both presidential and congressional action. In 1963 Congress enacted the Equal Pay Act. The 1967 executive order forbidding sex discrimination by employers holding federal contracts or subcontracts and the Education Amendments of 1972 followed. When combined with Title VII of the 1964 Civil Rights Act, these laws gave women the initial tools for legal redress and made court involvement inevitable. A multidirectional process ensued: President Johnson prohibited holders of federal contracts from discriminating on the basis of sex; Congress revised Title VII of the Civil Rights Act to include educational institutions receiving federal funds; the Court recognized the necessity for women to receive the same kinds of education available to men (*Stanton* v. *Stanton*); HEW fashioned and submitted to Congress new guidelines designed to equalize opportunities for women in schools and colleges. All of the branches of the federal government were involved, along with state and local governments, private industry, the media, the legal elite, and various pressure groups, in creating and articulating a still-evolving social policy.

Policy Response: The Court

While the movement has made demands on all the policy making subsystems, it has been particularly demanding of the courts. This is scarcely surprising, in part because any individual or small group that does not yet possess sufficient political influence to ensure legislative responsiveness can file suit before a court. In addition, however, the Supreme Court's recent openness to groups seeking change (e.g., civil rights, poverty law) made it a natural focus for yet another group whose goal has been alteration of basic social and political realities. As FDR nurtured the image of the presidency as a social problem-solver responsive to groups that felt excluded from other means of access to policy making, thus creating an image that outlasted its creator, so the Warren Court thrust itself into prominence as the advocate of underrepresented groups and their needs, and left its legacy for the Burger Court. It was only to be expected, then, that the drive for sexual equality would immediately involve itself in litigation designed to reach the Supreme Court, especially in view of the American society's proclivity for drawing the Court into its search for new truths. The unusual factor in this instance, however, was the importance of the influx of women into law schools and the resultant impact on the legal elite.

Role of the Legal Elite

The influx of women into the law schools in the 1960s was an integral part of the developments noted above. As they entered the law schools in increasing numbers, the law reviews began to reflect their presence by devoting more and more of their pages to various aspects of women's rights (Symposia 1970; 1971; 1973) and by admitting that to the extent that the law is not part of the solution it is indeed much of the problem. Journals from the *Harvard Civil Rights-Civil Liberties Law Review* to *Judicature* told their readers that it is not only the law that discriminates against women; it is the law schools and legal profession as well (Discrimination 1971; 1973; 1974). Included among the mea culpas were a number of articles devoted to discussion of the curriculum changes demanded by militant feminist student caucuses—changes that the reviews began to admit were desirable. Whereas no major law reviews had published articles about sex discrimination before 1966, 1970 saw 27 articles, including 2 entire issues, devoted to the topic. 1971 brought 84 articles, 5 entire issues. Between 1961 and 1971, the number of articles concerning women's rights increased by 430 percent (Cowan 1974, pp. 7-8). The Supreme Court began to cite the articles in its decisions, and as the decisions were handed down, they were dissected and applauded or criticized by the reviews. The Court and the reviews thus developed a dialogue about the Court's proper role in a major arena of social change.

In the area of sexual equality, then, the law reviews served as a particularly important channel of communication between the society and the Court. Reflecting the ferment within the law schools, which in turn was a reflection of the ferment in the society at large, the reviews must surely have surprised many of their older, more traditional readers with demands for legal sexual equality. Their treatment of the issue was itself a legitimation of similar demands appearing simultaneously in courtrooms and briefs.

The plethora of cases and briefs indicated that women law students and lawyers did not confine their attention to law reviews. Women students organized women's rights clinics at almost all the major law schools, and it was these clinics that began to generate much of the litigation that would filter through the lower courts up to the Supreme Court (e.g., the Columbia Law School Women's Rights Project and *Weinberger*). Responding to the sudden spate of litigation and anxious to organize it into a coherent attack on discrimination, the American Civil Liberties Union (ACLU) established the Women's Rights Project. This meant that litigants had not only the eager activists of the women's rights clinics to aid them, but the financial resources of the ACLU as well. They also had the aid of a growing pool of women lawyers. The Supreme Court found itself listening to women law school graduates such as Ruth Bader Ginsburg of Columbia Law School (in *Frontiero* and *Weinberger*), Harriet S. Shapiro of the Justice Department (in *Schlesinger*), and Kathleen Peratis of the ACLU (*Turner*). For the first time, the Court began to hire significant numbers of women as clerks. Justice Douglas had broken ground when he hired one woman clerk in 1944, but this precedent was ignored until Justice Black hired a woman in 1966, followed by Justice Fortas in 1968. In 1972 Justice Douglas hired two women clerks; in 1974 Justices Brennan, Marshall, and Powell each hired a woman clerk; in 1975 Justice Powell again hired a woman clerk and Justices Burger and Blackmun did the same. The Court's lone legal officer, a man, found in 1975 that he had acquired a woman colleague. The Court was infiltrated by aware and articulate women drawn from precisely the prestigious law schools that have experienced the most insistent surge of feminism within their student bodies. At the same time, similar law school graduates newly hired by a wide variety of government agenices began to urge them to use the judicial system for the redress of sex-related wrongs. The president of the Women's Bar in 1969 became the first woman ever to address the National Conference of Bar Presidents, exhorting the legal profession to involve itself in the movement (Sassower 1970).

Conclusion

The inconsistency of Court rulings is directly attributable both to the Court's haste in responding to a social movement peculiar for its immediate and insistent use of the judicial process and to society's continuing failure to generate definitive answers that could be translated into legal axioms. The relationship of the sexes is so basic to the entire social structure that it is scarcely to be expected that a complete alteration of that status could be accomplished without lengthy argument and rethinking. The justices were presented with problems for which the society had no consistent solutions and then denied the luxury of time that might have enabled them to spin out a chain of logical constructs. The Court decisions, by legitimizing the emerging demand for change, contributed to its impetus. The law reviews exacerbated the Court's difficulty with their cries for rapid response, but, simultaneously, they provided it with specific doctrinal alternatives. When the main thrust of the process of social change in this area has been completed, and no matter what value decisions it institutionalizes, the Court's holdings will show that the Constitution demanded the existence of such policies all along. As it normally does in times of dynamic social change, the Court now both reflects and encourages the move toward sexual equality. In this instance, a major factor in its involvement was the law reviews and the complementary activities of women law students and lawyers.

157

Cases

Cleveland Board of Education v. LaFleur, 414 U.S. 632 (1974).
Frontiero v. Richardson, 411 U.S. 677 (1973).
Geduldig v. Aiello, 417 U.S. 484 (1974).
Kahn v. Shevin, 416 U.S. 351 (1974).
Phillips v. Martin Marietta Corp., 400 U.S. 542 (1971).
Reed v. Reed, 404 U.S. 71 (1971).
Schlesinger v. Ballard, 419 U.S. 498 (1975).
Stanley v. Illinois, 405 U.S. 645 (1972).
Stanton v. Stanton, 421 U.S. 7 (1975).
Taylor v. Louisiana, 419 U.S. 522 (1975).
Turner v. Department of Employment Security, 96 S.Ct. 249 (1975).
Weinberger v. Wiesenfeld, 420 U.S. 636 (1975).

Statutes and Regulations

Education Amendments of 1972, Title IX, 20 U.S.C.A. §§1681-83.
Equal Pay Act of 1963, 20 U.S.C. §206(c) (1970).
Executive Order 11375, 3 C.F.R. 320 (1967).
HEW Regulations, 40 Fed. Reg. 24127 (June 4, 1975).

References

Bernard, Jessie. *Women and the Public Interest* (Chicago: Aldine).
Cowan, Ruth. 1974. "Litigation as a Strategy in Women's Rights Politics," paper presented to the American Political Science Association, September.
Discrimination: Doris L. Sassower, 1974, "Women and Judiciary: Undoing 'The Law of the Creator'," *Judicature*, 57, 282-288; Bradley Soule and Kay Standley, 1973, "Perceptions of Sex Discrimination in Law," *American Bar Association Journal*, 59, 1144-1147; Barbara Kirk Cavanagh, 1971, "'A Little Dearer Than His Horse': Legal Stereotypes and the Feminine Personality," *Harvard Civil Rights-Civil Liberties Law Review*, 6, 260-287; Judith T. Younger, 1973, "Community Property, Women, and the Law School Curriculum," *New York University Law Review*, 48, 211-260.

Freeman, Jo. 1973. "The Origins of the Women's Liberation Movement," *American Journal of Sociology*, 78, 30-38.

Ginsburg, Ruth Bader. 1971. "Sex and Unequal Protection: Men and Women as Victims," *Journal of Family Law*, 11, 347-362.

———. 1973. "Need for the Equal Rights Amendment," *American Bar Association Journal*, 59, 1013-1019.

Sassower, Doris. 1970. "The Legal Profession and Women's Rights," *Rutgers Law Review*, 25, 59-65.

Symposia: Rutgers Law Review, 25 (1970), 1-79; *Harvard Civil Rights-Civil Liberties Law Review*, 6 (1971), 215-287; *Women's Law Journal*, 59 (1971), 1-52; *Valparaiso Law Review*, 5 (1971), 203-488; *New York Law Forum*, 17 (1971), 335-598; *Trial*, 19 (1973), 10-27.

16 Assessing the Litigative Role of ACLU Chapters

Stephen C. Halpern

Statement of Problem and Purpose

Writing of the role of policy studies, Thomas Dye observed that if certain end values are desired, choosing the policies that would best implement those ends is a factual question that can be studied scientifically (Dye 1975, p. 4). Protecting civil liberties throughout the United States is a formidable goal. The American Civil Liberties Union (ACLU) is the nation's largest and oldest interest group working to protect general civil liberties. It has 250,000 members nationally, an annual budget of several million dollars, 49 affiliates in 47 states, local chapters in 325 communities, and 5,000 "cooperating attorneys" who volunteer to take cases for the organization without compensation. Yet, the ACLU's resources are meager when measured against the task it has set for itself. Consequently, the single most vital policy question the organization faces is how best to allocate scarce resources so as to maximize its capacity to protect civil liberties.

The ACLU has traditionally worked on the leading edge of the law, influencing the development of constitutional doctrine defining our fundamental rights. Appearing before the U.S. Supreme Court more frequently than any other private litigant, both the national organization and its affiliates have influenced judicial policy making in landmark cases dealing with school prayer, obscenity, and the rights of criminal defendants, juveniles, protesters, religious minorities, and mental patients. The test case, carefully chosen on the basis of the facts, litigants, jurisdiction, and "ripeness" of the issue raised, has been the ACLU's primary weapon. The organization's litigation strategy stresses what Jacob terms policy making as opposed to norm-enforcing cases. The latter affect the immediate case only, he notes, while the former establish new rules intended to be "guide posts for future actions" (Jacob 1972, p. 31).

As Dye's observation suggests, students of the policy process can offer recommendations to increase the capacity of ACLU chapters to help

The author gratefully acknowledges the support of the Christopher F. Baldy Fund of the State University of New York at Buffalo.

the organization achieve its goals. This chapter makes such recommendations. It assesses the role of chapters by analyzing the relationship between chapters and state affiliates and the considerations that affect the number and nature of cases chapters accept for possible legal action. The study is based on an examination of the civil liberties complaints lodged by citizens with an urban ACLU chapter over a period of six months and of communications during that time between the chapter and its state affiliate. Based on that analysis and the literature evaluating the impact of court decisions and programs providing legal assistance, specific changes in the strategies of the ACLU and functions of chapters are suggested and their implications discussed.

Chapter-Affiliate Relations

ACLU chapters are creatures of state affiliates. The affiliates recognize chapters, determine the parameters of their operating budgets, the manner in which they can raise money, and the nature of their power within the state organization. Chapters, which typically are run by a nonlawyer who works part-time, is paid poorly, and depends heavily on volunteers, usually receive only a small fraction of the membership dues raised locally. Most of that money is divided between the national office and state affiliates. In the state studied, for instance, approximately $4,000 was allocated for each of nine chapters, while nearly $400,000 was spent on the affiliate's special projects and appellate litigation. The uneven distribution of dollars between chapters and affiliates has been a continuing source of friction within the organization. Chapters run offices, mobilize volunteers, maintain old members, recruit volunteer attorneys and new members, and litigate—all with minimal financial support from the affiliate and national organization. Affiliates often establish self-serving regulations governing the manner in which chapters can raise funds to be retained solely for their use. In contrast to the precarious fiscal position of chapters, the ACLU constitution *guarantees* each state affiliate 60 percent of the membership dues and contributions collected from any of its constituents. They use these funds for litigation, and in industrialized, urbanized states also to lobby for policy reforms by supporting special projects in such areas as sentencing and parole; privacy; the rights of children, women, and prisoners. These affiliates have staffs that include full-time lobbyists and lawyers.

Significant decreases in the money the ACLU raised in 1974 necessitated cutbacks for all affiliates. How organizations revise priorities in a financial crisis tells much about what they value. The state CLU in this study economized by reducing the operating budgets of each of its chapters by nearly 50 percent, and terminating the staff counsel in the three chapters with such a position. There was no comparable cut in the staff or operating expenditures of the state affiliate. Officials of the affiliate believéd that the cases accepted by chapters duplicated the efforts of public legal aid and reflected the chapters' provincial perspective.

When test or policy making cases arise, the affiliates, not chapters, generally choose, sponsor, and manage the appellate litigation. Chapters are usually asked to notify the affiliate when such cases arise locally. Affiliates often encourage chapters to seek cases raising visible policy issues by compensating them for any expenses they may incur only when a case raises issues of statewide or national interest. Chapters also realize that their ability to discover such cases may affect the esteem in which they are held by the affiliate and hence the level of financial support the affiliate provides. In these ways and others, the power and priorities of affiliates influence the kinds of complaints chapters accept and the role chapters play in their communities.

Complaint-handling by a Chapter

Through their screening of complaints, chapters regulate the kinds of civil liberties problems raised as public policy issues in local communities and decided by courts. Because few chapters have a staff counsel, their capacity to take legal action is limited in the vast majority of cases not sponsored by affiliates. Most chapters depend entirely on the voluntary assistance provided by local cooperating attorneys. Actively engaged in private practices themselves, those attorneys are understandably not eager to spend a great deal of time providing free services. The scant resources provided chapters and the limited commitment cooperating attorneys make to them means that chapters are rarely able to investigate independently the facts and charges in a complaint or negotiate extensively about the outcome. A process of screening complaints results whereby chapters tend to accept cases in which the complainant has either gathered convincing documentation himself or alleges wrongs that are both manifest and grievous. Cases that have "good facts" and are easily won become the stock in trade. These considerations were evident in the way in which the chapter in this study reviewed the complaints lodged with it.

Few people brought cases that raised dramatic public issues or novel questions of constitutional or statutory interpretation. Of the 213 civil liberties complaints filed, 95 percent were enforcement cases, that is, cases in which a complainant alleged an infraction of a clear rule of law protecting a recognized legal right. The three most frequent categories of complaints involved allegations of police misconduct, discrimination by em-

ployers, and denials of the right to counsel. The chapter's ability to redress such grievances did not turn on its effectiveness in making constitutional claims in court, but rather on the quality of the evidence that it
could gather to document a complainant's allegations, and on its bargaining power and skill in informal negotiations with those against whom complaints were levied.

Most complaints were communicated to the chapter by telephone.
After a complaint was received and before the chapter took legal action, a
complaint passed through four stages: the initial telephone call between
the complainant and the chapter's executive director, a follow-up inter-
view in the office, a review by the lawyers' committee comprised of the
chapter's cooperating attorneys, and a review by the cooperating attorney
who accepted the case. Few complaints survived to the last stage.

As the chapter's only salaried employee, the executive director responded to all communications to the chapter, negotiated with state and
national ACLU officials about budgetary and policy matters, appeared
before community groups, lobbied local legislators, recruited cooperating
attorneys, and managed the chapter's finances. In deciding whether complaints warranted follow-up interviews, he learned to make quick judgments based on limited information. Three out of five complaints were
shut off from further consideration based upon his initial judgment.

In 38 percent of the complaints, the request for assistance was denied
and the complainant was not referred elsewhere (see Table 16-1). In these
cases the executive director either judged that the complaint was frivo-
lous, that the complainant lacked credibility, or that there was inadequate
documentation of the allegations. In 22 percent of the complaints, the request was denied but a referral given. The executive director usually believed these complaints to be more serious and credible than those in the
first category. Most often he decided to refer the complainant elsewhere
for two reasons: the chapter's limited resources and the existence within
the community of another organization that might remedy the complaint.
Referrals were made to such organizations as the State Commission of
Human Rights, the NAACP, the Epileptic Associaton, NOW, and a local
group working for the rights of mental patients. In a very few instances
complainants were referred to an elected official with a recognized interest in the subject of a complaint. In the 11 percent of the complaints in
which action was deferred, the chapter or complainant usually needed
time to gather additional information.

Although the chapter officially listed over 30 cooperating attorneys,
only one-half dozen or so regularly attended the monthly meetings of the
lawyers' committee. These same few attorneys did most of the chapter's
legal work. At the meetings the executive director presented nearly all of
the cases for which he had held personal interviews with complainants.

Table 16-1
Initial Disposition of Complaints by Executive Director

Manner of Disposition	Percent Disposed
Follow-up interview	29
Complaint rejected; no referral elsewhere	38
Complaint rejected; referral elsewhere	22
Action deferred	11
	100
	(n = 213)

Table 16-2
Summary of Actions Taken on Cases Accepted by Lawyers' Committee

Action	Number of Complaints
No lawyer found	5
Chapter subsequently withdrew	4
Complainant subsequently withdrew	2
Informally mediated	3
Litigated	1
Total	15

The lawyers discussed the facts and issues in the cases and decided by informal agreement whether the chapter should seek a cooperating attorney to accept the case.

During the six months of the study 58 complaints were presented to the lawyers. Forty-three of these requests, approximately 75 percent of the total, were rejected. The most important variables determining whether the lawyers decided to accept a complaint were the facts in the case and the likelihood of obtaining a cooperating attorney to do the work. These two considerations were not unrelated. Poorly documented cases with unfavorable facts involved more work for the attorneys, and were less likely to be won easily, if at all. Hence, they were less likely to be accepted.

Table 16-2 summarizes the actions taken on the 15 complaints the lawyers' committee thought the chapter should accept. It is striking that of the 213 civil liberties complaints lodged, the chapter ultimately took action against the target of a complaint in four cases, litigating only once. In that case the chapter was successful and the case was not appealed. In the other three cases the complaint was resolved informally.

Negotiating settlements was not uncommon. When a complaint was "accepted," the cooperating attorney often tried to arrive at an informal resolution before resorting to litigation. The chapter's threat to litigate, its public or private criticisms, or recommendations about a questionable practice were likely assessed by its adversaries, in part, on the basis of the chapter's record and reputation for taking effective legal action. To the extent that this was true, the chapter's limited capacity and willingness to act in more than just a few easy and unusual cases likely diminished its credibility as a combatant and its leverage to "persuade" accused parties to redress a complaint.

The Policy Implications of the ACLU Strategy

Affiliates and chapters both act on atypical complaints. Affiliates litigate in cases that raise innovative, visible questions of state or national importance while chapters do so when there have been flagrant or dramatic violations of rights in easily won and documented cases. Less than one in ten civil liberties complaints filed with the chapter in this study met these threshold requirements. The criteria for accepting a case neglect a wide range and sizable number of complaints that neither challenge existing policies about rights nor involve flagrant and dramatic violations of them. The ACLU's litigation strategy is biased against individuals who need help in documenting and articulating their case and who suffer unsensational violations of recognized rights in problematic cases. Insofar as most of the complaints filed with the chapter in this study fell into that category, we may conclude that the ACLU strategy does not reflect or respond to the civil liberties problems people commonly experience and lodge with the organization. The incongruity between the complaints lodged and cases litigated plainly results from the organization's litigation strategy.

Many problems are not dealt with as a direct consequence of a strategy allocating nearly all of the ACLU's resources for litigation to affiliates for a relatively small number of atypical and expensive cases. A former activist in the Office of Economic Opportunity's (OEO) legal services program estimates, for example, that for the cost and risk involved in one test case or class action suit, a legal defense organization could litigate perhaps several thousand enforcement cases (Brill 1974, p. 207). Although the group's officials are reluctant to say so, important organizational maintenance needs are met by its present strategy. The publicity surrounding test cases promotes the ACLU's visibility and enables it to maintain the traditional core of its clientele of liberal and conservative ideologues interested in cases raising sharp ideological and salient policy questions.

ACLU officials defend their litigation strategy by maintaining that it maximizes the organization's impact. They argue that the ACLU does not have the resources to provide general legal assistance. If it is to be effective, they insist, the ACLU must litigate only the most important cases. A strategy that emphasizes test cases is justified, as they see it, because victories in test cases, unlike those in enforcement cases, confer benefits upon large numbers of individuals and groups. Yet, research on the impact of court decisions calls into question that basic justification for the test case strategy.

The process by which behavior is changed only *begins* with a definitive ruling by the U.S. Supreme Court (Dolbeare and Hammond 1971, p. 133). It is now commonplace that many "victories" for civil liberties in both courts and legislatures often prove to be merely symbolic. New policies are simply not self-executing, and as Roscoe Pound observed one-half century ago, the life of the law is in its enforcement. The really difficult and important policy question often becomes whether and how local practices can actually be made to conform to new or long established national standards on questions of civil liberties. The U.S. Commission on Civil Rights took note of that problem when it concluded that the difficulties in protecting civil rights increasingly do not derive from inadequate legislation or unfavorable judicial precedents, but from the failure to enforce the strictures against discrimination where the law clearly prohibits it (U.S. Commission on Civil Rights 1972, p. iv).

The poor record in enforcing rules abut civil liberties should not surprise us. While there is strong public support for civil liberties in the abstract, support falls precipitously when questions are posed about specific and concrete cases (Prothro and Grigg 1960, p. 293). Furthermore, the law has greater influence on emotionally neutral, "instrumental" areas of activity than on expressive and evaluative areas of behavior (Dror 1959, 801). Since decisions about civil liberties often touch upon fundamental personal and societal values and enjoy strong public support only in the abstract form, perhaps the ACLU should anticipate that those decisions will require more extensive enforcement efforts than policies in other areas and adjust its litigation strategy accordingly. By emphasizing test cases, the ACLU has overvalued achieving official, public declarations of changes in policy and minimized the value of monitoring whether and how rights are enforced. Its strategy is not informed by empirical evidence indicating the nature of the civil liberties problems people actually experience or by the research documenting the limited impact test cases often have.

Policy Recommendations and Their Implications

Given the demand for assistance in protecting established rights revealed in this study and the emphasis that the literature suggests should be placed on enforcement, the ACLU might achieve more by reducing the resources provided affiliates for test cases and granting greater power and organizational resources to chapters to act on a larger number and variety of complaints than they now can. Litigating fewer test cases would free resources for chapters to represent many more people than they now can in enforcement cases.

Because few organizations working for civil rights and liberties at the state and national level are active at the local level, it is often easy for communities to resist implementing new court policies. Through publicity, litigation, the threat of litigation, and their general monitoring of local activities affecting civil liberties, chapters can increase the likelihood and extent of compliance with new policies. This contention is supported by William Muir's conclusion that greater compliance with the Supreme Court's ban on school prayer occurred, the more access citizens had to lawyers, the graver the danger of legal actions, and the more probable the invocation of judicial review in the event of noncompliance (1967, p. 133) and by Kenneth Dolbeare and Philip Hammond's observation that threatening local elites with the prospect of public controversy if they do not enforce the Court's policies may be "sufficient to bring them down on the other side of the fence" (1971, pp. 149-50). Enforcement cases can also deter violations of long-established policies by publicizing the fact that there exists locally an organization that investigates complaints and has the capacity to back up with legal action the rights the law protects (Appleby and Heifetz 1969, p. 104).

In order to maximize the potential of the union to protect civil rights and liberties at the local level, chapters might be given a guaranteed share of the organization's funds as are affiliates, greater leeway to raise money solely for local use, and incentives rewarding them for accepting complaints other than those involving manifest violations of law. Resources might be reallocated so as to enable more chapters to hire a staff counsel, bringing greater continuity and stability to the work of chapters, lessening their dependence on cooperating attorneys, and enabling them to take more cases requiring extensive legal work and investigation. Chapters might even be established in cities that do not now have one. Such changes could enhance the ACLU's capacity to translate declarations of reforms and rights into realities in local communities, something that would have a multiplier effect because enforcement cases can have an impact beyond the immediate dispute. Were the 300 ACLU chapters provided a larger share of the organization's resources and encouraged to accept a greater number of routine enforcement complaints, in addition to facilitating the implementation of new policies and deterring violations of long established ones, the reforms would enable chapters to educate and politicize many more citizens directly about their rights, enhance the power of chapters to persuade potential defendants out-of-court to discontinue or revise objectionable practices, and provide more and better feedback to policy makers about the inadequacies of existing policies and the difficulties that have arisen with their enforcement.

Conclusion

The criticisms levied here should not be interpreted to mean that the ACLU could more effectively protect civil liberties by eliminating testcase litigation. Rather they suggest that the organization's priorities and resources have been disproportionately weighted toward that kind of litigation by affiliates and that there are serious limitations to such a strategy. It affects the willingness and capacity of chapters to act on the large number of enforcement problems people experience and bring to them. Decreasing the organizational power and funds traditionally provided affiliates for test cases, while increasing the power and funds granted chapters to act on enforcement complaints, would reduce the imbalance in the ACLU strategy. It would make the organization more responsive to the civil liberties violations people most frequently and even routinely experience, which so often go unchallenged.

References

Appleby, Michael, and Henry Heifetz. 1969. "Legal Challenges to Formal and Informal Denials of Welfare Rights," *Justice and the Law*, ed. Harold Weissman (New York: Association Press), pp. 88-105.

Brill, Harry. 1974. "The Uses and Abuses of Legal Assistance," *Before the Law*, ed. John Bonsignore et al. (Boston: Houghton Mifflin), pp. 204-14.

Dolbeare, Kenneth, and Philip Hammond. 1971. *The School Prayer Decisions* (Chicago: University of Chicago Press).

Dror, Yehezkel. 1959. "Law and Social Change," *Tulane Law Review*, 33, 787-99.

Dye, Thomas. 1975. *Understanding Public Policy*, 2nd ed. (Englewood Cliffs, N.J.: Prentice-Hall).

Jacob, Herbert. 1972. *Justice in America*, 2nd ed. (Boston: Little, Brown).

Muir, William. 1967. *Prayer in the Public Schools* (Chicago: University of Chicago Press).

Prothro, James, and Charles Grigg. 1960. ''Fundamental Principles of Democracy: Bases of Agreement and Disagreement,'' *Journal of Politics*, 22, 276-94.

U.S. Commission on Civil Rights. 1972. *The Federal Civil Rights Enforcement Effort: One Year Later* (Washington: U.S. Government Printing Office).

17 Erotica and Community Standards: The Conflict of Elite and Democratic Values

Richard S. Randall

The obscenity question or, more appropriately, the degree to which depiction or communication of erotica is constitutionally allowable, is perhaps the most persistent and pervasive free speech issue the country has ever faced. No medium of communication and few if any individuals have been left untouched by changes in policy since the 1950s. In its first attempt to give obscenity legal formulation, in 1957, the Supreme Court said that the test was "whether to the average person, applying contemporary community standards, the dominant theme of the material taken as a whole appeals to the prurient interest" (*Roth* v. *United States; Alberts* v. *California*). In its 1973 decision, *Miller* v. *California*, the Court declared that "contemporary community standards," a concept that had never been satisfactorily explicated, referred not to the nation as a whole, as many had supposed, but to the state or local community. In this ruling the Court took an unusual step toward denationalizing a constitutional right; structurally it was also a step into the policy making past. If effective, it could result in a different balance drawn between elite, cosmopolitan values and local, popular ones, as well as a corresponding change in the distribution of costs and benefits from the familiar pattern of the last 20 years.

The Court's Dilemma

A majority of the Supreme Court has consistently refused to adopt an absolutist position on erotica, such as that championed by Justice Douglas, or a near-absolute one, such as that now advocated by Justice Brennan. Either of these positions would be a natural resolution for a progressively libertarian doctrine and would go far toward delivering the Court from the formulaic mire of its old decisions. However, either position also would almost certainly heighten tensions on the erotica issue. The fact that the Court has had to give substantive review to so many obscenity cases in recent years reflects both this difficulty and the disparity between its own cosmopolitan doctrine and local, popular values. By, in effect, delegating responsibility for making the substantive decisions to others, who would use the standards of their own communities, a five-member majority in the *Miller* case attempted to resolve this dilemma and get the Court out of the role Justice Black once described as that of the "Supreme Board of Censors." No doubt such denationalization was also intended to have a reallocative effect. This is all the more clear when the shift to local standards is coupled with the additional *Miller* reformulation that permissible erotica must have "serious literary, artistic, political, or scientific value," rather than merely not being "utterly without redeeming social importance," the more libertarian measure used in earlier cases. Nevertheless, the majority may yet be uneasy with denationalization and has given no indication of resigning the Court's opportunity to conduct its own review of erotic materials. Thus, a year after *Miller*, the Court was unanimous in finding "Carnal Knowledge" not obscene even though the film had been judged otherwise in Georgia, presumably through application of local standards (*Jenkins* v. *Georgia*).

Free Speech and the Decline of Local Sovereignty

The rise of erotica as a major public issue may or may not indicate policy making failure, but it does reflect a worrisome conflict between elite and democratic values that, perhaps inevitably, has come to mark many First Amendment and civil liberties questions. Throughout much of the American past, an individual's civil liberties, particularly his freedom of speech, were likely to be a coefficient of his political subculture (Roche 1963). In spite of diversity of opinion in the nation as a whole, there is little evidence of there having been great toleration of divergent opinion within local populations. In offering fraternity and security to those of like persuasion, the geographically isolated small community and its later urban counterpart, the culturally insulated ethnic or religious enclave, developed its own value ethos comparatively undisturbed. Early political settlements and legal arrangements reinforced this pattern. Not until the 1930s was there a higher law of personal freedom or liberty, to which a dissatisifed, censored, or prosecuted individual or group might appeal if a local or state right did not exist. One of the aims of the original constitutional settlement was that life in a state, including relations between individuals and state and local authority, was to be largely beyond reach of the central government. And the Bill of Rights, originally as much an expression of federalism as of libertarianism, was, if anything, an instrument to help effect that end.

Except for federal activity against suspected subversives during and following World War I, policy on free speech questions was for many decades mainly of state and local making. Yet, because of a censorial marriage of cultural homogeneity and well-developed majoritarian political institutions and processes in the community, it is unlikely there was much formal policy making on erotica even at state and local levels throughout much of the early American past.

Advances in transportation, mass education, and communications— particularly the appearance of new media and remarkable technological advances in older ones—helped to erode the cultural insulation of the local community at the same time that a new balance of power in the federal system was making the inner life of the states increasingly subject to national control. Inevitably, local values began to be challenged by those of other communities and, more particularly, by an incipient cosmopolitan culture. This exposure to the alien led to attempts to control its means of depiction. Early efforts often did not involve overt use of governmental power, but instead were based on a variety of social, economic, or political pressures brought to bear on local agents of the media. Elsewhere control could be exercised through advertisers who, needing to sell a product, were apt to be attentive to popular interests and generally cautious in their sponsorships. Although informal sanctions of this sort were often sufficient because of a still relatively high value consensus, government was formally available where needed, usually through the prosecution power, "traffic" or business regulation or, as in the case of the movies, institutionalized prior restraints in the form of censorship boards.

In spite of these arrangements, the community was no longer the culturally near-sovereign one of the more distant past. Instead, it was open to national power to which a loser in these local struggles might appeal instead of having to choose between conformity and exile. This power was also one that outsiders controlling the external communication media might find available against local restriction. Thus, by the time the Roosevelt Court began to judicialize civil liberties policy making in the late 1930s, the political, cultural, and technological requisites for nationalizing free speech policy awaited only an appropriate libertarian legal doctrine. This began to come forth on the erotica issue in the 1950s in *Burstyn* v. *Wilson*, extending First Amendment protection to movies, and in *Roth* v. *United States* and *Alberts* v. *California*, where the Court reformulated the test for obscenity and applied it to federal and state prosecutions, and was further accelerated in the 1960s. The progressively libertarian character of the doctrine in both its substantive and procedural aspects meant that erotica policy was determined by cosmopolitan, elite values rather than local, popular ones. The typical appellate obscenity decision that found local or state legislative or administrative action impermissible imposed or enforced an elite standard of tolerance on the local community. In doing so, formal judicial policy making favored local and national minorities as opposed to local and national majorities. Given the intrusiveness of erotica depiction, this was a pattern of policy making almost guaranteed to generate a high degree of stress.

"Community Standards"

In formulating its libertarian doctrine, the Court had not been able to develop a consensus on the question of which community—the national or the local—was referred to by the term "community standards." Its one formal attempt to define the measure, in *Jacobellis* v. *Ohio*, in 1964, found the justices almost evenly divided among those favoring the "national," those favoring the "local," and those opposed to any restriction on erotic depiction. Yet, in repeatedly sustaining the libertarian interest, the Court was operationally judging "community standards" by a referent that was neither popular nor local. Expert testimony on obscenity offered by the libertarian side was invariably based upon opinion of intelligentsia, few of whom were from the local community attempting restriction. Typically, witnesses were psychologists testifying to the harmless and possibly even beneficial psychic, attitudinal, or behavioral effects of the erotic material, or humanists, often professors of English, editors of journals of opinion, or literary, art, or film critics; the latter spoke to the artistic or intellectual worth of the material and testified that it was not regarded as undesirable or censorable in enlightened circles. Until the *Miller* case, appellate courts (the Supreme Court unfailingly) tended to accept such testimony over countertestimony that often embodied evidence of local standards of tolerance.

Yet, survey data would appear to indicate that the very concept "national standards" is misleading. The most systematic and probing nationwide study of attitudes toward erotica, undertaken before the *Miller* decision, revealed such a diversity of views that its authors concluded there was no such thing as "contemporary community standards." Nevertheless, the study did indicate that "public sentiment is more on the side of restriction than on the side of availability"(Abelson et al. 1971, p. 5; see also Wilson and Abelson 1973), a conclusion apparently understated in the light of the data presented, which repeatedly indicate large majorities opposing availability of many kinds of erotica found not obscene by the Supreme Court and other appellate bodies. For example, 74 percent of the 2,486 respondents agreed that sexual scenes aimed merely at entertaining, in contrast to being part of the story, should not be permitted in movies. Fifty-two percent thought such scenes should not be permitted even if they were part of the story. Fifty-four percent agreed that sexual materials should not be available in bookstores, while 66 percent agreed that "some people should not be allowed to read or see some things." Moreover, as an alternative to regulating erotica by law, 72 percent approved having "local boards of citizens from different walks of life keeping objectionable things out of the community" (Abelson et al. 1971). Thus, to whatever extent a nationwide standard could be said to exist, it would appear to offer little comfort to the libertarian position. In this light, the concept "national standards" as it has been commonly used actually refers to *nationally applied elite standards*, having their geographical referent, if any, in highly select communities. This means that policy making choice appears to be less one between "national" and "local" standards than between cosmopolitan, elite nationally enforced standards and local, popular ones, which may have varying degrees of cosmopolitanism in them.

If "community standards" refer to the local or the state community, then many complex questions of survey, evidentiary, and venue character arise. What is the "local community" and of whom does it consist? How are its standards to be known and measured? What is its threshold of unacceptability and how may it be determined? The leading study of local standards, involving 1,083 members of 38 community organizations ranging from church and PTA groups to the Sexual Freedom League, in a major metropolitan area (Detroit), is not reassuring on the question of consensus, providing little evidence of a common attitudinal position (Wallace 1973). Empirically, it would appear that local standards may or may not be clearer than national ones, may or may not indicate a high degree of consensus, particularly in large urban areas, and may or may not be more restrictive, although it is likely they will be more restrictive than nationally applied elite standards.

Costs and Benefits

Policy making on erotica involves a wide range of substantive ends of which the legal distributions of rights and obligations are only the most immediate. Beyond these are a number of more fundamental values, such as well-being, wealth, status, and enlightenment. The outcomes of erotica policy making, the actual operating conditions of freedom of speech and censorship, affect and are affected by both the immediate and underlying values.

The doctrinal shift from national to local standards is likely to influence both the mode and threshold of censorship action in the community. Prosecutors and local antipornography groups will find encouragement from increased chances of prevailing in court and from the overall symbolic effect of the *Miller* decision and later cases based upon it. It is significant that of the various elements in the pre-*Miller* test for obscenity, local prosecutors had cited "contemporary community standards" more often than any other except one as an obstacle to successful control of erotica. The most frequently mentioned was the other doctrinal element reformulated in *Miller*, namely, that offending material be "utterly without redeeming social importance" (Wilson et al. 1971).

The shift to local standards will probably have more impact in large cities than in smaller ones. Composed of a greater number and variety of subgroups and subcommunities, the former are apt to harbor a much wider range of values, attitudes, and behavioral norms. The absence of a single value structure on the erotica question in these communities means that legal controls and group action are less likely to be supported by informal sanction systems. In the past, it also meant that censorship action was more apt to be formal and overt and, therefore, more easily held in check by the courts. It is not surprising, then, that the libertarian doctrine with its elite standards of tolerance should have had its greatest operating effect in large communities. Nor is it surprising that prosecutors in such cities have been more likely to see erotica as a serious public problem and are also more likely to initiate legal actions. Antipornography groups, likewise, appear to have been active more frequently in large cities (Wilson and Abelson 1973).

In addition to increasing the likelihood that formal censorship will be more successful, local "community standards" place a legal premium on demonstrating what local standards, in fact, do exist. In turn, this may encourage greater activity on the part of local antipornography groups and give their efforts a less symbolic and more instrumental orientation. Where censorship interests are politically dominant, the restrictive standards they represent are likely to receive some legal effect. Where the interests are strong but not dominant, which is the case in many large cities, clear local standards of any sort may be difficult to establish. In these cases, erotica is likely to become a major local issue or, if already so, to remain one. In such cases, also, appellate courts, faced with no clear local standards, may find it easy to reapply the national elite standards of the pre-*Miller* period.

Apart from prosecutions and group activity, much effective censorship, especially in smaller communities, is self-imposed and normally unreported, and is thus hidden from view (Randall 1968). In a survey of censorship campaigns in 18 small- and middle-sized cities, more than half of the wholesalers of magazines and paperback books and nearly half of the retailers said they practiced some form of self-censorship. This restraint appeared to be less a matter of the proprietors' attitudes toward erotica than of their desire to conform to the general values of their communities or to respond to actual or anticipated coercion by authorities (Rodgers 1974). Since this mode of censorship depends largely on other modes and on perceived levels of tolerance in the community, its threshold, too, may be lowered by a shift from national to local standards.

Concern about *well-being* appears to be the most widely articulated underlying value or motive of those supporting restrictive policies, and it remains an important consideration even for those who do not. In the national survey mentioned earlier, 58 percent of the respondents indicated that their views on censorship were conditioned by whether or not erotica was harmful. A third of those favoring some form of restraint said they would change their minds were erotica shown not to be harmful, while two-thirds of those favoring no restraints would change their minds were erotica proven to be harmful (Abelson et al. 1971). Recent research has cast new doubt on the popular assumption that certain erotica—hardcore pornography, for example—has damaging effect on social behavior, attitude formation, or psychic development (Goldstein et al. 1973). Eventually, such findings could contribute to public opinion shifts on the policy question.

Yet, since the national survey also indicated that more than half of those favoring some kind of restriction would not change their views even if erotica were proven harmless, censorship may also have formidable symbolic meaning. If psychoanalytically oriented criticism is correct, the censorial disposition may reflect, at least in part, an interest in *self-control*. In this view, censorship is a projection onto the public world of repressions tightly imposed upon oneself as a means of controlling powerful but deeply recessed drives toward sexual expression and aggression. By censoring, one supposedly reaffirms self-control and increases the distance between the conscious self and disturbing impulses or temptations within.

The erotica issue may also harbor a symbolic interest of another sort: the defense of particularist *status values*. According to this theory, the status of the group or class with which identification is made and, indirectly, of oneself, can be seen as enhanced or depreciated by the degree to which the moral, ethical, or aesthetic standards or style of life of the group or class are "in force." This element of status politics, seen in earlier temperance movements (Gusfield 1963), appears to be present in many community censorship conflicts and may be the basis for local group action (Zurcher and Kirkpatrick 1971). At the same time, however, present-day antipornography activists, as individuals and members of their local community, appear to be relatively satisifed, socially unfrustrated citizens with a high sense of efficacy (Zurcher and Cushing 1971), temperate in use of tactics and somewhat embarrassed to be labeled "censors" (Rodgers 1974). In this sense, they may be less status discontents within the community than representatives of a local majority alienated from prevailing doctrinal values, in this case, those of a cosmopolitan, elite culture.

Free speech interests, though generally assumed to seek mainly values of *enlightenment* and *expressive opportunity*, may also have status investment in the erotica issue. Like their censorial counterparts, libertarian activists also tend to speak of pornography less as a single issue than as a symbolic representation of a much broader value arrangement (Zurcher and Kirkpatrick 1971).

Another major goal is *economic gain*. Allocations of rights and obligations under the libertarian doctrine have enabled the production and marketing of erotica to become a minor growth industry. As such, it has sometimes yielded spectacular profits and, it is believed not infrequently, to the hands of organized crime. Application of more restrictive standards could force many media proprietors specializing in such erotica out of business.

Extensive "Balkanization" of standards, a forbidding prospect to some proprietors of national media who seek uniformity of the marketplace, could impose heavy costs when such media deal with erotica. Such costs could result in production of erotica "versions" to fit different community standards or in adoption of some sort of "common denominator" content, such as that which occurred in movies when that medium was confronted with a multiplicity of state and local censorship boards (Randall 1976).

Proprietary losses or even a marginal lowering of profit, in turn, could affect erotica policy at both its doctrinal and operating levels. A willingness to risk prosecution to defend when indicted, to appeal when convicted, and, generally, to withstand informal pressures of local authorities or groups has usually required both material resources and willingness to use them however self-serving that may be. In fact, at the operating level, economic means have often been the free speech counterweight to the superior numbers of the censorship interest and to the fact that the latter is invariably more representative of community attitudes and opinion.

Conclusion

The distance between the Supreme Court's elite, cosmopolitan doctrine and local, popular values, reflected in repeated appellate victories for the libertarian side, could be shortened by either of two developments. Elite standards themselves could undergo modification as a result of some elite reactive response to perceived negative environmental by-products of the libertarian doctrine, in the same way that elite values have appeared to undergo modification in the civil rights and due process criminal justice issues. Perhaps a more likely possibility is a change in popular standards and attitudes in the direction of greater tolerance and acceptance. This already appears to have occurred to more than a small degree in the last ten years, only to be outstripped by further evolution of elite standards. The possibility of a continued liberalization in popular attitudes, which must compete with the possibility of further popular alienation, could be inhibited *or aided* by the denationalizing of "community standards." On the one hand, as we have seen, effective denationalization is likely to mean a more restrictive environment for erotica and offers some immediate encouragement to censorship interests. On the other hand, denationalization, effective or merely apparent, could also function as a Burger Court legitimation of much of the rapid libertarian output of the preceding Court and, in the long run, affect popular values in quite a different and more subtle way.

Cases

Alberts v. California, 354 U.S. 476 (1957).

Burstyn v. Wilson, 343 U.S. 495 (1952).

Jacobellis v. Ohio, 378 U.S. 184 (1964).

Jenkins v. Georgia, 418 U.S. 153 (1974).

Miller v. California, 415 U.S. 15 (1973).

Roth v. United States, 354 U.S. 476 (1957).

References

Abelson, Herbert, et al. 1971. "National Survey of Public Attitudes Toward and Experience with Erotic Materials," *Technical Reports of the Commission on Obscenity and Pornography*, Vol. VI (Washington, D.C.: U.S. Government Printing Office), pp. 1-138.

Goldstein, Michael J., et al. 1973. *Pornography and Sexual Deviance* (Berkeley: University of California Press).

Gusfield, Joseph R. 1963. *Symbolic Crusade* (Urbana: University of Illinois Press).

Randall, Richard S. 1968. *Censorship of the Movies: The Social and Political Control of a Mass Medium* (Madison: University of Wisconsin Press).

_____. 1976. "Censorship: From 'The Miracle' to 'Deep Throat'," *The American Film Industry*, ed. Tino Balio (Madison: University of Wisconsin Press).

Roche, John P. 1963. *Quest for the Dream* (New York: Macmillan).

Rodgers, Harrell D., Jr. 1974. "Censorship Campaigns in Eighteen Cities: An Impact Analysis," *American Politics Quarterly*, 2 (October), 371-392.

Wallace, Douglas H. 1973. "Obscenity and Contemporary Community Standards: A Survey," *Journal of Social Issues*, 29, 53-68.

Wilson, W. Cody, et al. 1971. "Gravity of the Pornography Situation and Problems of Control: A Survey of Prosecuting Attorneys," *Technical Reports of the Commission on Obscenity and Pornography*, Vol. V (Washington, D.C.: U.S. Government Printing Office), pp. 3-14.

Wilson, W. Cody, and Herbert Abelson. 1971. "Experience With and Attitudes Toward Explicit Sexual Materials" *Journal of Social Issues*, 29, 19-36.

Zurcher, Louis, and R. George Kirkpatrick. 1971. "Collective Dynamics of Ad Hoc Anti-Pornography Organizations," *Technical Reports of the Commission on Obscenity and Pornography*, Vol. V (Washington, D.C.: U.S. Government Printing Office), pp. 83-142.

Zurcher, Louis, and Robert G. Cushing. 1971. "Participants in Ad Hoc Anti-Pornography Organizations: Some Individual Characteristics," *Technical Reports of the Commission on Obscenity and Pornography*, Vol. V (Washington, D.C.: U.S. Government Printing Office), pp. 143-218.

Zurcher, Louis, et al. 1971. "The Anti-Pornography Campaign: *A Symbolic Crusade,*" *Social Problems*, 19, 217-229.

18 Civil Liberties in Revised State Constitutions

Albert L. Sturm and Kaye M. Wright

In general contemporary usage, the term *civil rights* is related to the protection of the rights of minorities; *civil liberties* applies to the rights and freedoms of individuals that are, or ought to be, protected by government. Their expression in legal documents is both positive and negative—positive in affirming the right of the individual to have something done *for* him and negative in stating the right not to have something done *to* him. The latter is more traditional and common. All American state constitutions include statements of the traditional rights of persons and property won through centuries of struggle against arbitrary and tyrannical governmental action. Most of the newer state documents also include provisions reflecting modern problems and conditions. These are usually positive rights, which guarantee governmental protection or intervention on behalf of particular interests or individuals, or certain material or social benefits to every person. Major changes in provisions concerned with civil liberties and civil rights in the newer state constitutions include the addition or extension of antidiscrimination or equal protection guarantees, modifications of traditional common law procedures, and inclusion of some social and economic rights. Few of the traditional provisions have been removed, although some are archaic and others are unenforceable statements of political theory.

This chapter focuses on guarantees of civil liberties and civil rights in 16 recently written or revised American constitutions. These include ten state charters that have become operative since 1950: Alaska and Hawaii (1959), Michigan (1964), Connecticut (1965), Pennsylvania (1968), Florida (1969), Illinois and Virginia (1971), Montana (1973), Louisiana (1975); the proposed extensively revised Texas document voted on and rejected in November 1975; the constitution of Puerto Rico (1952); and four state constitutions being revised by phases: California, New Hampshire, South Carolina, and Utah. The principal purpose of the following analysis is to summarize major rights and to identify principal changes in civil liberties guarantees in recently written or revised state charters designed by constitution makers to meet current and future needs.

This paper draws, in part, upon the analysis in Albert L. Sturm, "Bills of Rights in New State Constitutions," in *Law and Justice: Essays in Honor of Robert S. Rankin*, ed. Carl Beck (Durham, N.C.: Duke University Press, 1970), pp. 161-180.

State and Federal Guarantees

State constitutions commonly repeat most of the guarantees of civil liberties found in the Constitution of the United States. Some authorities declare that it is unnecessary for state constitutions to duplicate rights guaranteed in the federal Constitution, especially since judicial decisions in the last half century have moved the national and state governments toward a single protective standard for civil liberties. Others point out that, although the states cannot alter rights guaranteed in the U.S. Constitution, they can add to them so long as there is no conflict with the federal Constitution. Assertion of rights in a state constitution provides a basis for suits in state courts, and also expresses the philosophy of a state relating to individual liberty. In addition, some constitutional problems growing out of industrialization, urbanization, and expanding governmental activity can be met more effectively by the states, which have the primary responsibility for exercising the general police power to protect persons and property through the definition and enforcement of criminal law.

All of the recently revised state charters of government contain an enumeration of civil liberties. There is little disposition in the states to entrust their protection entirely to federal law and judicial interpretation. The 1974 general revision of the California Bill of Rights, for example, added due process and equal protection guarantees and a prohibition against laws respecting an establishment of religion. Writers of state constitutions have shown little tendency to omit traditional guarantees, and the excisions that have occurred are substantially outnumbered by adaptations of existing rights to modern conditions and by the addition of new guarantees. Since all traditional rights that the people desire to be protected are not safeguarded under the national Constitution, many revised state constitutions include additional rights or more detailed guarantees than those stated in the national document.

Classification of Civil Liberties

Traditionally, guarantees of civil liberties comprise a series of "thou shalt nots" directed toward government. Increasingly, however, they find expression in positive language. This is especially true of the emerging, newer rights, such as the rights to an education, to a clean and healthful environment, and to privacy. Moreover, some guarantees afford protection against private persons and groups, as well as against government. Although the categories of "substantive" and "procedural" rights are not always exclusive, most civil liberties provisions in constitutions can be categorized as one or the other, and these major categories are used in the following analysis. Substantive guarantees may include the right of participation in the political process, protection against encroachment upon social and economic rights, and a broad general category including guarantees of freedom of expression, inquiry, privacy, physical liberty, and other forms of private liberty. Procedural rights relate to the manner in which government must proceed in the protection of substantive liberties.

Political Theory and Inherent Rights

Most state constitutions contain provisions that affirm basic principles of American constitutionalism, which are intimately related to the protection of civil liberties. All 16 constitutions analyzed here assert the principle of popular sovereignty in language identical or similar to that of Alaska's "All political power is inherent in the people," and all expressly subordinate military to civil power. Most documents state the purposes for which government is instituted (12), and assert the people's right to alter it (9). All but 3 of the 16 constitutions declare that all persons have certain inherent rights, which include life, liberty, and the pursuit of happiness. New Hampshire, Virginia, and California guarantee the right to *obtain* as well as *pursue* happiness, and California names safety and privacy as coordinate basic rights. Acquiring, possessing, and protecting property are considered basic rights in 6 of the constitutions, and Pennsylvania's includes "protecting reputation." Enjoyment of the rewards of one's own industry is a stated basic right in Florida and Alaska. Assertion that citizens have duties and obligations as well as rights is a significant innovation in 5 new constitutions (Alaska, Hawaii, Illinois, Montana, and Virginia).

Substantive Personal and Property Rights

Religion and Expression

All constitutions considered here guarantee the free exercise of religion, and almost all forbid laws respecting an establishment of religion. Other common provisions relating to religion prohibit preference by law to any religious society (3), as well as religious tests for witnesses (4), jurors (2), and office holders (3). Public aid for religious purposes is expressly forbidden in 11 of the constitutions, but such a prohibition, which had been a part of the Louisiana constitution since 1864, was omitted from the 1975

document. Freedom of speech, press, petition, and assembly are expressly guaranteed in all the documents. The most recent additions were guarantees of freedoms of speech and press to the New Hampshire constitution
in 1968. Most constitutions (12) specify that the individual is responsible
for abuse of these freedoms. Also, most of the documents (9) provide that
the truth may be given as evidence in libel or defamation actions.

Equal Treatment

Of broader and more general character among the positive substantive
guarantees in constitutions are the "due process," "equal protection,"
"antidiscrimination," and "legal equality" clauses. The first two are well
known and are included in most of these constitutions—due process in all,
equal protection in ten. However, antidiscrimination and legal equality
clauses are relatively new provisions; they are mainly products of the
controversy over racial segregation and the U.S. Supreme Court's school
desegregation decisions.

Although protection against discrimination now exists under the national Constitution, the new and revised state organic laws reiterate
"equal treatment" or "antidiscrimination" guarantees, some more explicitly than others. Specific antidiscrimination statements are included in
10 of the documents reviewed here. Four constitutions that do not specifically guarantee against "discrimination" contain provisions that prohibit
persons from being deprived of rights (Florida); forbid discriminatory disqualification from entering or pursuing business, profession, vocation, or
employment (California); guarantee equal enjoyment of all civil, political,
and religious rights and privileges (Utah); or state that all free men have
equal rights (Texas). Six of the 16 constitutions here analyzed (Alaska,
Pennsylvania, Florida, Texas, Puerto Rico, and New Hampshire) contain
specific legal equality statements. The equal treatment provision in Montana's 1973 constitution is a broad statement specifically prohibiting discrimination by both public and private entities: "No person shall be denied the equal protection of the laws. Neither the state nor any person,
firm, corporation, or institution shall discriminate against any person in
the exercise of his civil or political rights on account of race, color, sex,
culture, social origin or condition, or political or religious ideas."

All state constitutions revised since midcentury, except Florida's and
Michigan's, prohibit discrimination based on sex. During the last five
years the prohibition was added by amendment to six of the documents:
Pennsylvania (1971), Alaska (1972), Hawaii (1972), Connecticut (1974),
California (1974), and New Hampshire (1974). A clarifying provision of

the 1971 Virginia constitution states that "the mere separation of the sexes shall not be considered discrimination." Other areas or subjects expressly covered by antidiscrimination provisions in one or more revised constitutions include mental or physical handicap (Illinois, Texas, Florida), physical condition (Louisiana), employment (Illinois, California), access to public areas (Louisiana), and sale or rental of property (Illinois). In Pennsylvania and Virginia, the antidiscrimination guarantee applies expressly to government.

Political Rights

The right of citizens to participate in the political process comprises a significant segment of their positive substantive civil liberties. All state constitutions specify basic eligibility requirements for voting, provide for the suffrage, the conduct of elections, office holding, and procedures for direct and indirect participation. Some recent innovations in state constitution making relate to the exercise of political rights. Illustrative are provisions for removal of disqualifications for voting. At least six documents (California, Hawaii, Illinois, Louisiana, Montana, and Puerto Rico) provide for automatic restoration of the right to vote upon termination of state and federal supervision following conviction for any offense.

The Louisiana and Montana constitutions expressly guarantee the rights to examine public documents and to observe the deliberations of public bodies. The latter document also states that "the public has the right to expect governmental agencies to afford such reasonable opportunity for citizen participation in the operation of the agencies prior to the final decision as may be provided by law." Furthermore, the Montana constitution provides that the "rights of persons under 18 include but are not limited to all fundamental rights" stated in the bill of rights "unless specifically precluded by laws which enhance the protection of such persons."

Traditional Substantive Guarantees

With a few exceptions, such as the "antidiscrimination" and "legal equality" guarantees, the rights discussed above are generally regarded as traditional. Other positive substantive rights of this character contained in most state constitutions are the right to bear arms (13) and the requirement of just compensation for property taken for public use (16). The more recent eminent domain provisions include one or more of the following additional requirements of compensation: property damaged (9), property destroyed (Texas), and lawsuit expenses when the property owner wins the suit (Montana).

Twelve of the 16 documents contain a savings clause, stating that enumeration of rights in the constitution shall not be construed to impair or deny others retained by the people. Other miscellaneous traditional substantive prohibitions retained in some revised constitutions, but deleted as obsolete, repetitious, or no longer relevant for modern conditions in others, apply to: slavery and involuntary servitude (5—omitted in the new Florida and Montana documents); impairment of contract obligations (13); quartering of soldiers (12—omitted in the new Florida constitution; efforts to remove this provision from the Alaska document failed); grants of special privileges and immunities (10), and hereditary emoluments (5).

Suits Against the State

Traditionally, the states and other governmental units have been immune from suit under the doctrine of sovereign immunity. Recent state constitutional revision, however, has eroded the traditional common law principle that "the king can do no wrong," from which the doctrine of sovereign immunity largely stems. Approximately half the new or revised state constitutions expressly provide for the right of individuals to sue the state and its political subdivisions.

Social and Economic Rights

Most positive guarantees of social and economic rights are nontraditional and appear only in some of the new or revised documents. A significant guarantee included in four of these constitutions is the right of employees to organize and to bargain collectively (Florida, Hawaii, Louisiana, and Puerto Rico). The Louisiana document limits these rights to classified civil service employees, and that of Puerto Rico to employees in private business. Florida's constitution includes a no-strike provision for public employees. A "right to work" provision is included in only the Florida and Louisiana documents, and in the latter is limited to classified civil service employees. Collective bargaining and right to work guarantees have been highly controversial as constitutional rights. They have been major issues in recent constitutional revision efforts, including those in Alaska, Michigan, and Texas.

Some of the other social or economic provisions included in at least one of the constitutions analyzed here are: employees' rights in the Puerto

Rico constitution (equal pay, a reasonable minimum salary, on-the-job protection against risks to person and health, and an eight-hour work day); the right to an education or equal educational opportunity (Montana, Puerto Rico, Texas, and Virginia); protection of individual dignity (Illinois, Montana, Puerto Rico); and preservation of historic, linguistic, and cultural origins (Louisiana). Specified as a concern of the state in the constitutions of Alaska, Hawaii, Michigan, and Texas is public health, and in those of Alaska and Hawaii, welfare of the people. Additional concerns in Hawaii include slum clearance and rehabilitation of substandard areas, including housing, for low-income persons. In most states, these matters are still regarded as more appropriate for statute.

Three new state constitutions (Illinois, Montana, and Pennsylvania) include a clean and healthful environment among their stated rights. Nine other revised state documents (Alaska, California, Florida, Louisiana, Michigan, Puerto Rico, South Carolina, Texas, and Virginia) declare protection of the environment and/or natural resources to be official state policy and mandate the legislature to enact appropriate implementing legislation.

Civil and Criminal Procedural Rights

Rights of Persons Accused of Crime

The rights of persons accused of crime are among the most basic and traditional of all. They afford protection against arbitrary police action, and require fair procedure in official action that may result in loss of liberty or property. Most affirmative procedural guarantees and prohibitions in state constitutions are also found in the federal document. Well-known affirmative rights commonly provided in all or most constitutions include the right to indictment by grand jury (12), habeas corpus (all), bail (14), speedy and public trial by impartial jurors (all), counsel (all except Virginia), information on the nature of the accusation (all), confrontation by witnesses (all), compulsory process to obtain witnesses (all except New Hampshire and Virginia), and change of venue to secure a fair trial (5). The constitutions of Hawaii, Louisiana, and New Hampshire require the state to provide counsel for indigents. In Virginia, instead of the usual "compulsory process" provision, the constitution guarantees an accused person the right "to call for evidence in his favor."

Modifications of these traditional rights in recently revised constitutions apply to indictment by grand jury, habeas corpus, and bail. Nine of the 16 documents provide for waiver of the right to indictment by grand jury, authorizing initiation of action by information; conditions for prosecuting by information are usually specified. With respect to habeas corpus, 3 state constitutions (Louisiana, Montana, Texas) contain absolute prohibitions against suspension of the privilege; the other documents permit suspension in cases of rebellion or invasion (or similar emergency) when the public safety requires it. Illinois forbids suspension in capital cases, and 4 documents (Connecticut, Hawaii, New Hampshire, Puerto Rico) authorize suspension only by the legislature. Puerto Rico's constitution makes no exceptions to the right of release on bail, although most (12) of the constitutions in this study provide for such release except in capital cases. Both the Hawaii and California documents vest in the courts the discretion to release defendants on their own recognizance; in Hawaii, expressly excepted are defendants charged with an offense punishable by life imprisonment.

All recently revised state constitutions protect against unreasonable searches and seizures and self-incrimination; most expressly forbid excessive bail (15) and fines (14), double jeopardy (15), cruel and unusual punishment (14), bills of attainder (12), ex post facto laws (14), and imprisonment for debt (12). Some documents, however, omit repetition of those guarantees stated in the federal Constitution. In the newer revisions there is some disposition to delete traditional prohibitions against corruption of blood and forfeiture of estate that seem less relevant in latter twentieth-century society. With respect to punishment, the Alaska and Montana documents contain significant innovative provisions that penal administration shall be based on the principle of reformation and upon the need for protecting the public. Similar statements regarding severity of penalties appear in the Illinois and New Hampshire constitutions, the latter providing: ''All penalties ought to be proportioned to the nature of the offense . . . the true design of all punishment being to reform, not to exterminate mankind.''

Searches, Wiretapping, and Privacy

Technological developments and the libertarian emphasis on the rights of accused persons have led to further additions to the prohibition against unreasonable searches and seizures, which is included in all recent constitutions. Puerto Rico forbids all wiretapping; typically, however, the new provisions that mention electronic surveillance authorize interception of private communications for reasonable cause. The Illinois document, for example, guarantees the people the ''right to be secure in their persons, houses, papers and other possessions against unreasonable searches, seizures, invasions of privacy or interceptions of communications by eaves-

dropping devices or other means'' and adds: ''No warrant shall issue
without probable cause, supported by affidavit particularly describing the
place to be searched and the persons or things to be seized.'' In addition
to the five documents (Florida, Hawaii, Illinois, Louisiana, Puerto Rico)
that prohibit unreasonable interception of private communications, seven
(Alaska, California, Hawaii, Illinois, Louisiana, Montana, South Carolina) either guarantee the right to privacy or prohibit the invasion of privacy.

The recent emphasis on the right to privacy, especially when applied
to accused persons, conflicts with another basic right: the protection of
life and property. Constitution makers considering expansion of searches
and seizures provisions face the continuing problem of finding the optimum equilibrium between human liberty and public order. The 1969 report of the Virginia Commission on Constitutional Revision exemplifies
such concern. After considering whether provisions against electronic
surveillance or a guarantee of the right to privacy should be included in
the proposed new constitution, the commission concluded that any such
revision "ought to be preceded by a thorough study of the techniques and
implications of modern surveillance devices, information-gathering systems . . . and other developments" and also should await further judicial
interpretation of search and seizure provisions in the national Constitution (Report 1969, pp. 94-95).

Other Procedural Guarantees

State constitutions contain fewer provisions relating to civil than to criminal procedure. Most recent revisions declare that the courts shall be open,
and that all persons shall have a legal remedy for injury. Most constitutions also continue to guarantee the right to trial by jury in civil as well as
in criminal cases, although many permit waiver of this requirement under
stated conditions. In Michigan, for example, trial by jury shall be waived
in all civil cases unless demanded by one of the parties. Other modifications of traditional common law requirements permit a smaller number of
jurors than is required for criminal trials. These range from a minimum of
5 permitted in courts not of record in Virginia to 12 jurors or any smaller
number agreed to in open court by the parties, which the California document provides. Deviations from the traditional unanimous verdict requirement vary from Montana's two-thirds to Pennsylvania's and Michigan's five-sixths. Alaska, Hawaii, Texas, and California authorize a verdict by three-fourths of the jurors. Some documents specify minimum dollar amounts before a jury trial is required: Hawaii, $100; Alaska, $250;
and South Carolina, $200 (increased in the 1970 revision from $100). At

least 5 state constitutions (California, Florida, Michigan, Montana, South Carolina) expressly forbid unreasonable detention of witnesses.

The Alaska and Michigan documents require fair and just treatment in legislative and executive investigations, thus providing citizens protection against abusive attacks on personal reputation, honor, and private life by these avowedly political branches of government. South Carolina's 1970 revision expressly extends to administrative proceedings the requirements of due notice and the opportunity to be heard, and mandates separation of the prosecution and adjudication functions.

A Concluding Note

The preceding content analysis of civil liberties guarantees in new and revised state constitutions has identified major substantive changes. They include: some omissions, exemplified in traditional prohibitions concerning quartering of soldiers in private residences in peacetime, corruption of blood, forfeiture of estate, titles of nobility, and hereditary emoluments; updating of traditional provisions, probably best illustrated by the new "legal equality" and "antidiscrimination" guarantees; and the addition of new rights, such as the right to an education or equal educational opportunity, and to a healthful environment.

Generally, these changes evidence not only an effort by constitution makers to achieve greater clarity and precision of statement in the fundamental law, but also a desire to express both new and traditional rights in flexible terms that permit adaptation to rapidly changing conditions and needs. Probably more than any other provisions in state organic laws, these guarantees manifest the continuing problems of balancing human liberties against requirements for maintaining public order. Changing needs and conditions will continue to require reevaluation and extension of both substantive and procedural traditional guarantees.

References

The Constitution of Virginia (Report). 1969. Report of the Commission on Constitutional Revision, January 1, 1969 (Charlottesville: The Michie Company).

Greenberg, Milton. 1961. "Civil Liberties," *Salient Issues of Constitutional Revision*, ed. John P. Wheeler, Jr. (New York: National Municipal League), pp. 7-20.

Konvitz, Milton R. 1968. "Civil Rights," *International Encyclopedia of the Social Sciences,* ed. David L. Sills (New York: Macmillan and Free Press), 312-317.

Rankin, Robert S. 1969. "Civil Rights," *Compacts of Antiquity: State Constitutions*, ed. Richard H. Leach (Atlanta: Southern Newspaper Publishers Association Foundation).

_____. 1960. *State Constitutions: The Bill of Rights* (New York: National Municipal League).

Sturm, Albert L. 1970. "Bills of Rights in New State Constitutions," *Law and Justice: Essays in Honor of Robert S. Rankin*, ed. Carl Beck (Durham, N.C.: Duke University Press), pp. 161-180.

19

The Supreme Court, Civil Liberties, and the Canadian Bill of Rights

Donald S. Dobkin

The role of Canada's highest court deserves increased public attention. This was the message of Canadian Supreme Court Chief Justice Bora Laskin in a recent address to the Canadian Bar Association as he exhorted Canadians to seek a better understanding of the Canadian High Court's function. Laskin's discourse also urged the media to upgrade their monitoring of the Court's activities by improving both the frequency and thoroughness of their reports. In encouraging the legal profession and the media as well as the public at large to recognize the Court as "expositor of the national legal conscience" (1974), Laskin was merely affirming the modest role that the Court has played in Canadian society during its first century.

One of the gravest consequences of the Court's underexposure has been a misconception, among both Canadians and non-Canadians, about just what civil rights Canadians do possess. Alert students of the Canadian judicial process have often observed that if the Court's policies were more widely disseminated, Canadians would be genuinely shocked to discover the limited range of their civil liberties. The sad and simple truth of the matter is that Canadians do not enjoy the legacy of civil liberties that have been bequeathed to their American neighbors, a reality that is seldom understood in Canada—or elsewhere. Nurtured by episodes of American detective and police stories on their television sets, Canadians often unconsciously equate their own rights with those they ingest through their viewing screens. Generally, they are ignorant of such facts as the lack of any provision in Canadian law requiring police to inform arrested persons of their right to remain silent—or their right to retain a lawyer. Indeed, it may be farther from "The Streets of San Francisco" to the Supreme Court chambers in Ottawa than many Canadians realize!

To understand better the inadequacies of civil liberties in Canada, it is necessary to examine the Canadian Bill of Rights (CBR) and its perceived defects, along with the Supreme Court's role in interpreting that document.

The Canadian Bill of Rights

It is important to point out first that nowhere in the Canadian Constitution (The British North America (BNA) Act) is there any explicit reference even vaguely approximating a guarantee of specific civil liberties. Historically, civil rights could be protected only through the ambiguities and uncertainties of the common law. Occasionally, however, the courts did participate in the civil liberties field in at least three indirect ways: by deciding cases on the distribution of legislation power under § 91 and 92 of the BNA Act, by awarding damages in private lawsuits, and by interpreting certain constitutional and statutory phrases.

The CBR was put into effect on August 10, 1960. Like its American counterpart, the CBR attempted to prescribe certain fundamental guarantees such as freedom of speech, press, assembly, and religion, and purported as well to ensure due process and equality *before* the law. Thus, it both recognized the failure of these earlier "indirect" techniques to encompass even a remote semblance of an egalitarian spirit and carried with it a hope that the inadequacies in the area of civil liberties would begin to be overcome.

From the very beginning, however, several serious problems arose. First to be exposed was the actuality that the CBR was enacted merely as an ordinary statute and not as an amendment to the Constitution. Consequently, this lack of constitutional status raised the theoretical possibility that a subsequent Parliament could repeal the Bill, although this has not and is not likely to happen.

Commentators writing in the 1960s cited this deficiency as the Bill's most distressing aspect. However, their primary dissatisfaction resulted from the fear that the Supreme Court would not give full effect to a document lacking full constitutional status. In any event, ensuing judicial decisions have proved that these early prophets were, at least partially, victims of misguided fears, because the Supreme Court has since declared that the CBR can be applied against federal laws in violation of its provisions (*Drybones* and *Lavell*). Unfortunately, the Court has applied this general doctrine of federal applicability both infrequently and cautiously.

Judicial Role and the Supreme Court

The Supreme Court's overriding policy has been that the CBR is not concerned with "human rights and fundamental freedoms in any abstract sense, but rather with such rights and freedoms as they existed in Canada immediately before the Bill was enacted" (*Curr* v. *The Queen*). In other words, key phrases are irrevocably rooted in their historical antecedents. This marked reluctance, shared even by the Court's more "liberal" thinkers, to give the Bill of Rights a significant degree of vitality has been the single most important factor in restricting the Bill's growth to date.

The High Court's position is not, however, a surprising one, given certain attributes of the Canadian legal tradition. The overwhelming premise is that Parliament is supreme over the other branches of government, and the concept of judicial law making is firmly rejected. The notion that courts might in any way be involved in the political process is usually denied by Canadian judges and lawyers alike, as well as by the press and the public (McNaught 1974). Clearly, one effect of this mental' prohibition against judicial law making has been to create a convenient vehicle for the Court's avoidance or superficial treatment of many key issues. The end result has been the repeated reinforcement of judicial restraint as the "honorable and proper" mode of judicial behavior.

Nor should it be overlooked that it was not until 1949 that the Supreme Court became the final court of appeal in Canada, thus ending a long and bewildering era of intervention by the Privy Council in England. However, it is seldom pointed out, let alone emphasized, that although direct British influence on Canadian courts was officially terminated, Canadians have yet to begin to discard the pervasive influences of the British legal tradition—a tradition hardly egalitarian and certainly without a history of dealing with the interpretation of written constitutional documents. There is little doubt that the mental processes of the present members of the Supreme Court are closer to Edmund Burke than to John Locke.

This influence has been reflected in the tenor of the commentary to appear on the Supreme Court; such commentary generally has embraced a cautious, apologetic, and surprisingly optimistic intonation (but see Weiler 1974). Unquestionably, British social mores, shunning overly critical or iconoclastic assessments of any kind and particularly of courts, are largely responsible for the current state of affairs. One should definitely not underestimate the impact that this "deferential reverence" has had on the Canadian judicial process as well as on the shaping of the general social fabric of Canadian society.

Foolish declarations that the Court is about to embark upon a new era of Canadian jurisprudence are widespread (Mitchell 1975), but wholly unsupportable. Not only do such contentions ignore all the mental and physical impediments discussed thus far, but in addition, there exists a failure to appreciate the manner in which constitutional cases are adjudicated. Specifically, constitutional cases are generally resolved in an atmosphere where the application of a legal doctrine to a particular set of facts emerges as the Court's primary duty. Considerations of policy, such as the effect that the contraction or expansion of a given legal rule or constitutional phrase might have on society, seldom appear in the text of the written decision. Characteristically then, decisions are written in what Karl Llewellyn termed the "Formal Style" of opinion writing as contrasted with the more informative and articulate "Grand Style." Decisions in constitutional cases are too often the products of the narrow, logic-chopping analysis traditionally used in private law cases (Miller 1969). The Supreme Court has yet to make the crucial distinction that, by definition, constitutional cases necessitate the use of a broader policy base than that applied in other areas of the legal process.

Recent appointments to the Court, including that of Chief Justice Laskin, have no doubt engendered the current wave of optimism concerning the potential for a new and expanded Canadian jurisprudence to surface. Laskin is particularly known for his centralist tendencies and notable contributions to the field of constitutional law in Canada (see particularly Laskin 1973). Nevertheless, the Court as a whole has been sharply divided on the question of the Bill of Rights. Even with the frequent dissents of Laskin, and occasionally others, it seems unlikely that in view of the Court's traditions, composition, and attitude, that we can expect much of a jurisprudential transition.

The Supreme Court and the Bill of Rights

After this introduction as to the character and composition of the Court, perhaps it is not terribly difficult to appreciate the reasons for the impotency of the Canadian Bill of Rights in providing adequate guarantees of civil liberties. Let us now turn to a sampling of specific areas prescribed in the Bill of Rights.

Perhaps the most accurate indicator of the success of a system's ability to ensure adequate civil liberties is the extent to which the system has been able to provide for certain First Amendment rights or for what Cardozo termed the "Honor Roll of Superior Rights." Thus far, it is difficult to say definitively to what degree these freedoms, "the matrix, the indispensable condition of nearly every other form of freedom" (*Palko* v. *Connecticut*), are guaranteed since there are no Canadian Supreme Court cases dealing specifically with the meaning of freedom of speech and press as they appear in the Bill of Rights.

Nevertheless, the strong traditions enshrined prior to the Bill of Rights indicate that a great many hurdles would need to be overcome for a pro-"preferred freedoms" position to emerge. Current laws such as those on defamation, sedition, obscenity, and censorship, arising principally from the Canadian Criminal Code, have been continuously upheld with little regard for possible free speech and press violations. The bulk of these restrictions were cultivated during a period when no written Bill of Rights existed. Hence, so-called First Amendment concerns could be protected only through the indirect methods mentioned earlier. Regrettably, flagrant disregard for freedom of speech and press claims continues to this day, especially in lower courts. For example, no principle analogous to the doctrine of "no prior restraint" as espoused in *Near* v. *Minnesota* exists in Canada today. In fact, it is possible to obtain an injunction to halt a scheduled radio or television broadcast or even to prohibit the publication of an article in a newspaper or magazine. All that need be met for the granting of such an injunction are the normal legal requirements that include injurious and irreparable harm (*Canada Metal* v. *The Canadian Broadcasting Corporation*).

Among the specific areas in which the Court has had to interpret the provisions of the Bill of Rights is freedom of religion. The Court's interpretation of this provision leads to the conclusion that there is no definitive separation between church and state in Canada. Although there is no official established Canadian religion, the complete separation of church and state has never been an avowed policy of Canadian legislators; in fact, many parts of Canada once maintained established churches (Tarnopolsky 1975).

Given the tolerance for religions having Sunday as the day of worship, as demonstrated by various members of Parliament, it is not surprising to see that the Supreme Court has reflected this position. In echoing the country's general religious reverence, the Supreme Court has repeatedly upheld the Lord's Day Act, an anachronistic statute forbidding business activities on Sunday (*Robertson and Rosetanni* v. *The Queen*). At first glance, this state of affairs should appear to be directly analogous to the American experience in *Braunfeld* v. *Brown*, where the argument that the statutes had a primarily secular purpose was used to validate Sunday closing laws. However, an examination of the Lord's Day Act would clearly reveal that its primary purpose is to preserve the sanctity of Sunday in support of Christian religious tenets. In the view of Justice Ritchie, the enactment of the Bill of Rights did not alter the meaning to be attached to freedom of religion; thus no argument that posited the unconstitutionality of the Lord's Day Act could be sustained. The possibility that the existence of this act might favor one religion over another received little attention; the majority of the Court was of the opinion that no such compelling interest as the likelihood of religious partiality could justify an alteration in their perceptions of what constituted religious freedom.

Apart from the policy of reinforcing beliefs and attitudes in existence prior to the birth of the Bill of Rights, the Court has in effect established the meaning of freedom of religion to include merely the "free exercise of religion." No establishment clause is found in the Bill of Rights and none has been read into the interpretation of freedom of religion. Unfortunately, no concrete definition of the meaning of free exercise has ever been advanced by the Court. The only guidelines to appear thus far as to its meaning have been by way of general analogies to the Australian and United States constitutions.

A further survey of the Court's activity in the civil liberties field indicates that, in just 15 years, the concept of due process of law has been dealt such a severe blow that it is difficult to envisage its immediate recovery. Essentially, due process has been limited to a position encompassing only *procedural* due process. The Court has flatly refused to incorporate the concept of substantive due process into the Canadian context for two principal reasons: the apparent confusion and controversy it has created in the United States, especially in economic matters prior to 1937, and, the CBR's lack of any provision similar to the Fourteenth Amendment of the United States Constitution (*Curr* v. *The Queen*).

Under § 2(c)(ii), the Bill of Rights provides for a "right to counsel." There have been several Supreme Court cases on this question, the most significant of which was the 1972 decision in *Brownridge*. Unfortunately, the Court was unable to reach a consensus as to the basis of this right, nor were specific guidelines as to the extent of this right outlined. At best, all that could be concluded from the decision is that there exists in Canada a general right to counsel, subject to the particular facts of each case.

Without question, there are major weaknesses in this right. The most glaring deficiency is the lack of any *Miranda* provision requiring police to inform arrested persons of their right to consult with counsel *before* questioning or testing of any kind commences. Naturally, few individuals are aware of their general right to confer with counsel. Hence, without this obligation to inform, the right becomes largely a symbolic one. Furthermore, there has been no indication from the Court as to what comprises a reasonable attempt by an accused to contact his or her lawyer, such that interference with the attempt would be a denial of counsel. Thus, at this juncture, we do not know whether an accused's inability to reach a lawyer could be considered a denial of counsel.

Perhaps the most alarming defect pervading the general area of search and seizure is that relating to illegally obtained evidence. By their decision in the *Wray* case, the Supreme Court has in effect removed the possibility that the American exclusionary rule could be established in Canada. Clearly, no such doctrine exists. As long as the relevance of the evidence is established, it is admissible, notwithstanding the fact that it was obtained through an unlawful search or seizure.

The Bill of Rights does provide for a privilege against "self crimination," with the wording here being somewhat different from that of the Fifth Amendment. Clearly, under the *Curr* decision this right is limited in several important ways. First, it does not apply to pretrial compulsions of police officers who force detained persons to submit to tests that might ultimately produce incriminating evidence against them. Second, even at the trial level, the privilege does not allow the accused to remain silent. He or she must answer the question asked, while at that moment raising the objection that such testimony might be incriminating. The Court will then acknowledge that the accused has invoked his or her right and thus theoretically, these answers may not be used against the accused in a subsequent judicial proceeding.

Setbacks comparable to those in the due process area have been inflicted on the "equality before the law" phrase in the Bill of Rights. Once again, the Court's policy has revealed a marked reluctance to give genuine effect to the Bill. Indeed, it has been continually emphasized by the Court that "this phrase is not effective to invoke the egalitarian concept exemplified by the Fourteenth Amendment of the United States Constitution" (*A.G. Canada* v. *Lavell*). Moreover, this phrase has been interpreted to convey the impression that discrimination per se is not sufficient grounds to constitute a violation of equality before the law. Specifically, the Supreme Court has said that in order for a violation to have occurred, there must have been discrimination *as well as* an infringement of those rights prescribed in § 2 of the Bill. The Court has therefore made the application of equality before the law considerably less broad and legally more difficult.

Conclusion

We have observed that as a consequence of a variety of factors, the presence of the Canadian Bill of Rights for the first 15 years has not resulted in the broadening of civil liberties to the extent desired by many. That the Bill was not enacted as a constitutional instrument has had its impact; so has the fact that some of the Bill's wording differs from the American Bill of Rights. Nevertheless, these factors should no longer be used to camouflage the true reason for the sluggish growth of the Bill, namely, the presence of a restrained judicial role on the Court. The question remains as to whether the Supreme Court can discard its present proclivities and instead allow a more liberal view of contemporary needs and social concerns to dictate the meaning of the Bill of Rights.

Cases

A.G. Canada v. Lavell et al. 38 D.L.R. (3d) 481 (1973).

Braunfeld v. Brown, 366 U.S. 599 (1961).

Canada Metal v. The Canadian Broadcasting Corporation [1974], 3 O.R. (2d) 1.

Curr v. The Queen, 26 D.L.R. (3d) 603 (1972).

Miranda v. Arizona, 384 U.S. 436 (1966).
Near v. Minnesota, 283 U.S. 697 (1931).
Palko v. Connecticut, 302 U.S. 319 (1937).
R. v. Brownridge [1972], S.C.R. 926.
R. v. Drybones, 9 D.L.R. (3d) 481 (1969).
R. v. Wray [1971] S.C.R. 272.
Robertson and Rosetanni v. The Queen [1963], S.C.R. 651.

References

Laskin, Bora. 1973. *Laskin's Canadian Constitutional Law*, 4th ed. (Toronto: Carswell).

_____. 1974. Speech to Fourth Atlantic Law Conference, in *Canadian Bar National*, 1, #11 (November), 1, 9-10.

McNaught, Kenneth. 1974. "Political Trials and the Canadian Political Tradition," *University of Toronto Law Journal*, 24 (Spring), 149-69.

Miller, Arthur S. 1969. *The Supreme Court and the Living Constitution* (Washington: Lerner Law Book).

Mitchell, C. Michael. 1975. "The Role of Courts in Public Policy Making: A Personal View," *University of Toronto Faculty of Law Review*, 33 (Spring), 1-17.

Tarnopolsky, Walter S. 1975. *The Canadian Bill of Rights*, 2nd ed. (Toronto: McClelland & Stewart).

Weiler, Paul. 1974. *In the Last Resort: A Critical Study of the Supreme Court of Canada* (Toronto: Carswell).

Additional References

Adams, George, and Cavalluzzo, Paul. 1969. "The Supreme Court of Canada: A Biographical Study," *Osgoode Hall Law Journal*, 7 (November), 61-86.

Beck, J.M., ed. 1971. *The Shaping of Canadian Federalism: Central Authority or Provincial Right?* (Toronto: Copp Clark).

Laskin, Bora. 1969. *The British Tradition in Canadian Law* (London: Stevens & Sons).

_____. 1970. "Constitutionalism in Canada: Legislative Power and a Bill of Rights," *The Fourteenth Amendment*, ed. B. Schwartz (New York: New York University Press), pp. 172-185.

Russell, Peter H. 1969. *The Supreme Court of Canada as a Bilingual and Bilcultural Institution* (Ottawa: Queen's Printer for Canada).

Van Loon, Richard J., and Whittington, Michael S. 1971. *The Canadian Political System: Environment, Structure & Process* (Toronto: McGraw-Hill).

**Part IV
Methodology and Civil
Liberties Policy**

20 The Applicability of Quasi-experimental Time-series Analysis to Judicial Policy Making

William Lee Eubank

During the past few years, one has had occasion to hear remarks of the general form, "The trend in Supreme Court decision making is. . . ." Usually what is meant is that, through the outcome of cases or through dicta, the Court has changed its "mind" on issues such as the criteria for standing, admissibility of certain types of evidence, the definition of obscene material, or rules of procedure for administrative agencies. Two propositions are implied by this type of remark: (1) in the recent past the Court has tended to act in a consistent manner with regard to a particular issue or set of issues, and (2) the Court's previously consistent behavior has changed in a specific way.

Political scientists, sociologists, and lawyers normally investigate the meaning of such remarks by adopting a case-by-case approach to judicial doctrine. Without question this methodology is important, for it tells us what these shifting criteria, definitions, and procedures were and are. However, another approach is available to students of the courts and it is the intent of this note to acquaint the reader with this approach and its applicability to the study of judicial policy making. Policy analysts concerned with either historical or contemporary judicial policy making should find it helpful in their efforts to determine if policy has changed and to offer explanations for that change.

Use of the Design

This approach to judicial policy making centers on the use of quasi-experimental research design and time-series data (Cook and Scioli 1972). The approach, which is quite flexible, has been used to assess the effects of policies as diverse as Connecticut's crackdown on speeders (Campbell and Ross 1968), the impact of legal reform on the divorce rate in turn-of-the-century Germany (Glass, Tiao, and McGuire 1971), and the effects of random "breathalyser" examinations of drivers on the accident rate in England (Ross, Campbell, and Glass 1970).

Using this approach, the investigator would take the decisions of the Court with respect to a particular issue to be a continuing affirmation of policy and would assume that a change in policy is the consequence of some event. A large number of propositions to this effect can be found in the literature. For instance, Robert G. McClosky (1972, p. 57) contends that the Vinson Court was decidedly less receptive to civil liberties than was its predecessor, the Stone Court, and demonstrates this through case analysis. To further substantiate his point, McClosky presents data in the nature of aggregate percentages of pro-civil liberties decisions by the Stone and Vinson Courts. The use of the quasi-experimental time-series approach allows one to specify clearly the "break point" between the two courts, which may not have come immediately with Vinson's accession to the chief justiceship, and to determine with more confidence than can be gained by the inspection of aggregate percentages whether the Vinson Court significantly reduced pro-civil liberties decisions. Thus, one can determine if the Vinson Court pursued a more conservative policy with regard to civil liberties claims than did the Stone Court. Another example is provided by the Warren Court's civil liberties decisions in the 1950s. It has been alleged that late in that decade the Court retreated from its previously favorable position on civil liberties claims, in the face of congressional reaction inspired by the Court's decisions in the areas of governmental control of Communist subversion, such as *Jencks* v. *U.S.*, and criminal law, such as *Mallory* v. *U.S.* (see Murphy 1962). The researcher could trace the Warren Court's pro-civil liberties decisions through that period and with this approach test whether there was a decrease in decisions favorable to the civil liberties claim, and if it was the congressional reaction that produced the effect it is contended to have had.

Of more contemporary interest is the impact President Nixon might have had on altering the Supreme Court's receptivity to civil liberties claims, especially those dealing with rights of the accused. President Nixon was elected in 1968 while running on a platform calling, in part, for a return of the balance of justice to the side of the police forces and away from the "criminal forces" and it is reasonable to assume he had this promise in mind when making his nominations to the Court (Levy 1974). Using the suggested approach, one would plot the annual percentage of pro-defendant decisions, starting with the Warren Court, and then determine if that percentage had decreased significantly after the appointment to the Court of Chief Justice Burger and the other Nixon nominees. One would thus be able to judge the president's success in remaking the Supreme Court's policy.

One may also use the proposed approach to detect the impact of judicial policy making on local legal systems. In a recent study, Barton L. Ingraham, using a nationwide survey, assayed the effect on local prosecutors and defenders of *Argersinger* v. *Hamlin*, in which the Supreme Court extended to all defendants facing imprisonment the right to counsel guaranteed in *Gideon* v. *Wainwright*. Some questions of impact raised by Ingraham, including the decision's effect on the number of not guilty pleas in misdemeanor cases, the increase in time between arrest and resolution, and the differential impact of the decision on indigent and nonindigent defendants are amenable to analysis with the time-series quasi-experimental approach. For example, by use of local records, one could test whether the assignment of counsel to misdemeanor cases and the number of not guilty pleas had increased following *Argersinger*, or if after the decision, the number of indigents awaiting trial on misdemeanor charges had increased while the number of nonindigents awaiting trial had remained stable.

Design

Quasi-experimental time-series designs are particularly appropriate for investigating issues like those above because they are most useful when the researcher lacks a full range of experimental manipulations available in "pure" laboratory designs (Campbell and Stanley 1963, p. 34), such as control over the introduction of the experimental intervention, random selection of subjects or random assignment of subjects to treatment and control groups (Caporaso and Pelowski 1971, p. 420). The basic form of the design is as follows:

$$O_{n-i} \ldots O_{n-3}\, O_{n-2}\, O_{n-1}\, O_n \quad I \quad O_{n+1}\, O_{n+2}\, O_{n+3} \ldots O_{n+j}$$

In this design, each "O" represents an observation of the experimental unit taken at equally spaced intervals in time, such as the proportion of civil liberties claims decided favorably by the Supreme Court each year. In theory these observations may be extended indefinitely in time, but the nature of the research question and practical considerations will limit their number. The "I" represents the experimental intervention introduced into the series midway between O_n and O_{n+1}, with those observations prior to "I" termed prechange observations and those following "I" postchange observations. The expectation is that after the experimental intervention has been introduced, a discontinuity will be evident between the pre- and postchange observations, and that the appearance of a discontinuity may be taken as evidence that an effect predicted as a consequence of the intervention has occurred.

In the examples noted earlier, the interventions are respectively, the change in composition of the Stone Court, congressional reaction to the Warren Court, President Nixon's nominations to the Court, and the *Argersinger* decision. However, as a practical matter, the investigator may find that it is difficult to locate precisely the intervention in the time series. Consider again, for instance, the example of the Warren Court and civil liberties in the 1950s. In this case the intervention quite obviously is the political reaction by Congress to certain of the Warren Court's judgments. However, the intervention's exact position in the time series is hard to define because the reaction continued for some period, although it was manifested by individual pieces of court-curbing legislation. In this instance the researcher is faced with the question of when the intervention "occurred" and also where in the series the intervention had its effect. The researcher must decide whether that effect occurred at the beginning of the reaction, at some point half-way through the period of reaction, or at the point at which the researcher determined the reaction to be most intense. (If the precise location of an intervention is obvious but there are good, theoretical reasons to expect a delayed effect, it is permissible to move the intervention forward in the time series.)

An additional difficulty, which may be encountered in specifying an intervention, is found when the intervention is an event that cannot be directly measured and an event that can be directly measured must be designated as the intervention. The issue of President Nixon's impact on Supreme Court policy is a case in point. The policy of the Nixon administration with regard to the Court's civil liberties policy is the intervention, but since the administration's policy cannot be definitely specified as an event, it is necessary to substitute President Nixon's nominations to the Court as the intervention. Thus, the president's impact on the Court's policy acts through the change in Court personnel.

Clearly some research questions that use the quasi-experimental time-series design are more subject to these problems than are others. For example, with respect to the impact of *Argersinger* the intervention is obvious and its location in the time-series is clear. The point is that while the investigator will not have full control over the intervention and although he should designate an event as the intervention before data analysis in order to avoid posthoc hypothesis formation, he must be willing to select an event and be content to live with what may seem to be an unacceptable degree of imprecision.

After the intervention has been introduced into the time series, one expects to see an intervention effect, a discontinuity, in the postchange observations. There are two basic kinds of discontinuities that can be anticipated as the result of the intervention's impact on the series: abrupt changes in series level (intercept differences) and in trend (slope differences). Some of the possible intervention effects are no change in level but change in trend of the series; temporary change in level; change in level but no change in trend; and change in both trend and level (Campbell and Stanley 1963, p. 38; Glass, Willson, and Gottman 1972, pp. 45-52).

Thus, one might look for a dramatic change in level for favorably decided civil liberties cases from the Warren Court to the Burger Court, a more gradual change (change in slope), or the presence of both intervention effects.

The interpretation of intervention effects and series discontinuities may be erroneous if the researcher does not account for several potential sources of invalidity to which all quasi-experimental designs are subject (Campbell and Stanley 1963, pp. 5 ff; Glass, Willson, and Gottman 1972, pp. 53-70; Neale and Liebert 1973, pp. 35-41). The most likely source of potential invalidity in these quasi-experiments, especially when applied to political and social events, is history. This means that there is the danger that an event or events other than the one designated as the experimental intervention is the likely source for series discontinuity. Making matters somewhat more complicated is that although invalidating events can be approximately coincident in time with the intervention, that is not necessarily the case. To guard against this type of threat to validity, one should, in the initial stages of research planning, try to account for plausible rival hypotheses that offer alternative explanations for changes found in the series. For example, with respect to the impact of *Argersinger*, one may need to account for such events as a change in the state law reclassifying some offenses from felonies to misdemeanors, an industry-generated population increase that could lead to an increase in the number of misdemeanors, or long-term judicial vacancies that might increase the time between arrest and resolution for misdemeanants.

Tests for Interpretation

To aid in interpreting the time-series quasi-experiment's results, the investigator may select from among several statistical procedures (Caporaso 1973; Sween and Campbell 1965; Wilson 1973). When using these procedures for testing the significance of series discontinuity and in the determination of the experimental intervention's effect on the series, the researcher should be guided in his choice of an appropriate test by such theoretical considerations as the nature of the particular research question asked and the predicted intervention effect. Should he decide that more than one test is appropriate, the researcher can lessen the likelihood of drawing incorrect conclusions by using multiple tests to assess the series' behavior and to test for predicted series discontinuity.

Three tests in particular are well suited to the kinds of questions that are likely to be asked by those concerned with the impact of changes in legal policy and with the use of quasi-experimental time-series analysis: the Mood test is appropriate for judging the immediate impact of an intervention. With this test the investigator estimates a least-squares regression for the prechange observations and predicts the value for the first postchange (O_{n+1}) observation. Whatever difference there may be between the predicted and actual value for the first postchange observation ($O_{n+1} - \hat{O}_{n+1}$) is evaluated by a t-test, and if the results are significant, that is, if the results require the rejection of a null hypothesis of no difference, one can infer that the intervention had an immediate effect. This test might be most useful if the investigator wished to determine as soon as possible what impact a new policy, say *Argersinger*, had on a local court system. Adopting this test, he could judge whether the decision had an immediate effect on the time between arrest and the resolution of the defendant's cases, for instance. One might also use this test to determine the impact of an intervention when there are only one or two observations in the postchange period, such as the effect of congressional reaction on the Supreme Court's civil liberties policy during the 1950s.

The second and third tests that the researcher may find useful for judging the outcome of time-series quasi-experiments are two tests of the analysis of covariance model (Walker and Lev 1953; Schuessler 1971), which have been elaborated for use with this design by Joyce Sween and Donald T. Campbell. These two tests are referred to as Walker-Lev test 1 and test 3. The first, Walker-Lev test 1, is a test of the difference in slope for two regression lines, one fit to each time period. Notice that this test, as does Walker-Lev test 3, differs from the Mood test in that the investigator is concerned with a number of observations in the postchange period and he may have to apply the test well after the judicial or legal policy change has been adopted. If the F ratio is significant, the researcher can reject the null hypothesis of equal slope in each time period (H_0: $\hat{B}_1 = \hat{B}_2$) and draw the inference that the intervention has had an impact on the series, which is reflected by a change in trend. Whether this change in trend is positive or negative can be determined by an analysis of a graph of the date. As an example, Walker-Lev test 1 could be appropriately applied to determine if the Nixon administration was successful in changing Supreme Court policy in the area of criminal law. President Nixon's appointment of "law-and-order" judges to the Court was intended to decrease the percentage of pro-defendant decisions by the Court, that is to change the trend of the Court's criminal rights policy, and Walker-Lev test 1 would be the correct test to use in detecting that change.

Walker-Lev test 3 is a test of the hypothesis that a single regression line fits, that is, describes, both time periods and thus the entire time period under study. If the null hypothesis is rejected the judgment can be made that two regression lines, one each for the pre- and postchange periods, are necessary to describe the series and the unit under observation.

This test is quite useful for determining changes in series level, that is intercept differences, and especially whether the level has increased or decreased by a specific amount, or increment, following the intervention. For instance, Robert G. McClosky's contention that there was a difference in civil libertarian policy between the Stone and Vinson Courts can be stated as a hypothesis of change in level. McClosky (1972, p. 57) notes specifically that in no term of Stone's Court did the percentage of favorable civil liberties decisions fall below 50 percent, whereas in only one term of the Vinson Court did the percentage of favorable civil liberties decisions rise above 50 percent. Here the implication is that there was an incremental change between the two courts, and for anyone concerned with this hypothesis Walker-Lev test 3 would be the appropriate procedure.

Cases

Argersinger v. Hamlin, 407 U.S. 25 (1972).
Gideon v. Wainwright, 372 U.S. 335 (1963).
Jencks v. U.S., 353 U.S. 657 (1957).
Mallory v. U.S., 354 U.S. 449 (1957).

References

Campbell, Donald T., and H. Laurence Ross. 1968. "The Connecticut Crack-down on Speeding: Time-Series Data in Quasi-Experimental Analysis," *Law and Society Review*, 3, 33-53.

Campbell, Donald T., and Julian C. Stanley. 1963. *Experimental and Quasi-Experimental Designs for Research* (Chicago: Rand McNally).

Caporaso, James A. 1973. "Quasi-Experimental Approaches to Social Science: Perspectives and Problems," *Quasi-Experimental Approaches: Testing Theory and Evaluating Policy*, ed. J.A. Caporaso and Leslie L. Roos, Jr. (Evanston, Illinois: Northwestern University Press).

Caporaso, James A., and Alan L. Pelowski. 1971. "Economic and Political Integration in Europe: A Time-Series Quasi-Experimental Analysis," *American Political Science Review*, 65, 418-433.

Cook, Tom, and Frank Scioli. 1972. "Policy Analysis in Political Science: Trends and Issues in Empirical Research," *Policy Studies Journal*, 1, 6-11.

Glass, Gene V., George C. Tiao, and Thomas O. McGuire. 1971. "The 1900 Revision of German Divorce Laws: Analysis of Data as a Time-Series Quasi-Experiment," *Law and Society Review*, 6, 539-562.

Glass, Gene V., Victor L. Willson, and John Mordechai Gottman. 1972. *Design and Analysis of Time Series Experiments* (Boulder: Laboratory of Educational Research, University of Colorado).

Ingraham, Barton L. 1974. "The Impact of Argersinger—One Year Later," *Law and Society Review*, 8, 615-644.

Levy, Leonard W. 1974. *Against the Law: The Nixon Court and Criminal Justice* (New York: Harper and Row).

McClosky, Robert G. 1972. *The Modern Supreme Court* (Cambridge, Massachusetts: Harvard University Press).

Murphy, Walter F. 1962. *Congress and the Court: A Case Study in the American Political Process* (Chicago: University of Chicago Press).

Neale, John M., and Robert M. Liebert. 1973. *Science and Behavior: An Introduction to Methods of Research* (Englewood Cliffs, New Jersey: Prentice-Hall).

Ross, H. Laurence, Donald T. Campbell, and Gene V. Glass. 1970. "Determining the Social Effects of a Legal Reform: The British 'Breathalyser' Crackdown of 1967," *American Behavioral Scientist*, 13, 493-509.

Schuessler, Karl. 1971. "Covariance Analysis in Sociological Research," *Sociological Methodology 1969*, ed. Edgar F. Borgatta (San Francisco: Jossey-Bass Inc.).

Sween, Joyce, and Donald T. Campbell. 1965. "A Study of the Effect of Proximally Autocorrelated Error on Tests of Significance for The Interrupted Time-Series Quasi-Experiment," unpublished paper, Department of Psychology, Northwestern University.

Walker, Helen M., and Joseph Lev. 1953. *Statistical Inference* (New York: Holt Rinehart and Winston).

Wilson, L.A., II. 1973. "A Review of Statistical Techniques Appropriate for the Analysis of Time-Series Quasi-Experiments," *Policy Studies Journal*, 2, 118-123.

21 Comparative Rights Policy: The State of the Art

Richard Pierre Claude

Comparative research in the field of rights policy can make three contributions to our efforts to understand the legal order as one facet of the human experience. The first contribution is to direct our attention to the basic questions of *institutional development* by clarifying the relationship between institutional forms—the formulated and developed concepts and structures of law—and the legal order's institutional arrangements structuring man's efforts to provide a just and workable ordering of human affairs. The second contribution is to forward understanding of specific problems of *public policy* having a bearing on civil liberties and human rights. We will benefit by the accurate description of alternative approaches to the practical problems of liberty, equality, and human welfare that are common to many countries. The third contribution is to clarify some of the difficult questions relating to the *theoretical dimensions* of the interaction of law and society. Social science research techniques are now sufficiently sophisticated to make material contributions to the systematic study of civil liberties.

Whether the focus of research is upon institutions, policy, or behavior, ideological context, of course, must be taken into account. Both the liberal concept (Rawls 1971) and the contrasting socialist concept (Szabo 1966) of human rights set up an equivalence between human needs and rights. However, in the liberal concept, rights depend for their realization upon their assertion by individuals (hence the primacy of free expression), while rights in the socialist concept are said to depend for their realization upon the anticipation of need (hence the primacy of party interest aggregation and articulation). Given these points of contrast, it is not surprising that the liberal concept is most faulted for failing to respond to the needs of the unorganized and the dispossessed (Lichtman 1969), while the socialist view is said to be weakest in failing to respond to individual grievances (Medvedev 1975).

Ideological differences worldwide, no less than philosophical differences among individuals, result in widespread disagreement about how to evaluate standards of rights and liberties. For example, enforcement of the Foreign Assistance Act (which Congress amended in 1974 to reduce arms aid to countries engaged in "gross violations" of human rights) foundered on the inability of the State Department to find any adequately objective way to make distinctions of degree between rights violations from nation to nation ("U.S. Blocks Rights Data on Nations Getting Arms," *New York Times*, November 19, 1975, pp. 1, 14). Not only are normative problems in this case extremely complex, but basic analytical tasks designed to facilitate systematic policy evaluation remain untended by scholars.

Institutional Analysis

A comparative approach to civil rights and liberties can aid political and institutional analysis (see Becker 1970; Schubert and Danelski 1969; Abraham 1975; and Grossman and Sarat 1975). A salient point of comparison at the institutional level is whether specified rights are fixed in documentary constitutional terms requiring extraordinary amending processes ("entrenched rights"), and whether such limits are applied to government by virtue of judicial review or some comparable mechanism for enforcement. (See Table 21-1.) Although the rights of British subjects are precisely defined in law, they are neither entrenched nor enforced by judicial review (de Smith 1975). English-speaking countries generally omit from their listings of rights desirable but unenforceable rights; by contrast, francophone states tend to bundle economic and political rights together. Although beginning from quite different ideological sources, the European People's Democracies have all followed France in adopting a written constitution. These constitutions are comparably rigid in their binding force over ordinary legislation and in requiring special procedures and special majorities for amendment. With the sole exception of Yugoslavia, they also follow the French model of not recognizing judicial review (*New York Times*, October 22, 1974, p. 13).

In the United States, a rigid constitution entrenching various specific

Table 21-1
Comparison of Entrenched Rights and Use of Judicial Review

		ENTRENCHED RIGHTS	
		Yes	No
JUDICIAL REVIEW	Yes	United States	Canada
	No	France	Great Britain

rights and liberties is combined with a system of judicial review. Going beyond the "preventive control" available to the French Conseil Constitutionnel, the American system is famous for the capacity of the Supreme Court to nullify legislation and administrative action as void, thereby placing the Court in a policy making position at both the federal and state levels. The American model is found in many countries, albeit with noteworthy modifications. The Federal Republic of Germany relies upon a written constitution and a centralized system of judicial review. Since 1951 it has even provided for a special proceeding called "constitutional recourse" (*Verfassungsbeschwerde*) whereby the individual may directly attack any governmental action in the Federal Constitutional Court after the exhaustion of ordinary remedies. A comparable "special recourse" procedure (*judicio de amparo*) is also available in Mexico and other Latin American countries (McWhinney 1969). To date, no systematic comparative impact studies have been done to discern the relative effectiveness of these varied enforcement approaches to comparable civil liberties issues (Wasby 1974).

Judicial review is thought by many, especially Americans, to be an indispensable support for various civil liberties. Nevertheless, the French, British, and Canadian models noted above suggest that this need not be the case. Clearly, there are nonjudicial institutions equipped to enforce rights such as ombudsmen in Scandinavia, commissions of inquiry in Canada, and hearing boards in Great Britain. The pressures for decentralization, which partly explain the unique position of Canada in Table 21-1, draw attention to the extent of government centralization as an independent institutional variable affecting review. The impetus behind judicial review appears, in the first instance, to be associated with a general governmental centralizing tendency. The effort to create uniformity in civil, social, and political rights throughout a country may be more a part of a centralizing strategy than a libertarian movement. Centralization of the rights-defining and rights-adjudicating agencies has the effect of positioning the mass of citizens as legal equals in a direct unmediated relationship to the central political authority. This proposition, first advanced by de Tocqueville and recently carried into comparative analysis by Stein Rokkan (1970, p. 28), deserves further research.

Human Rights Policies

Just as the range of possible institutions concerned with civil liberties is great, the variety of "human rights" policies is also extensive. Included are legally binding guarantees beneficial to the individual in his citizenship

Table 21-2
Liberal Model of Human Rights Development

	Twentieth Century SOCIOECONOMIC RIGHTS	Nineteenth Century PARTICIPATION AND CIVIL RIGHTS	Eighteenth Century or earlier CIVIL LIBERTIES	Seventeenth Century or earlier POLITICAL FREEDOM
Against private persons & groups	Protection from environmental pollution Security from economic coercion Protection of children	Protection from involuntary servitude	Protection from libel	Protection from bodily harm
Private Rights	Artistic expression Life style Inquiry Information Participation in cultural life Privacy Marriage Choice of birth control strategies	Teaching Travel	Security against unfair criminal procedures Security against unfair civil procedures Security against arbitrary administrative action	Life Physical liberty Religious belief and practice
Political Rights	Political asylum Right to retain citizenship Right of egress	Voting Political candidacy Association Organization	Political discussion Assembly Petition Publication	Security against arbitrary government action
Equality Rights	Freedom from unfair discrimination based on: sex, age, literacy, wealth	Equal opportunity Civic equality Freedom from unfair discrimination based on: race, language, ethnic and national origin	Equality before law Freedom from unfair discrimination based on: religion, status of nobility	
Economic Rights	Nondiscrimination in government benefits and services	Labor organization	Possession and use of property Occupation Buying and selling Contracting Copyright	
Positive Rights	Adequate income Health services Housing Employment Insurance against: financial risk of: work injury unemployment retirement ill health old age	Education		
	Centralized Processes	Bargaining Processes	Market Processes	Feudal Transition

Left-margin groupings: Human Rights — Negative Rights (Against private persons & groups; Against government) and Positive Rights.

Source: Richard P. Claude, ''The Classical Model of Human Rights Development,'' *Comparative Human Rights*, ed. R. P. Claude (Baltimore: The Johns Hopkins University Press, 1976), ©The Johns Hopkins University Press.

and private roles and to groups seeking status equality, nondiscrimination, and inclusion in the social, economic, and political process. As claims against government, groups, and private individuals, the resulting entitlements (including civil liberties) may be characterized as negative rights. Guarantees to socioeconomic welfare policies are claims upon government and other organizations that, as positive rights, are typically implemented by a system of administrative support. This analysis is reflected in Table 21-2, which also is organized on the basis of a development scheme roughly classifying by century the period during which various rights policies emerged (Claude 1976).

What brings the experience of countries in the liberal tradition together in the schema presented by Table 21-2 is that three varieties of human rights policies can be clearly linked with three categories to which political economists refer as "public choice processes": market choice, bargained choice, and centralized choice (Elkin 1974). Thus, property rights, liberty of contract, free expression, the right to petition, and related civil liberties are developed side by side with processes of choice involving a largely decentralized exchange of goods, services, and ideas concomitant with relatively free market conditions. The political and civil rights stage of policy development that followed was associated with changing processes that emphasized collective choice: competing labor, political, associational, and social groups engaged in a variety of bargaining processes including competition, compromise, persuasion, and electoral participation. The positive socioeconomic rights policies emphasizing health and welfare considerations have become associated in a subsequent stage of human rights development with centralized choice processes where authority is concentrated and where the hierarchical choice processes emphasize planning.

In terms of their eighteenth-century origins, civil liberties offered the promise of minimizing individual insecurity wrought by government interference. Without the security of expectations ensured by the law in the form of the institutions of property and civil liberties, people are seen from the liberal perspective to be less motivated to work, save, and invest. But just as insecurity among the mass of citizens promotes economic stagnation, so does privilege among the few. Electoral rights that encourage participation and civil rights that extend equality and freedom from discrimination help to break down privilege and vested interests that dampen the incentive to attempt change, entrepreneurial risk, and economic development (Kuznets 1969). Modern economic development associated with industrialization requires the aggregation of capital. Where, for purposes of concentrating capital, multiple sources of private financial reserves contribute to the aggregation needed for investment, processes of public choice may usefully rely upon market and bargaining interactions.

But what of developing countries that lack pluralized private investment sources? Where the accelerated concentration of capital must rely upon hierarchical choice processes, traditional civil liberties and civil rights may not be seen by government elites as congenial to economic development (Cooray 1969). David M. Trubek draws the general conclusion: "Today, when laissez-faire has been abandoned in the West, and development command economies exist in the Socialist bloc, contemporary developing nations almost inevitably lean toward a degree of government economic involvement." (1968, p. 36) Whether government economic planning in developing countries necessarily advances at the expense of liberal-style civil liberties and equality rights is a subject that urgently demands future research (Barry 1973).

Mapping the range of rights and liberties is unfinished business for research. To date the most elaborate academic effort to map the policy fields involved in human rights is that made by Myres S. McDougal, Harold D. Lasswell, and Lung-chu Chen (1963 and 1976). They have brought a policy-oriented approach to bear upon international law through their conceptual framework, although it has been subject to the criticism of producing confusion as well as clarity by its tendency to "formalism" (overconcern for definitional precision) and "discursiveness" (Symposium 1974). Although the McDougal-Lasswell-Chen enterprise has offered rather little explicit guidance to the comparative study of rights and liberties, it could serve as the appropriate core for the comparative study of various rights, both in terms of problem solving and theory building.

Theory Building on Human Rights Policy

Forward movement concerning institutional analysis and public policy studies has not been matched by the systematic study of human behavior linking personality and other individual causal factors behind discrete decisions affecting civil liberties. Reviewing various trends in comparative and international research in the 1970s, one observer wrote, "It is the social sciences which, precisely because of the techniques which they have developed recently, now permit research on certain aspects of reality bearing importantly on the subject of human rights." (*Human Rights Journal*, p. 109) However "technique rich" research cognate to the study of rights policy may have become in recent years, the field remains "theory poor" (Spinrad 1970). The reasons are multiple.

The undernourishment of the study of comparative civil liberties policy is partly attributable to the lack of available data. There is a dearth of reliable information about rights developments from country to country. A lesson can be taken from the United Nations' experience with information gathering in connection with implementation of the Universal Declaration of Human Rights. The Declaration, adopted by the General Assembly in 1948, was to be strengthened according to a 1966 plan calling for government-composed reports on domestic human rights developments. However, the triennial reports to the United Nations Commission on Human Rights have been selective and fragmentary and do not coalesce to form a realistic, reliable, or complete picture. Moses Moskowitz, faulting the reporting sources rather than the commission, has complained sharply: "The irrelevancies contained in the reports are only exceeded by their omissions." (1968, pp. 93-94)

In 1967 Milton Konvitz called for the development of American social indicators, to include a civil liberties report. Unfortunately this suggestion for an annual inventory of noneconomic data has not been taken seriously. Currently, however, the social indicators movement in Great Britain, Scandinavia, and the United States presages the development of rights-related data (see Sheldon and Freeman 1970). Trends and national reports on free expression are published monthly by the International Press Institute in Zurich. More systemic cross-national data on civil liberties (freedom of the press) has been developed by the Yale University World Data Analysis Program. Extensive discussion is supplied by Taylor and Hudson regarding the reliability and validity of the attribute data reported in the *World Handbook of Political and Social Indicators*. Reliance may also be placed upon the *Freedom House Survey of Human Rights* (Gastil 1973), but caution is needed because of lack of definitional clarity. Especially promising is work currently underway at Stanford University to assemble social and legal development indicators (SLADE) from 1945 to 1970 for Chile, Costa Rica, Italy, Mexico, Peru, and Spain (Merryman 1974).

The study of comparative rights policy has been weakened partly by the methodological disparities between research on law and the social sciences. Consequently, two distinct perspectives have emerged: an institutional perspective concerned with rule making and rule adjudicating functions associated with legal institutions (e.g., Cappelletti and Tallon 1973) and a public policy perspective preoccupied with rule application and its social and political consequences (e.g., Duchacek 1973). Applied to the problems of civil liberties, such bifurcation results in emphasizing one dimension of rights policy at the expense of others. Cooperation among scholars in many disciplines is needed to initiate study of so broad a field as comparative rights and liberties policy. However, because scholars in such varied areas as law and the social sciences have tended to use quite different professional vocabularies and to employ incompatible methods of analysis, cooperation will not be without its difficulties.

The problem of developing an integrated theory of human rights addressed to questions of explanation also derives from basic difficulties not fully resolved by the philosophy of social science. Should the foundation for explanatory theory be elicited from the ways whereby men understand and justify their behavior, or should the measurable externalities of behavior form the basis for theorizing? Should the focus be upon personal motives or social effects? Social science inquiry into civil liberties, like social science inquiry generally, may be conducted at two levels. At one level, observation of behavior is carried out by considering the actions studied in the perspective in which it has meaning for the actor. Ths psychological (Gallatin 1976), cultural (Grossman and Sarat 1975), and indeed moral (Danelski 1966) dimensions of the actions are taken into account by reference to the individual participant in the social process. Second, observation is pursued in terms of the empirically verifiable features of human interaction that sustain or nullify hypotheses framed to explain the larger processes of change in society at large. The political, economic, and perhaps anthropological dimensions of the actions studied are taken into account by reference to decisional and societal processes. A fully developed program of research along these lines would ask both genetic questions using diachronic data—What are the origins and stages of rights development? (Schwartz and Miller 1964)—and functional questions using synchronic data—What are the conditions requisite for sustaining effective civil liberties? (Nixon 1950).

In the effort to progress beyond case studies to the scientific comparison of rights policies, communications theory may supply a fruitful framework for inquiry linking free speech, civil liberties, and socioeconomic development. To foster economic development, governments must rely upon the law, which is the filter through which policy becomes practice. Since economic modernization is a type of social change, it is peculiarly dependent upon communication. The trade-offs involved between civil liberties and free speech on the one hand and rapid economic growth on the other should be examined in subsequent research. Appropriate descriptive beginnings have been made by David Bayley and Robert Martin, but further work is now timely. Such inquiry should examine the variety of approaches of the elites who organize the industrialization and modernization process from country to country. Research should also focus on the role of culture in adaptations of society to changing patterns of rights consciousness, and should link social stratification and cleavages to questions about the beneficiaries of free speech and civil liberties policies. With such questions left untended, it remains the case that the field of rights and liberties as a matter of any but parochial national concerns is "an untrodden area of systematic research" (Moskowitz 1958, p. 21).

References

Abraham, Henry J. 1975. *The Judicial Process*, 3d ed. (New York: Oxford University Press).

Barry, Brian. 1973. *The Liberal Theory of Justice* (Oxford at the Clarendon Press).

Bayley, David H. 1964. *Public Liberties in the New States* (Chicago: Rand McNally).

Becker, Theodore L., ed. 1970. *Comparative Judicial Politics* (Chicago: Rand McNally).

Cappelletti, Mauro, and Denis Tallon, eds.. 1973. *Fundamental Guarantees of the Parties in Civil Litigation* (Dobbs Ferry, New York: Oceana Publications).

Claude, Richard P. 1976. "The Classical Model of Human Rights Development," *Comparative Human Rights*, ed. Claude (Baltimore: The Johns Hopkins University Press), chap. 1.

Cooray, Joseph A.L. 1969. *Constitutional Government and Human Rights in a Developing Society* (Colombo, Sri Lanka: The Colombo Co.).

Danelski, David J. 1966. "A Behavioral Conception of Human Rights," *Law in Transition Quarterly*, 3 (Spring), 63-73.

de Smith, S.A. 1975. *Constitutional and Administrative Law*, 2d ed. (London: Penguin, Foundations of Law Series).

Duchacek, Ivo D. 1973. *Rights and Liberties in the World Today* (Santa Barbara: The American Bibliographic Center—Cleo Press).

Elkin, Stephen L. 1974. "Political Science and the Analysis of Public Policy," *Public Policy*, 4, 399-422.

Gallatin, Judith. 1976. "The Conceptualization of Rights: Psychological Development and Cross-National Perspectives," *Comparative Human Rights*, ed. Richard P. Claude (Baltimore: The Johns Hopkins University Press), chap. 12.

Gastil, Raymond D. 1973. "Comparative Survey of Freedom," *Freedom at Issue*, No. 17 (January), and subsequent issues.

Grossman, Joel B., and Austin Sarat. 1975. "Political Culture and Judicial Review," *Comparative Juridical Review*, 12, 181-209.

Human Rights Journal (Revue des droits de l'homme). 1973. Symposium on the Methodology of Human Rights Study, "Droits de l'homme et droit comparé," 6, 43-115.

Konvitz, Milton. 1967. "Civil Liberties," *Annals*, 371, 20-37.

Kuznets, Simon. 1969. *Modern Economic Growth* (New Haven: Yale University Press).

Lichtman, Richard. 1969. "The Facade of Equality in Liberal Democratic Theory," *Inquiry*, 12, 170-208.

Martin, Robert. 1974. *Personal Freedom and the Law in Tanzania* (Nairobi: Oxford University Press).

McDougal, Myres S., Harold D. Lasswell, and Lung-chu Chen. 1963. "Human Rights and World Order: A Framework for Policy-Oriented Inquiry," *The American Journal of International Law*, 63, 237-269.

_____. 1976. *Human Rights and World Public Order,* unpublished ms.

McWhinney, Edward. 1969. *Judicial Review*, 4th ed. (Toronto: University of Toronto Press).

Medvedev, Roy A. 1975. *On Socialist Democracy* (New York: Knopf).

Merryman, John Henry. 1974. "Comparative Law and Scientific Explanation," *Law in the U.S.A. in Social and Technological Revolution*, eds. John Hazard and W. Wagner, Vol. 6, 80-104.

Moskowitz, Moses. 1958. *Human Rights and World Order* (Dobbs Ferry, New York: Oceana Publications).

_____. 1968. *The Politics and Dynamics of Human Rights* (Dobbs Ferry, New York: Oceana Publications).

Nixon, Russell B. 1950. "Factors Related to Freedom in National Press Systems," *Journalism Quarterly*, 37, 13-28.

Rawls, John. 1971. *A Theory of Justice* (Cambridge: Harvard University Press).

Rokkan, Stein. 1970. *Citizens Elections Parties* (New York: David McKay).

Schubert, Glendon, and David J. Danelski, eds. 1969. *Comparative Judicial Behavior* (New York: Oxford University Press).

Schwartz, Richard D., and James C. Miller. 1964. "Legal Evolution and Societal Complexity," *American Journal of Sociology*, 70, 159-69.

Sheldon, Anor B., and Howard E. Freeman. 1970. "Notes on Social Indicators: Promises and Potential," *Policy Sciences*, 1, 97-111.

Spinrad, William. 1970. *Civil Liberties* (Chicago: Quadrangle Books).

"Symposium on the Lasswell-McDougal Approach." 1974. *Virginia Journal of International Law*, 14, 387-586.

Szabó, Imre. 1966. *Socialist Concept of Human Rights* (Budapest: Akadémiai Kiadó).

Taylor, Charles Lewis, and Michael C. Hudson, eds. 1972. *World Handbook of Political and Social Indicators*, 2d ed. (New Haven: Yale University Press).

Trubek, David M. 1968. "Toward a Social Theory of Law," *Yale Law Journal*, 82, 1-50.

Wasby, Stephen L. 1974. "The United States Supreme Court's Impact: Broadening Our Focus," *Notre Dame Lawyer*, 49, 1023-1036.

Table of Cases

Index

abortion, 95, 101-106; conscience clause, 101, 103-104; consent, 101, 103-104; hospitals, 103-104; Medicaid, 101, 103-104; unanswered questions, 103-105

access: to documents, 183; to media, 6-10, 130; to records, 122-125. *See also* media; newspapers

Administrative Procedure Act, 129, 131

advertising: effect on media, 3-4; television, 28

aggression, and television, 15-18, 28-29

American Civil Liberties Union, 57, 85, 155, 159-167; chapter-affiliate relations, 160-161; complaint-handling, 161-162; criticism of strategy, 164-167; internal operation, 162-164; internal structure, 159-161, 166; recommendations for change, 165-166; and Supreme Court, 159; types of cases, 159, 161-167

American Psychological Association, methodological standards, 70-71, 73

Amish, Old Order, 64

antidiscrimination provisions, 69-76, 153-154, 179, 182-183

antipornography groups, 174-175

antitrust laws, 97; and media, 4-5

Areopagitica, The, 3, 30

armed services, sexual equality, 151-152

arms, right to bear, 183

assembly, freedom of, Canada, 192; state constitutions, 182

association, freedom of, 38-40. *See also* unions

audio-visual material. *See* television

bail, 185-186

banishment, 115

bargaining. *See* collective bargaining

Barron, Jerome, 6, 130

Bellah, Robert, 49-50, 53

Bible reading, 57, 61

Bill of Rights, ix, 51, 91, 95, 98, 107; and federalism, 170; "New Bill of Rights," 92-98. *See also specific amendments*

Black, Hugo, 54, 96, 156, 170

blacks, treatment of, 79-80, 84-85

boycotts, 37, 44-45

Brandeis, Louis, 119-120

British North America Act, 191-192

broadcasting. *See* media; television

Buckley Amendment, 124-125

Burger, Warren, 74, 130, 154, 156, 177, 204

cable television, 10, 21, 25, 27, 30

Canada, 191-197, 212-213. *See also* Supreme Court of Canada

Canadian Bill of Rights, 191-197; constitutional status, 192; equality before the law, 197; free speech, 194-195

cases, types of, 159-167. *See also* Table of Cases

censorship, 19-21, 25-27, 29, 169-177; self-censorship, 174-175. *See also* erotica; Federal Communications Commission

Chicanos: and media, 8-10; and Texas Rangers, 80, 84; treatment of, 79-80, 84

children: effects of television, 15-22, 28-29; children's programming, 28. *See also* juveniles; television

China, travel to, 141-144

church-state relations, ix, 49-55, 57-66; church-state settlement, 58-59; judicial doctrine, 60-66; policy making, 57-60; Supreme Court, 57, 60-67. *See also* Bible reading; civil religion; freedom of religion; nonestablishment of religion; parochial schools; school prayer; tax exemption

citizen groups, and the media, 7-10, 25, 28-30. *See also* consumer groups; interest groups

civil liberties, in Canada, 191-197, 212-213; comparative research, 211-218; conflicts of values, x, 169-177; defined, 179; in developing countries, 216, 218; differential treatment, 79-85; and economic development, 215; expansion of, 79, 91-98, (*see also specific subjects*); negative, 179; normative approach, xi; and other policy areas, x, portrayed on television, 191; positive, 179, 184-185; remedies, 96-97; scholars' interests, ix-xi; scope, ix; social indicators, 217; in state constitutions, 179-188; substantive due process, 92-98; Supreme Court's role, 91-92. *See also* human rights; rights; *specific topics*

civil religion, 49-55; relation to First Amendment, 50-54; Supreme Court, 52-54

229

235

Universal Declaration of Human Rights, 139-140, 216-217
universities. *See* collective bargaining; teachers
unwed fathers, 93, 151

validity, types of, 70-71
values: conflict between, x, 169-177; cosmopolitan, 169-177; democratic, 169-177; elites, 169-177; enlightenment, 173, 176; status, 173, 175-176; well-being, 173, 175
Veterans Administration, 120
Vinson Court, 204, 209
violence: social indicators, 19; and television, 15-22, 28-29

Voting Rights Act of 1965, 91

Walker-Lev tests, 208-209
"wall of separation," 52. *See also* church-state relations
Warren, Earl, 115, 130, 154, 204
welfare recipients, 92, 96
whipping, 108-109
wiretapping, 186
women: in law schools, 154-155
women's movement, 85, 152-153
women's rights, 79, 81; abortion, 101-106. *See also* sexual equality
work: right to, 93, 184

zoning, 98

About the Contributors

Larry C. Berkson is Assistant Professor of Political Science at the University of Florida. He received the B.A. from Doane College, the M.A. from the University of South Dakota, and the Ph.D. from the University of Wisconsin. He has contributed articles to several law reviews and political science journals, and is the author of *The Concept of Cruel and Unusual Punishment*.

Thomas C. Britton is a third-year law student at the Southern Illinois University School of Law and is a staff assistant in the Office of the Board of Trustees of Southern Illinois University. He received the M.A. in higher education from Southern Illinois University at Carbondale in 1973.

Richard Pierre Claude is Associate Professor of Government and Politics at the University of Maryland, College Park. He received the Ph.D. from the University of Virginia in 1964. He is the author of *The Supreme Court and the Electoral Process*, and editor of *Comparative Human Rights*.

Donald S. Dobkin is currently an LL.M. candidate and James Nelson Raymond International Fellow at Northwestern University School of Law. He holds a law degree from the University of Windsor (Ontario) and is an M.A. candidate in political science at Wayne State University. His immediate research interests include constitutional law, civil liberties, law and the social sciences, and judicial politics. He is presently working on a book entitled *The Political Role of the Supreme Court of Canada*.

William Lee Eubank is a graduate student in the Department of Political Science, University of Oregon, whose major field of interest is judicial behavior and the American legal system; he has an additional interest in research methodology and political recruitment.

Daryl R. Fair is Professor of Political Science at Trenton State College. He received the Ph.D. from the University of Pennsylvania and has written articles that have appeared in the *Wisconsin Law Review, Rutgers-Camden Law Journal, Western Political Quarterly*, and elsewhere. He is currently working on a study of nonestablishment of religion doctrine and the politics of the *Everson* v. *Board of Education* case. He has served as president of the New Jersey Political Science Association and as a member of the council of the Northeastern Political Science Association.

Marilyn Falik received the Ph.D. from New York University. She has taught at Lehman College and American University. She was a Research Fellow at Brookings Institution in 1973-74, served as research director of a university affirmative action study project, and is a legislative assistant to a member of Congress. Her research interests include health care policy making, bioethics, and civil liberties issues.

Stanley H. Friedelbaum, Professor of Political Science at Rutgers University, received the B.A. from Brooklyn College, the M.A. from Rutgers, and the Ph.D. from Columbia University. He teaches constitutional law at the graduate and undergraduate levels. He is the author of *Contemporary Constitutional Law* and a contributor to a number of journals, including *The University of Chicago Law Review* and *The Supreme Court Review*.

Werner F. Grunbaum is Professor of Political Science at the University of Missouri—St. Louis. His research interests include civil liberties and computer applications. He has published in the *Journal of Politics, Frontiers of Judicial Research, Houston Law Review, Journal of Applied Psychology, Public Opinion Quarterly,* and *Harvard Educational Review*.

Stephen C. Halpern is Assistant Professor of Political Science at the State University of New York at Buffalo, where he teaches courses in judicial process. He is the author of *Police Association and Department Leaders*. Currently, he is engaged in research on the Office of Solicitor General, and on the Civil Rights Division of the Department of Justice.

Jerome J. Hanus, Professor of Government and Public Administration at The American University, received the M.A. from the University of Washington and the Ph.D. from the University of Maryland. He is presently on leave as a Social Science Analyst, Governmental and General Research Division, Congressional Research Service, Library of Congress. He teaches in the fields of public law, public policy, and American government, and has contributed to several journals and law reviews.

Donald W. Jackson is Associate Professor of Political Science at Texas Christian University. He received the B.A. and the J.D. from Southern Methodist University and the Ph.D. from the University of Wisconsin in 1972. He spent the academic year 1974-75 as a Judicial Fellow in the Office of the Administrative Assistant to the Chief Justice of the United States. His research and teaching fields focus on judicial process and public law. His current research emphasis is on legal professional socialization and law school curricula.

Francisco J. Lewels holds a masters degree in education from Troy State University and a doctorate in journalism from the University of Missouri. After working as a communication consultant for the Community Relations Service, U.S. Department of Justice, he became chairman of the Department of Journalism, University of Texas—El Paso, and is presently chairman of the Department of Mass Communication there. A past editor of the Freedom of Information Digest and Report, he is the author of numerous articles about mass communication and of *The Uses of the Media by the Chicano Movement*.

Emmet V. Mittlebeeler (J.D., University of Louisville; Ph.D., University of Chicago) is Professor of Government and Public Administration at The American University, Washington, D.C. He was Assistant Attorney General of Kentucky and assistant to Congressman John M. Robsion, Jr., of Kentucky, and has served as a consultant to the House Committee on Government Operations and to the Administrative Office of the United States Courts. He has been a visiting professor at universities in Rhodesia and Nigeria, and is the author of *African Custom and Western Law*.

Richard E. Morgan, William Nelson Cromwell Professor of Constitutional Law and Government at Bowdoin College, was trained at Columbia University and taught at Columbia College before serving as a Fellow in Law and Government at Harvard Law School in 1968. He is the author of *The Politics of Religious Conflict* and *The Supreme Court and Religion*, editor of *The American Political System: Introductory Readings*, and is a contributor to several journals and collections. He is presently research director of a Twentieth Century Fund Study of CIA and FBI spying on American citizens.

Richard S. Randall, chairman of the Department of Politics, New York University, holds a Ph.D. from the University of Wisconsin—Madison. He is the author of *Censorship of the Movies: The Social and Political Control of a Mass Medium (1968); Self-Regulation in the American Film Industry*, for the Commission on Obscenity and Pornography, 1971; and other articles on freedom of speech and civil liberties policy.

Deanna Campbell Robinson is Assistant Professor in the Department of Communication, The Ohio State University. She received the Ph.D. from the University of Oregon in 1974 and her work has been published by the *Journal of Broadcasting* and *Communication Research*. Her major research interest is how and why people use the mass media. Currently, she is studying how adults process audio-visual information.

Raleigh W. Smith, Jr., is Assistant Professor of Political Science at Miami University—Hamilton where he teaches political science and criminal justice studies. He received the Ph.D. in politics and literature from the University of Dallas. He has contributed to *Mississippi Quarterly*, *Intercollegiate Review*, *Renaissance Quarterly*, *Journal of Police Science and Administration*, and *Political Science Reviewer*.

Philippa Strum received the B.A. from Brandeis, the Ed.M. from Harvard, and the Ph.D. from the New School (1964). She is presently Professor of Political Science at CUNY—Brooklyn College. In addition to several articles, she is the author of *Presidential Power, American Democracy*, and *The Supreme Court and "Political Questions,"* and has contributed an article on "The Supreme Court and the Vietnamese War" to *International Law and Vietnam*, ed. Richard Falk. She is currently engaged in work on a biography of Justice Brandeis.

Albert L. Sturm is University Research Professor of Political Science at Virginia Polytechnic Institute and State University. He is the author of books, monographs, articles, and reports on state constitutional development and revision. Among his most recent publications are *Trends in State Constitution-Making: 1966-1972*, and *State Constitutions and Constitutional Revision, 1945-1975: A Selective Bibliography*.

Meredith W. Watts is currently Associate Professor of Political Science at the University of Wisconsin—Milwaukee. He has co-authored books on *Legislative Roll Call Analysis* and *State Legislative Systems*; and has contributed articles to the *American Political Science Review*, *American Journal of Political Science*, *Experimental Study of Politics*, *Political Methodology*, *Social Science Quarterly*, and *Teaching Political Science*. His work is generally in the areas of political behavior and attitudes and his current research deals with the psychophysiology of aggressive attitudes and the socializing effects of media.

Kaye M. Wright is a research assistant at Virginia Polytechnic Institute and State University. Active in civic affairs and organizations, she is the first woman elected to the Blacksburg, Virginia town council. She served as a member of the Blacksburg charter commission.

About the Editor

Stephen L. Wasby, Professor of Political Science at Southern Illinois University at Carbondale, received the M.A. and the Ph.D. from the University of Oregon. He was a Russell Sage Post-Doctoral Resident in Law and Social Science, University of Wisconsin—Madison (1969-70). He is the author of *Political Science: The Discipline and Its Dimensions, The Impact of the United States Supreme Court,* and *Continuity and Change: From the Warren Court to the Burger Court.* He is a member of the editorial boards of *Policy Studies Journal* and *Justice System Journal,* and is engaged in research on the communication of legal decisions.